POST-VICTORIAN MUSIC

POST-VICTORIAN MUSIC

WITH OTHER STUDIES AND SKETCHES

BY

CHARLES L. GRAVES

KENNIKAT PRESS
Port Washington, N. Y./London

134279

POST-VICTORIAN MUSIC

First published in 1911
Reissued in 1970 by Kennikat Press
Library of Congress Catalog Card No: 71-102838
SBN 8046-0754-0

Manufactured by Taylor Publishing Company   Dallas, Texas

TO

C. M. H. AND H. P. G.

NOTE

THESE papers, with some alterations, are reprinted from the *Spectator* by the kind permission of the proprietor.

CONTENTS

CONTENTS

I

THE SYMPHONIA DOMESTICA

Richard Strauss has come and gone. He has conducted the second performance of his *Symphonia Domestica* in such a way as to throw a certain amount of new light on his intentions by adopting *tempi* and *nuances* of expression differing from those adopted by Mr. Henry Wood, to whose exertions in training the band and preparing the work he paid a handsome and well-deserved tribute of gratitude; he has had an enthusiastic reception; and he has convinced everybody that whether he is an inspired creator or not, he is at least *verflucht pfiffig*, as Wagner said of Berlioz. More than that, he has exhibited his talent, on the whole, in so much more engaging a light than in some of his recent works—notably *Ein Heldenleben*—that were it not for his programme, one might well abandon the rôle of fault-finding, and hail the new work as a pledge of further and more wholesale renunciation of the cult of extravagance and eccentricity. In face of that programme, however, such an attitude is unhappily impossible. We shall endeavour as briefly as may be to justify our regret that he should have saddled his work with this amazing incubus of egotism and absurdity.

Into the details of the programme—occasionally quite Gampish in their Teutonic homeliness—we have no intention of entering. But it is surely permissible to ask a plain question. If Strauss finds it necessary to supplement the ordinary full orchestra by at least twenty extra players, including a quartet of saxophones, in order to depict a normal day—devoid of any exciting incidents—in the home life of a young married couple, how large an orchestra and how many unfamiliar instruments will he need to delineate a really tragical episode ? By employing the fullest possible amount of musical machinery to render justice to a tranquil and idyllic theme, he has left himself no margin, no reserve to cope with the needs of a soul-shaking crisis. Armageddon is reduced to the same level as a baby's bath, and the friendly argument of fond parents over the education of their "young hopeful" is raised to the plane of a conflict of Titans.

But then, it may not without good grounds be objected, this is *not* a musical picture of a normal day in the home life of a normal young couple. It is a day in the life of a Great Genius, *videlicet* Strauss himself. If you think otherwise, you have only to read the dedication, the annotations in the score, the sketch programme by the composer and the full programme, based on his own hints, which he has never disclaimed or condemned as a false interpretation of his meaning. We reluctantly grant that this may be so ; reluctantly, because it brings us back to our old cause of complaint against *Ein Heldenleben*, that never before had a musician of commanding talent advertised himself in his works with such unblushing complacency. If Strauss is ever to justify completely the panegyrics of his admirers, and do something really and sanely great or consistently noble — it is not enough to be able to give us occasional pages as gorgeous in their colouring as peacocks' tails— he will have to emancipate himself from the paralysing effect of these introspective and self-advertising programmes. Great geniuses are seldom untainted by egotism : their work must be coloured by their own experiences. But this labelling process is undignified and ignoble. It is a degradation of the symphony to turn it into a *roman à clef*. It may be necessary to submit to interviewing, but one does not like to think of a "Celebrity at Home" acting as his own interviewer.

Whether Strauss will in the end extricate himself from the thraldom of this present formula remains to be seen. That he may do so must be the sincere desire of all lovers of an art of which he is so immensely gifted, so influential, and so disconcerting an ornament. It will be a relief, again, to his whole-hearted admirers, many of whom must find the process of interpreting and justifying all his *lustige Streiche* a somewhat arduous task. But the omens are not altogether reassuring, and if one theory of his aims and plan of campaign is correct, there is not much chance of his ever completely emerging into the Olympian atmosphere of the really great masters. The theory, which has at any rate the merit of providing a working explanation of his aims and methods, is briefly as follows. Strauss is sincerely desirous of achieving a position of such independence that he will be able to write exactly and entirely as he pleases — to indulge his genius without thought or regard for public opinion. But in order to reach that enviable position, he believes it to be necessary first of all to impress and attract the public, and since *populus vult decipi*

—*decipiatur*. In other words, he realises that for him the shortest cut to popularity and success is in the deliberate resort to eccentricity—much like Disraeli's audacities of speech and costume in the early stage of his public career. The method has answered admirably, for he is certainly the most talked about and the best abused of living composers ; indeed, the only drawback is that it has answered too well. The nature of his works and the choice of his subjects have necessarily involved a good deal of literary commentary, initiated by the composer himself, but carried out with great zeal and industry by those who take him seriously. Thanks to their indefatigable hermeneutics, the eccentricities of Strauss have achieved such a resounding success as to eclipse his beauties. His disciples have justified him with such uncompromising loyalty that if he were now to compose a symphonic poem on a broomstick they would find it palpitating with cosmic emotion. In these circumstances, it would be an act of treachery on his part to go back on them ; indeed, it is by no means certain that they have not so far reacted upon him that he no longer knows himself whether he is in jest or in earnest. A style which was originally adopted to arrest attention and to make the public " sit up " has now become a second nature ; and by the Nemesis which waits upon all who are not true to the best that is in them, instead of doing what he meant to do, he is unable to resist doing what is expected of him.

The foregoing theory may possibly be doing a grave injustice to the aims and methods of Richard Strauss, but at least it illustrates the dangers attendant on the composition of programme music when the composer, instead of giving explicit indications as to his intentions, contents himself with furnishing hints for the encouragement of fantastic interpreters. According to some accounts, Strauss wishes his Symphony to be judged simply as absolute music. But his own sketch programme and annotations have rendered such an attitude impossible. He cannot have it both ways, and by refusing to disavow the grotesquely circumstantial details of his analysts, he has seriously impaired the enjoyment which a great deal of his latest work is capable of causing if it be regarded, according to Beethoven's dictum, as *mehr Ausdruck der Empfindung als Malerei.*

April 22, 1905.

II

ELEKTRA

GENIUS—modern musical genius—according to the witty perversion of a well-known composer, may be defined as "an infinite capacity for giving pain," and no better illustration can be found than the work in which Strauss has bedevilled Hofmannsthal's squalid perversion of Sophocles's drama. That he should have based this monstrosity on the Sophoclean in preference to the Euripidean version is at first sight hard to understand, for Euripides is generally supposed to be much more modern, romantic, and emotional. But a very brief examination of the *Electra* of Euripides will show that here for once Euripides has provided fewer opportunities for realistic treatment. The whole episode of Electra's relations with "Autourgos" and his chivalrous treatment of her is singularly ill adapted for the pathological development in which a writer of

Hofmannsthal's stamp excels.   Then there is the
case of Pylades, whose amiable devotion, immortalised in the strains of Gluck, would be
ludicrously out of place in the Royal slaughter-
house of Mycenae.   Euripides not only gave him
a part, but designated him as Electra's bridegroom.
This deplorably tame " happy ending " is endorsed
by the judicial words of the great Lemprière :
" Some have imagined that Aegisthus had married
her to a man of obscure birth, but the more
probable account is that, as a proof of his gratitude
and affection, Orestes gave her in marriage to his
friend Pylades."   Pylades is a *persona muta* in
Sophocles, and he is very properly eliminated
altogether from the cast of Hofmannsthal's play.
There is no room for chivalry, or magnanimity,
or happy endings here.   Electra has been trodden
into the dirt, and dirt she has become.   Her
attitude in the opening scene is expressly compared
to that of a wild cat.   She spits at the maid-
servants, who replace the Chorus, and spends her
time, when she is not " howling " for her father,
in crawling " where carrion stench is worst " and
digging in search of " an ancient carcase."   (We
quote from the careful English version of Mr.
Alfred Kalisch, which, if it errs at all, errs on the
side of diluting the crudities of the German.)
And Electra is not merely the incarnation of hate,

but she is consumed body and soul by haemato-
mania, with which it is her desire to inoculate
her craven sister Chrysothemis. The dialogues
between the two sisters have no dignity, but in
their abandonment suggest the mutual " barging "
of a pair of epileptic fishwives. The degradation
of Clytemnestra reaches an even lower depth of
loathsomeness. She has a " sallow bloated face
. . . the lids of her eyes," swollen with disease,
" are larger than is natural, and it seems to cost
her an unspeakable effort to keep them from falling." Her " whole body is tainted," and her
whole life is spent in the ceaseless torture of
victims, of which we are given a typical specimen
in the procession which rushes and staggers past
with stifled cries, hissing whips, and the struggling
of fallen men and beasts. In this series of scenes
from the shambles we are spared the sight of
Clytemnestra's death agonies, but not the hideous
sound of her dying shrieks. We are allowed, however, to see Aegisthus dragged away to his death
and struggling frantically at a window.. Electra
remains outside, and when the deed is done
celebrates her triumph in a " nameless dance."
As a matter of fact, it is not nameless at all. It is
a long sequence of those reptilian contortions and
convulsions extremely popular at the modern
music-halls under the title of Apache dance,

Vampire dance, or some such lurid designation. It is also a dance of death, for at the climax of her uncontrolled exultation Electra drops dead, and Chrysothemis is left battering the door of the palace and crying out for Orestes.

There is of course a ready-made defence of this bestialising of the εὐκολία of Sophocles. The Greek classic drama, it will be urged, so far from being a true representation of life, was a highly artificial, conventional, and restrained version of the old legends of Greece, and with fearless and splendid sincerity—those are the invariable epithets by which these exploits are dignified—the modern dramatist abandons the, principle of selection, and gives us the real primitive passions of humanity in all their magnificent and palpitating actuality. And it will no doubt be further urged that Wagner put his own gloss· on the *Nibelungenlied*. These arguments open up a wide field of discussion ; it may suffice for the moment to say that the fearless-return-to-Nature view will not work very smoothly in face of the difficulties presented by Hofmannsthal's conception of Clytemnestra. Compared with Lady Macbeth, she is a type of the most sophisticated decadence. Again, there is a considerable difference between recasting a rough-hewn legend and barbarising a consummate classic.

Beethoven may or may not have been a great dramatic composer, but it is a curious fact that he, with all his rebellion against forms, was repelled from this field of composition by the difficulty of finding a congenial theme. Beethoven was not squeamish, but he strongly disapproved of the levity of Mozart's libretti. His solitary venture into the domain of lyric drama takes the form of a eulogy of conjugal devotion and womanly tenderness. Richard Strauss, unfettered by such old-fashioned prejudices, has experienced no difficulty in the choice of themes for operatic treatment, and in his latest work he has at any rate clothed Hofmannsthal's drama in a singularly appropriate musical garb. Causeless suffering, as Aristotle pointed out—and, we may add, causeless degradation—is not fear-inspiring or piteous, but simply odious. And Strauss brings to bear an unrivalled equipment on the delineation of whatsoever things are sinister, uncomfortable, *macabre*. Schumann happily said that the instruments in Schubert's Symphony in C Major were like human voices. In *Elektra* the entrails of the orchestra are laid bare, and the instruments suggest the cries of sick or wounded animals or *obscenae volucres*. This is quite in keeping with the element of the θηριῶδες which pervades the play, and it also serves another useful purpose. If you compose a long stretch of exceedingly complicated and ugly music, and then suddenly strike the chord of C, the effect produced is one of ineffable relief and heavenly beauty. This method—the oasis method, as it has been called—has already been assiduously cultivated by Strauss, and he reverts to it once more with undiminished success in *Elektra*. By far the most impressive effects are attained by these occasional lapses from contorted and highly organised discord into straightforward, genial, and, if the truth be told, commonplace melody. For the quality of the later Straussian melody, when stripped of all its magnificent orchestral upholstery, is often quite Early Victorian in its bland banality. The fact that it is so extravagantly extolled by his admirers is only a proof of this. If you proscribe melody as a rule, an extra charm attaches to your occasional deviations into it. This frugal use of his genial moments is certainly one of the cleverest things about Strauss. If he were to indulge his amiable mood con-tinuously, he might run the risk of being classed with his Viennese namesake. But the very rarity of these excursions into the normal adds to their grace. Of themes in the technical sense there are of course no lack, but apart from the dexterity and ingenuity shown in manipulating and juggling with them, apart too from the *outré* choice of subjects with which they are associated, they are neither distinguished nor important. It is impossible to avoid a comparison between the intrinsic nobility or beauty of the motives of Wagner and those coined by Strauss ; at the same time it is difficult to avoid noticing how much the passion of *Tristan* has coloured the turbid and intermittent stream of Strauss's inspiration. Energy and violence are here, and the repulsive aspects of the new version of the *Electra* have their native ugliness intensified by the music. It is a strenuous, stimulating, and exciting entertainment, and as a whole provides as good a substitute as modern civilisation can offer to fashionable audiences for the delights of the ancient amphitheatre or the modern bull-ring.

The efficiency of the performances at Covent Garden, whether one regards the mounting, stage management, and scenery on the one hand, or the skill, endurance, and energy of the singers, players, and conductor on the other, has been quite wonderful. *Elektra* has been the event of the season so far—*grande et conspicuum nostro quoque tempore monstrum.* But there must be not a few who regard with feelings akin to dismay the squandering of this prodigious amount of talent and energy on a work which is saturated with the spirit of decadence, and from which the authentic tragic temper is entirely eliminated. *Elektra* is a sickening disappointment to those who have hoped against hope that Strauss would still extricate his great talent from that slough of calculated eccentricity in which it has been too long submerged.

March 12, 1910.

III

SALOME

For the mainspring of the drama of *Salome*, which is virtually identical with the libretto of Strauss's music drama, there is no authority whatever either in the New Testament or in the pages of Josephus. But it has not even the merit of originality. It is simply a tertiary deposit—a perverted expansion of the folk-legend which Heine condensed into the memorable ballad given in chap. 19 of *Atta Troll.* According to the legend, Herodias—not Salome, who could have been little more than a child at the time of the death of John the Baptist—was condemned to eternal penance for her guilt in procuring his death, and roamed everlastingly over the face of the earth, carrying the head of the man whom she had loved. Heine's poem is a masterpiece of laconic simplicity. There is something *macabre* in the situation, but it is handled with a classic restraint, a mordant brevity, which purge the story of its sensual taint.   It was reserved for a modern writer, oblivious of the maxim of Tacitus, *puniri debent scelera, abscondi flagitia*, to reconstruct the legend in such a way as to aggravate its monstrosity by insisting on the ferocity and animalism of the central figure. Indeed, " whatsoever things are impure, whatsoever things are hateful, whatsoever things are of evil report, if there be any vice, and if there be any infamy,"—all these things are to be found in the character of Salome as portrayed in the drama which, we gather, has achieved considerable success in Germany.   Those who have noticed the corrupt Neo-Byzantinism of a section of German art, or who have been shocked by the ferocious and sinister humour of *Simplicissimus*, will not be surprised, but it would be unfair to judge of Germany as a whole by this cult of the θηριῶδες in art and letters.   It is the corruption of the best that is the worst, and the corruption cannot have gone very far in an age which gives us *Hänsel und Gretel*.   Still, it is of evil augury that the most conspicuous living German musician should choose for his guide, on the occasion of his first and only incursion into the domain of Biblical narrative, a writer

> cui fervens
> Aestuat occultis animus semperque tacendis.

Beethoven's initial difficulty in writing an opera was to find a sufficiently noble theme. As it has been well said of him,

the connection between the music and the words and dramatic situation was so close in his mind that he could not bring himself to write music to anything ignoble. . . . His gift was too sacred to be desecrated. . . . In this he is the greatest type of high and unyielding honour ; for the idea of degrading and cheapening his precious art seems to have been so entirely impossible to him that he probably never allowed himself even to consider it for a moment. In this respect German musicians have always been patterns to the world.

These words, written by a distinguished British musician more than twenty years ago, remain true of Beethoven, but not of German composers. The difficulty with Strauss seems to be to find something sufficiently ignoble, and if the record of history or literature does not provide him with something adequately degraded, it has to be decorated, or perverted to suit his requirements. Beethoven, who ultimately fixed upon a story of pure and unconquerable womanly devotion for his subject, held a view of the function of opera which corresponds exactly with that of Dr. John Brown : —" Great works of art elevate public feeling. They tend, like all productions of high and pure genius, to the glory of God and the good of

mankind : they are a part of the common wealth."
Strauss, on the other hand, has chosen in *Salome* a
heroine whose sole claim to distinction is the
eminence of her infamy, the persistence with
which she commits the crime of *lèse-majesté*
against womanliness. Salome, in the words of
one of the most thorough-going admirers [1] of the
libretto and the music, is " fundamentally sensual."
But, according to the same authority, " such
questions do not concern us in regarding a *work
of art*. What matters is the artistic, the creative
representation of the whole, and it is only when
we approach the work without moral ' ifs ' and
' buts ' that it can unfold its beauty." Again,
" the essence of opera, if rightly conceived, is an
elevated, intensified feeling and acting of uncommon persons, which proceeds from the depths
of the soul and surpasses the ordinary measure."
Inability to appreciate the artistic beauty of a
character which has scaled the topmost pinnacle
of infamy is the sign of a defective intelligence.
If we contemplate her aright, Salome does not
lack " sympathetic and purely human traits,"—
this of a woman who is so absorbed in her guilty
passion that when her neglected lover stabs himself in her presence, she pays no more attention

---

[1] *Salome*.   Words and Music Explained by Alfred Schattmann.   London :
Breitkopf and Härtel.   [6d.]

to his bleeding corpse than if he had never existed. Indeed, when, in addition to the assemblage of infra-human qualities which she displays, we are bidden to admire her "sympathy," the effect is overwhelming, and, as Macaulay said of Barère when his biographer claimed him as a good Christian, " we sink under the contemplation of such exquisite and manifold perfection." The fact is that these musical revolutionaries, like the Corcyraeans of old, no longer use familiar words in their old acceptations. They speak of " elevation " where the plain person only sees sensuality ; "sympathy" becomes a convenient euphemism for desire ; " humanity " connotes only the attributes of the *bête humaine*, not the fullest and most harmonious culture of all the human faculties and powers ; and the epithet " uncommon" lends distinction to the possession of depraved or perverted instincts. The eccentricities of official eulogists must of course be discounted to a certain extent, and it is possible to be merely amused when Herr Alfred Schattmann naïvely remarks that " nobody ' thinks of Wagner ' when hearing the music of *Salome*," or when he, or rather his translator, observes, *à propos* of Strauss's courage in combining unrelated keys, " in this respect *Salome* is unique and of unprecedented geniality." But what are we to say of the taste of a composer

who apparently sanctions the issue by his
publishers of picture postcards showing the
headless figure of a man bearing on a dish the
head of Richard Strauss, as it would appear in
death, with gouts of blood, disguised as musical
notes, dropping from the dish and spirting from
the neck ? The likeness is unmistakable, and
the name Richard Strauss is printed at the
foot. Truly the wit of the post-Wagnerians is
" unique and of unprecedented geniality."

The " correct " and reverential attitude which
one ought to assume before Strauss's opera is
clearly indicated by the faithful Schattmann.
" His work takes such gigantic forms, and its
effect is nevertheless so extraordinary, that we can
stand before this phenomenon only with admiration and amazement. Let us rejoice in the opera
Salome, an opera so boldly conceived and possessing
innumerable passages of surpassing beauty, a work
which by reason of its grandeur, beauty, and
aesthetic meaning appears indeed to be destined
to live as a lasting work of art." Herr Schattmann
does not " stand " at all. He approaches the
work of Wilde and Strauss on all fours. Admiration, however, cannot be commandeered in this
way, and, speaking from the point of view of
those whose limited intelligence prevents them
from appreciating the " fascination of corruption "

presented by the book, the transcendental gymnastics of this redoubtable musical athlete leave us
cold.   The opera has, however, one great negative
merit—it only lasts an hour and a half.   Here is
no *himmlische Länge*, but rather a brevity which,
in view of the heroine's character, may correctly
be styled infernal.   But it would be most unjust
to Strauss to convey the impression that his music
in any way reinforces the sensuality of the text.
Herr Schattmann boldly declares that "nobody
thinks of Wagner when hearing *Salome*."   With
all respect, we venture to differ.   There must
have been not one but several persons present
during the recent representations of *Salome* who
felt that if the opera had been set to music as
full-blooded and passionate as Wagner set to the
story of *Tristan und Isolde*, it would have blown
the roof off Covent Garden, and rendered it
impossible for anybody to sit out the performance.
By mere virtue of contrast with the extravagantly
restless musical characterisation of Salome, the
phrases assigned to the Prophet have a certain
dignity and breadth, much in the same way that
the scale of C major sounds beautiful after a
surfeit of Debussy ; but the "motives" throughout, apart from their millinery, are extremely
insignificant.   The claims, so passionately advanced by his admirers, on behalf of Strauss's

momentous psychological methods are irreconcilable with continuous inspiration. What is wrong with Strauss is that he has a cold heart and an emotional head. He presents the strange, if not unique, spectacle of a composer who is capable of being hysterical with his intellect. This may enrapture the limited public which delights in the later novels of Mr. Henry James, but it will never begin to satisfy the great majority who still, as in the days of the author of *The Spleen*, can only be "tarantulated by a tune." Hardly any concession, again, is made in respect of local colour, the only obvious use of Oriental idiom being in the much-talked-of "Dance of the Seven Veils," the music of which would do almost equally well for seven phylacteries. The score is much more scrappy and less impressive than that of *Elektra*—which has its dazzling moments—and more is left to the acting to stall off tedium. Thus the balance of the arts is not preserved, and for all Strauss's consummate skill as an orchestral prestidigitateur, his score seldom rises above the level of an ingenious rather than an appropriate commentary. It is a curious fact that where he attempts realism or imitation he is more often outrageous than striking. The scene of the five Jewish doctors is a *reductio ad absurdum* of ineffectual cleverness. When Herod declares that

he will not deliver up the Prophet, for he is
a man that has beheld God, the Jews raise a
great dispute. In the words of the inimitable
Schattmann, "it is illustrated in a delightfully
drastic movement full of polyphonous audacity.
Five Jews, each drawn in characteristic lines,
shout confusedly. Each attempts to outdo the
other by sustaining high notes. This movement
is built up with unmitigated realism by means
of intentional cacophonics produced by the wild
medley, a use of contrapuntal dramatic possibilities
that has not its equal." To put it crudely, the
transcendental genius of Strauss is exhausted in
producing an effect quite inferior to the artless
shrieks of five cockatoos. In other passages he
makes the instruments snarl like sick or wounded
wild beasts, but there is nearly always an element
of freakishness in his treatment of the horrible.
Indeed, if we may again quote Macaulay on
Barère, "there is something peculiarly tickling
and exhilarating to his mind in the grotesque
combination of the frivolous and the terrible."
There are moments when one is sorely tempted
to fall back on the theory of *nomen omen*, and
account for the Jekyll-Hyde dualism of Strauss
by the strange mischance which linked his Christian
name with the composer of *Parsifal* and his
surname with the Viennese *Walzerkönig*.

The musical world owes so much to the spirited, if somewhat undiscriminating, enterprise of Mr. Thomas Beecham that we regret to be unable to see anything heroic in his persistence in securing a hearing for *Salome* in London. The "booming" of the opera has been tremendous—quite equal to that of one of Mr. Hall Caine's plays—but this sort of booming, like the bombination of the Chimaera in Erasmus's famous problem, generally ends in the void. It may be that the wish is father to the thought, but we do not think that the opera-going public will take a permanent pleasure in seeing the resources of a great musical organisation lavished on the glorification of erotomania. But Mr. Beecham has undoubtedly succeeded in making the Censorship ridiculous. The modifications insisted on by the Lord Chamberlain, with their puerile and ostrich-like evasions, have struck a heavy blow at this office. Had the Censor refused to sanction the opera, he would, we believe, have met with general support. Had it been possible to allow the unexpurgated version to be performed, we believe that public opinion would have confirmed the verdict of New York and Chicago. The compromise arrived at in the case of *Salome*, concerning which it is open to doubt whether it would have been permitted for the benefit of any

British composer or playwright, while [slightly abating the bestiality of the closing scenes, only serves to show that the Censor has neither courage nor consistency. The amount of talent expended on the production has been immense. Mr. Beecham has again proved himself a conductor of uncommon accomplishment. As for Mme. Ackté, her rendering is too steeped in modernity to suggest a barbaric or elemental passion, but it is so vivid as to distract attention from the music, though she sings the part with amazing skill. Mr. Whitehill sang finely as the Prophet, but there was no hint of the zealot in his acting. He bore himself with a somewhat wooden dignity ; though allowance must be made for the hampering effect of a costume which, as a writer in the *Westminster Gazette* truly observed, suggested a sort of prehistoric evening-dress. The Herod of Herr Kraus was strangely undistinguished and undignified. But his spasmodic gestures and utterance may have been due to a conscientious desire to illustrate the peculiarity on which Herr Schattmann insists, that he is "a neurasthenic person."

December 24, 1910.

IV

PELLÉAS ET MÉLISANDE

WHATEVER may be said in disparagement of the
Opera Syndicate, they have certainly deserved
well of the musical public by their production of
Pelléas et Mélisande, one of the most vehemently
canvassed operas of our time, and, like all French
music of any account, most severely criticised in
France itself. But apart from being a focus of
controversy, Debussy challenges attention on a
variety of grounds. To begin with, though
extremely modern and unconventional, he has
arrived at his present stage of development after
a thorough and sympathetic study of the classics,
towards whom, moreover, he feels no hostility.
Again, though it would be absurd to say that he
had learned nothing from Wagner, his indebtedness to that master is less manifest than in the
case of most of his contemporaries. On the
other hand, his divergence from the methods of

Richard Strauss is even more marked. Among modern composers of note Debussy is conspicuous for his frugal use of the orchestra, for his abstinence from excessive sonority and violent dynamic contrasts. He does not find it necessary to reinforce the band, but gets his best effects from the employment of its normal resources. And the undeniable charm which he often exerts is not the result of resort to the oasis principle—*i.e.* the alternation of long stretches of deliberate ugliness with little scraps of commonplace melody, which sound lovely, just as ditch-water might taste delicious to a man perishing of thirst—it is intrinsic and inherent in his music.

It was a happy choice, certainly, that led Debussy, with his delicate bizarre talent, to turn *Pelléas et Mélisande* into an opera. He is by temperament attuned to the crepuscular atmosphere, the dreamy mysticism of Maeterlinck's play. Its vague mediaevalism, so far removed from "actuality," must have appealed to him with singular force. For here there is no suggestion of any epoch or reign. As in the *Ring*, we have to deal with people who only possess one name apiece; but while Wagner shows his *dramatis personae* at meals, slaking their thirst with deep draughts, one cannot possibly imagine the characters in *Pelléas et*

Mélisande eating or drinking. The impressiveness of the play largely depends on omissions. In many ways it is the very antithesis of realism. It would be hard to find any historic justification in the records of the early Middle Ages for the psychology of the characters concerned. Jealousy in those days was a plant of swift growth, and Golaud's long-drawn methods are too sophisticated for a primitive society. But such tests are inapplicable to a drama of so ethereal a texture. The question for us to decide is how far Debussy's music enhances the magic of the play and emphasises its poetic content. There can, we think, be little doubt as to how that question must be answered. There is much in the drama that reminds one of a dream, and the music has a curious narcotic flavour that assists this hypnotic influence. The action, phantasmal in itself, is rendered even more so by being enveloped in an impalpable mist of sound, so vague that the vast majority of listeners will not find the slightest vestige of anything that they can carry away. Even an intelligent musician will not glean much in the way of positive impression beyond the recurrence of a peculiar scale. Of melody or definite phrases—we do not say in the manner of Mozart, but such as we are familiar with in the works of Wagner—there is hardly a trace.

And this applies not only to the orchestra, but also to the voice parts, which are for the most part chanted or intoned, the variations in pitch being probably based on the inflections of the voice in actual speech. The "leading motive" system is discarded altogether. It is typical of Debussy that, for all his disregard of convention and tradition, there is a good deal of method in his madness. You cannot call music meaningless which is invariably appropriate, or chaotic which is so curiously reserved and consistently unobtrusive. Even his eccentricities are so strictly controlled that one would probably cease after a very few hearings to be troubled by them. As a matter of fact, quite long passages occur which even at a first hearing are genial and grateful to the ear, while the character of the score throughout is wonderfully homogeneous. On its unassertiveness we have already commented. Indeed, one could well imagine an unmusical spectator intently following the course of the play without being in the least distracted by the music. This is perhaps negative praise, if not approximating to musical disparagement. But, speaking for ourselves, we should be inclined to say that, although the musical setting does not reinforce the emotional poignancy of the play, or emphasise the sufferings of the unhappy lovers *quos durus amor crudeli tabe peredit,*

it certainly does add to its phantasmal glamour. It is hard to imagine that the opera will ever be widely popular, nor can we profess to desire such popularity. Negatively we ought to be grateful to Debussy for his delicacy and restraint. But we do not want music to be consistently of subnormal temperature any more than we want it to be consistently inflammatory and over-stimulating, and the elimination of all pronounced rhythm, sustained melody, and clear-cut outlines gives the music of Debussy an invertebrate and emasculate character. It has been fancifully compared to a mixture of olives and caramels, but a better comparison is to some strange and insinuating opiate. It soothes, but it lowers the vitality of the hearer. The atmosphere of Debussy's opera is not that of high noon, but the spectral twilight of sombre autumnal glades.

There was very little to criticise in the production, which was extraordinarily good all round. The scenery, apart from some unnatural greens and pinks and a pond that looked like a pincushion, was thoroughly appropriate, and the lighting was excellently managed. The artist who took the part of Golaud was inclined to exaggerate his suspiciousness and roughness ; otherwise the cast was of rare excellence, and

the enunciation of the text a model of distinct-
ness. A hundred years ago so well equipped
a critic as Lord Mount Edgcumbe—" the Old
Amateur"—had hardly a good word for French
operatic singers. Their superiority at the present
day over all comers in works which call for
elegance, distinction, and purity of diction is once
more incontestably shown in the representations
of Debussy's opera.

June 12, 1909.

V

ELGAR'S FIRST SYMPHONY

A NUMBER of circumstances combined to lend
peculiar significance and interest to the production
of Sir Edward Elgar's symphony. To begin with,
there was Sir Edward Elgar's popularity and
prestige, attested not only by the ample recognition of his fellow-countrymen, but by the
esteem in which he is held by foreign critics,
composers, and conductors. Again, though he
has attained distinction in many of the higher
walks of composition, this was his first essay in
what is generally regarded to be the most exalted
and exacting of all. But apart from the expecta-
tion naturally aroused by the character of the
work, the circumstances of its production were
exceptional, if not unique. It was to be performed by the most famous of living conductors,
to whom it had been dedicated, and the full
score was already engraved in a cheap miniature

edition before its production, so that intelligent amateurs had the privilege of following the performance, not merely with an analytical programme, but with the complete record, so far as musical notation goes, of the composer's intentions. Produced for the first time at the Hallé Concerts in Manchester by Dr. Richter on December 3rd, 1908, it was repeated, under the same conductor, by the London Symphony Orchestra on December 7th and December 19th, and by the Queen's Hall Orchestra, the composer conducting, on January 1st. A further performance has also been arranged for January 7th. Thus the new symphony will have been given five times in the space of five weeks, and each time by a first-rate orchestra. Never in all the annals of modern music has a composer enjoyed such splendid opportunities for familiarising the public with a work of this description in his lifetime— for the great "boom" in Tchaikovsky's *Symphonie Pathétique* began after his death—and Sir Edward Elgar is to be heartily congratulated on his good fortune. He is to be congratulated, also, on the enthusiasm with which his work was received. We all know the saying that what Lancashire thinks to-day, England thinks to-morrow. But in this case England, or at

D

any rate London, endorsed the verdict of Lancashire with even greater applause. "From whatever point of view we look at it," writes the
Manchester Guardian of December 8th, "Manchester will be glad to learn that it has preserved
its reputation for coolly critical judgment, for
whereas on Thursday night Sir Edward Elgar
was recalled three times, he had to appear seven
times last night—once after the first movement,
twice after the slow movement, and four times
at the close." The summoning of a composer
to the platform after the first movement of
a new symphony, so far as we know, constitutes a musical "record"—certainly for this
country.

The welcome accorded the new work has not
been confined to demonstrations of approval in
the concert-room—demonstrations in which the
conductor and orchestra cordially joined, and of
the sincerity of which there can be no doubt. It
has been no less strikingly manifested, with a few
exceptions, in the Press. The symphony has
been acclaimed in certain quarters as the greatest
achievement in English music. The musical
critic of the *Manchester Guardian* declares that
the composer has "refertilised the symphonic
form by infusing into it the best ideas that
could be gathered from the practice of the writers

of symphonic poems," and, speaking of the introduction to the last movement, observes : " If there is such divine consolation to be found, then we may go through whatever there is to fear without trembling." Instances of eulogy equally unreserved might be multiplied from Press notices or from the analytical programme, the author of which, discarding the more judicious conception of his function, assumes the immortality of the work as beyond question, and describes it as

> a music, deep as love or life,
> That spread into a placid lake of sound,
> And took the infinite into its breast,
> With Earth and Heaven, in an embrace at rest.

A minority of the critics, on the other hand, have expressed disappointment with the symphony, and treated it with a certain asperity. Whichever may be the true view, the vehemence of partisanship excited by music is an interesting evidence of the hold which the youngest of the arts takes upon the modern world. We do not find literary likes and dislikes expressed with such freedom nowadays. People write and talk of Strauss as if he were either a divinity or a criminal. · As a modern novelist puts it, " possibly rant is a sign of vitality " ; and again, " the kingdom of music is not of this world : it will accept those whom breeding and intellect and culture have alike rejected,"—Dvorák, for instance.

After hearing the symphony twice under Dr. Richter, we regret that we cannot share the view of those who pronounce it a great masterpiece or an epoch-making achievement, though it is beyond doubt a work of high and serious purpose, marked by unfailing command of orchestral resource. Occupying longer in performance than Schubert's great Symphony in C, its length is not a *himmlische Länge*—there is too much deliberate strenuousness, and even harshness, about it for that—nor is it devoid of *longueurs*. In combining the essential structural features of the symphony with the fundamental principle of the symphonic poem— resort to the device of thematic metamorphosis— Sir Edward Elgar has, according to one critic, settled "all the quarrels of Brahms and Liszt." Thus not only is there a " motto " theme which reappears throughout the entire work, but the first subject of the second movement—a theme for the most part in racing semi-quavers, and accurately described by the analyst as marked by " bustling energy "—reappears almost note for note as the principal subject of the slow move- ment *Adagio cantabile*. In this *tempo* it has undoubted melodic charm, and with the aid of rich and vivid instrumentation forms the chief beauty of the symphony. But when given at racing speed, its melodic grace vanishes in a sort of steeplechase for the violins. Such an economy of material is not easily reconcilable with the fervour of inspiration, and gives a handle to those cynical critics who allege that the device of thematic metamorphosis is merely an ingenious trick to conceal a dearth of ideas.

The second criticism that occurs to us in dealing with the symphony is concerned with the themes themselves. No musical composition, certainly no symphony, can be pronounced great which is not based on the bedrock of noble melody. Just as the grand style in literature depends on verbs and nouns rather than epithets, so melody forms the bones and sinews of the grand style in music. If this canon be accepted, we cannot accord the title of greatness to the new symphony. The chief or " motto " theme, which runs through the entire work, is marked *nobilmente e semplice* ; but its character—so, at least, it appears to us—is sentimental rather than noble, and it owes its effect more to harmonisation and presentation, to orchestral trappings and dynamic contrasts, than to its intrinsic majesty or beauty. The same remark applies to most of the other themes, though an exception may be made in favour of the fresh and graceful melody of the

Trio in the second movement. The ingenuity shown in development and "working out" is unquestioned ; but it borders at times on feverishness. The human ear is only capable of absorbing a certain volume of sound at a single hearing, and the continuous sonority of this symphony, which eschews those pauses and silences which furnish some of the most eloquent and affecting moments in the works of Beethoven and Schubert, begets a sense of physical fatigue. Of colour and atmosphere, ornament and embroidery, Sir Edward Elgar makes a use that, without being ever tawdry, is at least lavish. To revert to a former parallel, he is stronger in his epithets than in his nouns and verbs. And thus it comes about that the work is not likely to satisfy what is perhaps the truest and most exacting test of all. It will not endure the ordeal of reduction, in the way in which a great masterpiece of painting in the imperfect form of an engraving or a photograph will convey a distinct impression of its beauties to those who have never seen the original. It may be objected that this test will rule out a great deal of modern music, and so it undoubtedly will. But it certainly can be applied with satisfactory results to all the most abiding work of the last sixty years—to the *Meistersinger* as well as to *Carmen*, to the symphonies of Brahms and Dvorák,

to *Hänsel und Gretel*, *Parsifal*, and the *Ring* itself.
It is the melody that counts in the last resort,
melody which remains in the mind apart from all
suitable or gorgeous embroidery, and the memory
of which can be refreshed by the simplest pianoforte arrangement.

For all these reasons, while heartily admitting
the high aims and the immense skill shown by
Sir Edward Elgar in his new symphony, we
cannot recognise in it an advance in essentials on
the high standard reached by him in *The Dream of
Gerontius*, the *Cockaigne* overture, and above all
the masterly " Enigma " Variations. Sir Edward
Elgar was once described as a musical Melchisedek,
in that his artistic lineage was unknown ; but
although there is much that is distinctively
Elgarish in the symphony, its individuality is
less strongly marked than in the works we have
mentioned. The treatment of the basses reminds
one of Tchaikovsky, and the influence of Berlioz
and of Wagner may be occasionally traced. We
are glad to note that the composer has refrained
from committing himself to a programme, and it
is worthy of remark that, in spite of the great
complexity of the work, there are comparatively
long passages in which he confines himself within
the limits of the diatonic scale. The test of time
alone can determine whether the symphony is

made of the stuff that endures or not. In demurring to the view that he has permanently enriched the literature of the orchestra by his latest composition we are only expressing an individual opinion, and have no desire to belittle his earlier achievements or imply any doubt of his capacity to equal or surpass them in the future.

January 2, 1909.

VI

ALFRED RODEWALD

The past week has been marked by two events of personal interest in the musical world—the tardy official recognition of August Manns's fifty years' work at the Crystal Palace, and the death of Alfred Rodewald, the founder and conductor of the Liverpool Orchestral Society. Of the splendid services rendered by Sir August Manns as a musical educator we have already spoken (*Spectator*, November 16th, 1901), on the occasion of the reorganisation of the Crystal Palace Saturday Concerts over which he had so long and brilliantly presided. Sir August Manns, *iam rude donatus*, has since that date withdrawn from the active pursuit of his profession, carrying with him into his retirement the good wishes and gratitude of all musicians and music-lovers. But while the occasion for a reference to him at this moment is a matter for general rejoicing, it is far otherwise

in the case of Mr. Rodewald, who has been struck
down in the prime of life and vigour, to the deep
and abiding regret of all who prized him as a
friend or admired the rare union of gifts which
lent him a position almost unique in the musical
world.   The sphere of his activities lay in
Liverpool, and though he was well known to the
leading members of the musical profession all over
the country, his very name is probably unknown
to the great majority of our musical readers.   It
is to remedy an ignorance inevitable in the
circumstances, and to give some faint sketch of
what he was and what he did, that the following
lines are written.

Alfred Rodewald, who was born in 1861, was,
as his name indicates, of German extraction ; but
he was born and bred in England, educated at an
English public school, and in manners, speech,
and sentiments was a thoroughgoing Britisher of
the most robust and genial type, the soul of good-
fellowship, and a striking figure in any company
by reason of his commanding stature, his energetic
gestures, and his resonant voice.   He had learned
to play the piano and begun to study the violin
before he went to Charterhouse, but he never
received a professional musical training, and was
conspicuously free from the airs and graces, the
affectations and mannerisms, so often observable

in executants. It was thoroughly in keeping with his robust and impressive personality that the instrument of his choice should have been the double-bass, which he learned at school, and on which he attained a considerable proficiency, playing from time to time in the orchestra at the Niederrheinische Festival, and more than once coming all the way from Liverpool to Charterhouse to assist in performances of oratorios. Soon after leaving school he settled in business in Liverpool, where he was well known and highly respected in the commercial world, not merely as the head of a firm of cotton merchants, but as an intelligent student of economics and currency questions. Though fond of open-air pastimes, and with a thoroughly British love of games, he associated himself as early as 1884 with the movement initiated by Mgr. Nugent, which aimed at the establishment of free concerts of instrumental music in Liverpool as a counter-attraction to the public-house. The orchestra was composed at the outset of some five-and-twenty amateurs, but under Rodewald's inspiring direction—he became conductor in the season 1886-87—the numbers ultimately increased to about seventy, and when the People's Orchestral Society Concerts were discontinued his forces were re-embodied as the Liverpool Orchestral Society, of which he remained the conductor till the day of his death. Latterly the professionals, largely recruited from the famous Hallé band at Manchester, were in the majority of at least two-thirds, and the standard of excellence was so high that the statement of the *Liverpool Daily Post* may be readily accepted that the band was beyond question the most efficient orchestra in this country to which amateurs were admitted. Over this organisation Rodewald held sway with a mixture of enthusiasm, skill, and discrimination which won the admiration of all who had the good fortune to attend its performances. The programmes included the most intricate and elaborate examples of modern symphonic music, but they were chosen with admirable catholicity of taste. In this respect Rodewald was emphatically *nullius addictus iurare in verba magistri*, whether native or foreign. It would have been hard to say whether he admired Wagner more than Brahms, Dvorák than Humperdinck, Richard Strauss than Tchaikovsky. And it was just the same with the works of native composers, with most of whom he was on terms of close personal friendship. The present writer had the good fortune to hear him conduct an admirable performance of the " Enigma " Variations of Dr. Elgar (who dedicated to Rodewald another of his works), and will not easily forget the enthusiasm with which Rodewald spoke of Hubert Parry's "Job" after a performance at Gloucester. And while Parry's and Stanford's symphonies figured in his programmes, he did not neglect the claims of the younger men. His *camaraderie* was agreeably shown by the fact that he played the double-bass in another orchestra conducted by his own first violin, while his keen interest in orchestral music did not tend to any narrowness of outlook. He hardly ever missed attending the chief festivals, was a fervent lover of the great choral masterpieces, especially those of Bach, had a great sympathy with Irish folk-music, and secured the services of the best singers to lend vocal relief to his programmes. But though his aims were high, he hugely enjoyed a joke, even at his own expense, as when a musical friend, while staying under his roof, hired a piano-organ to serenade his host with the inter-mezzo from *Cavalleria Rusticana*, a piece that Rodewald held in peculiar abhorrence.

Music was undoubtedly the ruling passion of his life, but he had many resources and interests—it may be mentioned incidentally that he acted as secretary to the Bimetallic League in Liverpool—and was a great reader of German as well as English philosophy and *belles-lettres*. He was thus entirely free from the "shoppiness" notice-

able in musicians who are entirely absorbed in
their art, and yet, in spite of this many-sidedness,
he attained by sheer force of merit—for he never
thrust himself forward, and was singularly free
from anything approaching conceit or self-satis-
faction—a position which can best be described
by saying that he was perhaps the only British
amateur, certainly the only amateur conductor,
with whom the leading members of the profession
associated as one of themselves. For Dr. Richter
he had the deepest affection, and the closeness of
their friendship may be measured by the fact that
the great conductor has expressed his desire to
direct a special memorial concert to be given by
the Liverpool Orchestral Society on December
5th. Rodewald's popularity with his band was
immense, and his ability as a trainer is sufficiently
shown by the fact that many players who entered
his band as amateurs ultimately won their way to
distinction as professionals. Moreover, being in
easy circumstances and of a generous disposition,
he contributed freely towards securing the all-
round efficiency which was the distinguishing
mark of the concerts of his Society, at which
many promising executants obtained engagements
as soloists which led to their recognition elsewhere.
It is only since his death that it has become
known how often needy or struggling musicians

were assisted by his unobtrusive and tactful liberality.

The career of Alfred Rodewald cannot be erected as a precedent to guide those who are distracted by the rival claims of art and affairs. His case was exceptional, for he united rare gifts of talent and temperament with material advantages which rendered it unnecessary for him to look to art as a means of livelihood. But his case raises the interesting question whether he would have achieved a more enduring work if he had abandoned commerce and devoted himself entirely to art. The temptation must at any time in the last ten years have been strong, and it is stated on good authority that he was encouraged by some of the most distinguished members of the musical profession to take the step. For ourselves, we are inclined to think that his services to art were not impaired, and that his life was probably rendered happier by his resolve to retain the amateur status. The fact that he was so constituted as to be able to lead a life in two compartments, so to speak, and to attain efficiency in both, furnishes perhaps the true answer to the question. Not all people are so constituted ; the call of art in many cases is too peremptory ; the rival pursuits overlap and paralyse each other. But there are cases—and Rodewald was a noticeable instance—in which the routine of a fixed business occupation acts as a steadying alternative to the cultivation of the artistic and emotional instincts. He turned to his music with the ardour of a schoolboy leaving the schoolroom for the playground — an ardour which never flagged, as it might perhaps have done if he had made art the sole aim and object of his existence. Matthew Arnold might have been a better poet if he had not been obliged to make his living as a school-inspector, though the point admits of dispute. But we have little doubt that Alfred Rodewald exerted a wider and more stimulating influence, and did more to promote good-fellowship between musicians and music - lovers, by leading the strenuous and honourable dual existence so prematurely closed on Monday.

November 14, 1903.

VII

ANTONIN DVORÁK

It was a favourite theory of the late Sir George
Grove that the days of the uncultured composer
ended with the eighteenth century. From Weber
onward, as he was fond of pointing out, they were
all men of general education, extending in the case
of Mendelssohn to an Admirable Crichton-like
versatility. And Grove in his periodical addresses
to the pupils at the Royal College always
encouraged them to widen their range of intellectual resources, believing that they would be all
the better musicians in consequence. While
prepared in the main to endorse the soundness
of Grove's rule, we may point out that it has
admitted of two very extraordinary exceptions, one
at the beginning and one at the end of the nineteenth century—Schubert and Dvorák. In the
case of the latter, whose death occurred on May
1st, lack of culture, though it undoubtedly

hampered him in certain directions, was compensated by a certain ingenuous naïveté particularly refreshing in a sophisticated age. There were no 'ologies in Dvorák's work; his compositions needed no elaborate programmes, and he was never engaged in the furthering of any polemical propaganda. He was born a peasant, and remained in essentials a peasant to the end—a shy, unaffected, half-articulate person who was so destitute of small-talk that when a colleague complained of this speechlessness to a great conductor he was asked, "Did you try him with pigs?"— Dvorák's father having been a pork-butcher.

The annals of modern music are full of splendid examples of "from log cabin to White House": indeed, there is no calling in which a career is more open to talent; and after Verdi, there is no more striking example of a rise from obscurity to fame than Dvorák. It is said that all Bohemians are born fiddlers; but Dvorák was a born composer as well, and, like another great orchestral writer—Dr. Elgar—he was practically self-taught. It was a case of *per aspera ad astra*, however, and Dvorák had a severe struggle before he could gain more than a bare living by his composition. It is pleasant, therefore, to remember that it was Brahms—who happens to be at the present moment specially singled out for depreciation by

"enlightened" critics—who gave Dvorák the
great lift of his life, by recommending him as a
fitting recipient of Government bounty. The
episode is in itself a sufficient answer to all the
ignorant and afflicting balderdash that is talked
about Brahms's pedantry, coldness, austerity, etc.
The sympathy and appreciation of Brahms, backed
up later on by the powerful encouragement of
Richter, opened the door to Dvorák in Vienna,
where, after Prague, his genius has been more
cordially recognised than anywhere else on the
Continent. In Germany his unintellectuality has
no doubt stood in his way. There is too much
scene-painting, too little psychology and philosophy, in his music to satisfy the serious Teuton.
In France he is practically unknown ; but in
France the unexpected always happens—Tchaikovsky, for example, being far less known and
infinitely less appreciated in Paris than in London.
But in England, though Dvorák has been latterly
somewhat eclipsed by newer idols, the instructed
public, thanks to the lead given them by Sir
August Manns, Sir Charles Hallé, and Dr Joachim,
had the good taste to appreciate his music almost
from the first, and one of his choral compositions,
the *Stabat Mater*, has passed into the British
repertory of standard works, happily dislodging
Rossini's setting in the process. The appreciation

of the music of Dvorák by the British public is one of those things that one accepts gratefully without attempting to explain. Exotic and extra-European as it is in many ways, with its barbaric colouring and its strange alternations of childlike exuberance and poignancy, one might well have imagined that it would disconcert the staid British oratorio-going public as something "pagan, I regret to say." Certainly these contrasts are less vivid in the *Stabat Mater*, the most dignified and classical of all Dvorák's choral works, than in the *Requiem*, where the composer's "profuse strains of unpremeditated art" are occasionally impossible to reconcile with the spirit of the words, and almost tempt one to believe that Dvorák could not have understood the meaning of the Latin text.

The recognition of Dvorák's genius in England, where more than one of his most ambitious works were produced for the first time, and the desire of Festival Committees in the middle and late "eighties" to secure novelties from his pen, exposed him to a temptation which somewhat injuriously influenced the development of his genius. In the *Spectre's Bride*, a cantata based on a Bohemian variant of the legend which Bürger familiarised in his ballad of *Lenore*, he was most happily inspired, and the result was a work of true romantic feeling, great melodic charm, rich orchestral colouring, and a vivid appreciation of the *macabre* element in the story. One felt that he was indulging his genius without any regard for his public. But in *Ludmila* he set himself to write an oratorio for an oratorio-loving people, and the result was a strange and kaleidoscopic amalgam, in which echoes of classic exemplars alternated with characteristic national rhythms and melodies. The work had some fine moments and delightful snatches of melody, but it was killed by its length, its reminiscences, and its jumble of styles. It was much as though a poet had written a tragedy interspersed with lyrics in dialect. The limitations of Dvorák's equipment, and his lack of self-criticism, were never more conspicuously illustrated. But if Dvorák's relations with England were somewhat mixed, what are we to say of the curious episode of his sojourn in the United States ? The facts of the case were very simple. Dvorák was offered the post of Director of a Conservatoire established and endowed in New York by a munificent American lady. He was a poor man, dependent on his compositions for a very modest income, and the salary attached to the post was handsome. He could therefore hardly be blamed for consenting to this well-remunerated expatriation. The most perfunctory inquiries must have made it clear that he was singularly unfitted for the administrative duties of such a post. He was not a man of affairs, he had no capacity for organisation, no social gifts, no general education. But the authorities at New York were presumably aware of all this ; it was enough that he was a famous European composer, and they imported him as a picturesque figure-head. Yet in the short space of time — 1892-95 — during which Dvorák remained in New York he showed a faculty of adapting himself to his new surroundings, and an artistic loyalty to the country of his temporary adoption, for which few would have given him credit. His aims and achievements are briefly but lucidly expressed in Mr. Louis C. Elson's interesting *History of American Music* (Macmillan and Co.), published only a few weeks ago. After referring to Dvorák's efforts to promote the renascence of Bohemian music, Mr. Elson continues :—

On Dvorák's coming to New York, he began with composition classes at the National Conservatory at once, and many prominent young musicians became his pupils. He desired, however, to evolve something distinctly American on his own account, and at once sought to discover what American folk-song was like. He must have been somewhat disappointed at first, for he found only the Indian music (unfamiliar to almost every American) and the plantation music of the South, the product of an alien race. Yet, as the latter portrayed phases of American existence and was recognised and understood by almost all the people (a prime necessity of folk-song), he proceeded to employ this material in classical composition. Music for a string quartet, a sextet, and a symphony were the results of the search for native material. The symphony " From the New World " has given rise to considerable contention. Some maintain that it is no more American than Dvorák's own painful attempts in the native language. One may disagree with such a dictum ; the symphonic language is not itself a local dialect, but it may properly be founded on local themes. It is not a Bohemian masquerading as a plantation darky that we find in this work, but an idealization of the typical music of the South, developed, as this epic form demands, yet entirely recognizable. The chamber-music on American figures is still more frankly plantation-like in its vein. But the American Symphony (in E Minor, Op. 95) will always remain Dvorák's chief achievement in this country. The whole proceeding was a demonstration, on the part of a great composer, that the roots of the music of a nation are to be found in its folk-songs ; should there be no such inspiration to draw from, the result will be more generally eclectic and less typical. For that reason it is still a mooted point as to whether a distinctively American school can ever arise, even amid a host of talented native composers.

Mr. Elson goes on to state that although Dvorák was the first to call the attention of Europe to the possibilities of plantation-music, he was not the discoverer of this foundation of classical music, Mr. G. W. Chadwick in the *scherzo* of his Second Symphony having already recognised the adaptability of this material before Dvorák came to New York. He omits to mention, however, in his enumeration of Dvorák's American pupils, whether any of them were of negro extraction, a point of interest in view of the talent shown by coloured musicians in the more ambitious fields of composition of late years. *In Dahomey*, the piece which, after being a great success in New York, has recently drawn the town in London, was not only written but composed by men of colour, and in the piquant orchestration of the songs and dances one seemed to recognise a good deal of the spirit of Dvorák's treatment of similar themes.

After his three years' sojourn in New York, Dvorák returned to take up the directorship of the National Conservatoire at Prague, where he died a fortnight ago in his sixty-third year. His creative impulse, if not dormant, had not shown any remarkable activity of late years; but there was at least no serious falling off in the quality of his more recent compositions, and his death removes the most refreshingly unconventional, and at the same time most genuinely musical, of modern

musicians. He essayed every form of composition, and achieved distinction in the symphony, in
choral work, in chamber-music, and in his songs.
Of his numerous operas—belonging more or less
to the category of the *Singspiel*—which attained a
considerable vogue in his native country, we cannot speak, none of them having been brought to
a hearing in England. But two of his symphonies—notably the beautiful work in G, with
lovely Schubertian *Allegretto*—will certainly
live, as well as the exhilarating Symphonic
Variations, the joyous *Carnival* overture, and the
delightful Slavonic Dances and Legends. It was
his privilege to invest the classical forms with a
certain fresh and primitive grace, which expressed
itself by turns in artless melody and luxuriant
harmonies. With Spohr the use of the chromatic
scale led to a cloying sweetness : with Dvorák, on
the other hand, it gave a quasi-Oriental or tropical
piquancy to his music. He wrote, in short, like
an inspired rustic ; and it is perhaps that very fact
which renders his music so peculiarly welcome at
a period when composers are so assiduously
engaged in the attempt to de-simplify the processes
and the products of the art.

May 14, 1904.

VIII

EDWARD DANNREUTHER

THE cry of "England for the English" is periodically raised in the musical world, but of such importations as the late Mr. Dannreuther England can never have too many. As a matter of fact, he could be almost claimed as one of ourselves—*noster utinam nostras*—for though born and, apart from a brief sojourn in the United States, educated in Germany, he settled in England just fòrty years ago, made his home in London, and without losing any of the best traits of the land of his birth, definitely cast in his lot with the country of his adoption. In noticing the first volume of the new edition of Grove's *Dictionary* we expressed regret that his long and faithful services to the art he served so well in the country of his adoption had not been more adequately recognised. This, however, was perhaps inevitable, because he was not a composer,

for many years he had not figured on the concert
platform, and when the volume appeared he was
still an active member of the profession he so
conspicuously but so unobtrusively adorned.   It
was not that he was lacking in social gifts.   His
talent and his interesting personality secured for
him an immediate welcome in the best artistic
society of London on his first arrival in our midst.
He was admitted to the friendship of William
Morris, Rossetti, and others of the Pre-Raphaelite
brotherhood, and in the mid "sixties" was
already a familiar figure at the brilliant gatherings
of musicians, men of letters, and artists who used
to frequent the house of the late Mr. Frederick
Lehmann.   But his studious nature and his
professional engagements caused him to give up
to art what was meant for mankind.   He was not
a figure who loomed large in the public eye.   Yet
the influence he exerted on the elect was deep
and abiding, and the range of his activities was
only equalled by the width of his sympathies.
More than perhaps any musician of his generation,
he combined a devout admiration for the classical
composers with a fervent championship of those
who trod the new paths.   From the very first he
recognised the commanding genius of Wagner,
with whom he was on terms of intimate personal
friendship ;   but he was never betrayed by his

belief in the ultimate triumph of the music-drama into the acrimony of partisanship, or the depreciation of antagonistic methods. He was content to spread the light without resorting to controversial tactics or invidious comparisons. He never tried to force his views on others, but did his pioneer work in an eminently conciliatory spirit. This large and wholesome sanity, this discreet enthusiasm, was a special mark of the man, and rendered him a living disproof of the belief still held by many educated persons in this country, who, generalising from the eccentricities of semi-educated *virtuosi*, hold that the pursuit of the musical career necessarily exerts an emasculating and unhinging effect on those who embrace it. The true antidote is to be found in general culture, and Mr. Dannreuther belonged, to that increasing class of musicians whose artistic influence is fortified and enhanced by the wide range of their interests. He was a great musical scholar, but he was no pedant ; he was a Professor and attached to the staff of the Royal College of Music, but in view of his championship of Wagner and the modern Romantic school, not even the most rabid of our musical Jacobins ever ventured to label him as an "academic." He was the first to play the concertos of Tchaikovsky, Grieg, and Liszt in public in London ; he founded the

Wagner Society thirty-three years ago—in the same year, by a significant coincidence, in which H. F. Chorley died ; translated Wagner's *Music of the Future* and *On Conducting*, and received him as his guest in 1877. But it was in the same house in Orme Square where he entertained Wagner that he used to give year after year those delightful concerts of classical chamber music of which his finely intellectual readings of Bach and Beethoven were so welcome a feature. He had been a brilliantly distinguished pupil at the Leipzig Conservatorium, where he studied under Moscheles, Richter, and Moritz Haupt-mann, and no one ever better realised the motto given to that institution by Mendelssohn, *Res severa est verum gaudium.* For forty years he was a pianoforte teacher, but the inevitable drudgery associated with that department of his calling never blunted his enjoyment of good music or dulled his appreciation of good work. There have been more effective trainers in the gymnastics of agility, but for any one anxious to obtain an insight into the deeper meaning of the classics and to assimilate the best traditions, and prepared to subordinate desire for display to respect for the composer's intentions, there have been few more stimulating or helpful masters than Edward Dannreuther.

But besides being a pioneer, propagandist, interpreter, and teacher, Mr. Dannreuther rendered a great deal of valuable assistance to the cause of musical education in a variety of other ways. We have already spoken of his admirable translations of two of the most important of Wagner's *brochures*. In addition to this, he was one of the most illuminating contributors to Grove's *Dictionary of Music and Musicians*. Here the help that he rendered was twofold : first, by his admirable articles on Wagner, Tchaikovsky, and Chopin ; and second, by laying his exact scholarship and expert technical knowledge at the disposal of the original editor. Grove, with all his enthusiasm and wide range of interests, had his limitations. But he was fully conscious of them, and always ready to supplement his deficiencies by consulting musicians better equipped than himself. Of all those whom he referred to during the course of his editorial labours, there was none on whom he leant with greater reliance than Mr. Dannreuther. Indeed, for months at a time—in particular, when Grove was engaged on his monograph on Beethoven— hardly a day passed without his writing to consult his friend on some point or other where he distrusted his own unaided judgment. Nor was Grove's an isolated case. Many other musicians regarded him as their mentor and adviser-in-ordinary, and in particular Sir Hubert Parry has placed on record his deep sense of indebtedness to the instruction, the criticism, and the encouragement of Mr. Dannreuther. For the last eight years he had been attached to the professorial staff of the Royal College of Music, where, in virtue alike of his great ability, his fine character, and his commanding influence, he was held in the highest esteem by his colleagues and pupils, and where, long after his physical strength had begun to fail, his strong sense of duty and loyalty kept him at his post. Indeed, he may almost be said to have died in harness, for his last lesson was given less than a week before his death. He was only sixty years old, and his greatest ambitions had been altruistic ; none the less, he had achieved a great and peculiar position, for the best judges would probably agree that in the liberal and stimulating influence which he brought to bear on the progress of higher musical culture in this country he was excelled by none of his contemporaries.

February 18, 1905.

IX

ARTHUR JOHNSTONE

LANCASHIRE music recently sustained a severe loss by the premature deaths—they both died at forty-three, and within a year of each other—of Alfred Rodewald, the founder and conductor of the Liverpool Orchestral Society, and Arthur Johnstone, the musical critic of the *Manchester Guardian*. It would be difficult to imagine a greater contrast than that presented by the two men in physique or temperament — Johnstone being slight, small, rather saturnine in appearance, and reserved in manner, while Rodewald was a genial giant with an eminently forthcoming disposition. Yet, in spite of superficial differences, the two men were not only excellent friends, but were united by their common love of the art they served so well. They were at one in combining a deep veneration for Bach with a most sensitive appreciation of any composer, no matter how *outré* or anarchical, who honestly endeavoured to enlarge the horizons of the art. And they both cordially detested insincerity, charlatanry, claptrap, and vulgarity. Rodewald, as became a man with a greater gift for friendship, was more catholic in his tastes, less uncompromising in his dislikes; but in the main they saw eye to eye in matters musical, and the work of the one was complementary to that of the other, Rodewald educating his audiences by the performance of programmes chosen in accordance with the principle enunciated by Johnstone when he wrote : "Music is an art of expression, and all thoroughly and richly expressive music is good music, no matter what the informing emotion or underlying idea." And if Johnstone exercised the rôle of critic somewhat too consistently in the spirit of the gadfly, it must be admitted that he had great excuse in his antecedents, and considerable provocation in the state of British public opinion even in so musical a centre as Manchester.

Arthur Johnstone, who was born in 1861, was the son of an Anglican clergyman, and was educated at a high Anglican school and a high Anglican College—Radley and Keble—but his nature refused to take the colour of his surroundings ; its bent was ingrainedly secular and artistic, and he became by reaction anti-clerical, though, as his biographers correctly note,[1] he "continued to appreciate the value of religion, chiefly through art and music." He was out of sympathy with the public-school spirit, none of his numerous accomplishments being such as could ensure him prominence in the playing-fields ; while his genuine passion for art and beauty, coupled with a certain eccentricity in attire, probably caused him to be confounded by the unobservant with the votaries of pseudo-aestheticism. He tried for the Indian Civil Service and failed, because "he made no serious attempt to succeed," the prospect of an examination with him proving to be the reverse of an incentive to work. He had to earn his living, however, and, leaving Oxford without taking a degree, supported himself by teaching for a few years, until a small legacy enabled him to realise a long-cherished ambition and study music at a foreign conservatorium. He worked hard for a year at Cologne—long enough to enable him to realise that he could never hope to achieve anything great as a player or composer, to convince him that the career of music teacher was intolerable drudgery, and to bring to light his unexpected gift for modern languages. He returned to Oxford to take his degree in 1888 as a member of

[1] *Musical Criticisms.* By Arthur Johnstone. With a Memoir of the Author by Henry Reece and Oliver Elton. Manchester : at the University Press. [5s. net.]

Balliol, "the college which should have sheltered him from the beginning," where he foregathered with Farmer and impressed Jowett—by his skill as a conjurer, which was certainly remarkable. For six months he acted as tutor in the family of a Russian Prince in Podolia—the neighbourhood was a "paradise of gypsies," who appealed in every way to Johnstone's antinomian instincts—and then studied Russian seriously at Odessa until he was driven home by want of funds, though he contrived to pay a visit both to Bayreuth and the Passion Play at Oberammergau on his way home. In 1890 he accepted a Mastership in Modern Languages at the Edinburgh Academy, which he held until he left Edinburgh for Manchester in January 1896 to join the staff of the *Manchester Guardian*, and Manchester was his home until his death after a short illness in December 1904.

One cannot expect the foregoing brief sketch to make it clear wherein consisted Johnstone's peculiar fitness for the calling in which he did his best work. But it may be at once asserted that to a technical equipment possessed by few musical critics he added a gift of incisive literary expression and a fearlessness surpassed by none. His contempt for charlatanry and sentimentality and his sardonic wit occasionally prompted him to use phrases which gave more pain than he realised or intended.   Thus he once compared the style of an immensely popular singer to that of a bank-holiday trombonist on Blackpool sands.   But he never descended to the truculence which has disfigured the criticism of some of his colleagues, and vigorously protested against onslaughts on certain composers by writers " who attacked without regard either for the facts of the case or even for common decency."   Even where he was out of sympathy with the methods employed by a composer or his animating purpose, he never failed to recognise high aims and earnest endeavour.   As his biographers most truly say, " he thought instinctively more about ideas and purposes than about persons, so that he sometimes ignored persons and therefore dissatisfied them." It was characteristic of the man that some of his friendships began in controversy, even in a quarrel. Having himself fought and suffered for his unorthodoxy, he had an instinctive sympathy with the spirit of revolt, with the untrammelled expression of individuality.   In literature it was the same : " he had a swift preference even as a boy for all that was fresh, vehement, and strange in modern drama and fiction."   His sympathy with anarchical tendencies, however, was more aesthetic than political ; he associated with Russian refugees, and enrolled himself among the Friends of Russian

Freedom, but held that "a paternal Government was required in Russia, and that his countrymen as a whole were to blame for their harsh judgment of a civilisation merely because it ran counter to their own political ideals." So in music his frank admiration for the primitive and barbaric element in Dvorák and Tchaikovsky did not blind him to the rodomontade, the lack of dignity and of deep intellectuality, by which their works were often marred. His profoundest admiration, his most unstinted praise, were reserved for Bach, as may be gathered from the following really noble tribute :—

Bach represents by far the greatest stimulating influence that has ever existed in the musical world. His stupendous industry, resulting in a body of first-rate work that may be reckoned among the greatest wonders of the world (it is not possible for a modern to know it all) ; his awe-inspiring union of very great talent with very great character ; the completeness of his human nature and the absolute purity of his life and art,—these things unite to make of Bach's personality something truly august, something that administers a quietus to the ordinary critical, fault-finding spirit. Glancing over the huge library of his collected works and knowing the glories that a few of them contain, one is fain to say, "There were giants in the earth in those days." Yet "giant" is scarcely the word. For the astounding sinew and sturdiness of the man were quite secondary in the composition of his character to that quality, in virtue of which he worked on throughout a long life as though in perpetual consciousness of something higher than ordinary human judgment ; not waiting for full appreciation, which did not come till about a century after his death (very much as in Shakespeare's case), but perfectly realising the great ethical ideal of Marcus Aurelius—the good man producing good works, just as the vine produces grapes.   No greater praise can be bestowed on Handel than to say that in his very best moments he is almost worthy of Bach, as, for example, in the choral section " The Lord hath laid on Him the iniquity of us all," or in the tenor of the recitative " He looked for some to have pity on Him, but there was no man ; neither found He any to comfort Him."

Nor was his attitude to Beethoven less wanting in reverence or in appreciation of his Michelangelesque *terribilità*.   Speaking of the *Missa Solennis*, he writes :—

It is, beyond question, the most austere of all musical works—a product of Beethoven's quite inexorable mood. At the period when it was written the composer had become a sort of suffering Prometheus.   Even apart from his deafness, it is wonderful that Beethoven's persistent ill-fortune, his isolated and unhappy life, should not have discouraged him and checked the flow of his creative energy.   But that the mightiest of his compositions should have been produced when he was stone-deaf—that is surely one of the most perfectly amazing among well-authenticated facts !   So far as we know, there never was any other case in which deafness failed to cut a person off altogether from the world of music.   With Beethoven it only brought a gradual change of style. As the charm that music has for the ear faded away he became more and more absorbed, aloof, austere, and spiritual. The warm human feeling of his middle-period compositions gave way to a style of such unearthly grandeur and sublimity as are oppressive to ordinary mortals. Of that unearthly grandeur there is no more typical example than the " Missa Solennis." Not only in regard to the composition but even in regard to a performance the ordinary language of criticism is at fault. Who ever heard a " satisfactory " performance of the " Missa Solennis " ? A spirit of sacrifice is demanded of the performers ; for the music is written from beginning to end with an utter want of consideration for the weaknesses and limitations of the human voice. Of course that would be intolerable in an ordinary composer. Handel's combination of German structural solidity with Italian courtesy, sense of style, and delight in rich vocal rhetoric is the ideal thing. By comparison with the reasonable and tactful Handel, Beethoven is a kind of monster, from the singer's point of view, but a monster of such genius that his terrible requirements must occasionally be met. The quartet was best in the astonishing " Dona nobis pacem " section, where the composer seems to represent humanity as endeavouring to take the Kingdom of Heaven by violence, protesting against all the oppression that is done under the sun, and sending up to the throne of God so instant a clamour for the gift of peace as may be heard amid the very din of strife. For that prayer for peace sounds against the sullen rolling of drums and menacing clangour of trumpets, the voices having now a mighty unanimity, now the wail of this or that forlorn victim. One looks in vain through the temple of musical art for anything to match that

tremendous conception marking the final phase of the
" Missa Solennis."

One merit of Johnstone's criticisms, as may be
readily understood from the above extracts, was
that they appealed not merely to musical, but to
non-musical readers. He seldom wrote a notice
without introducing some happy literary or artistic
parallel or starting some interesting psychological problem. His tone was often peremptory,
and at times recalled the schoolmaster ; we well
remember one notice of a work of Tchaikovsky
which he prefaced with a long and somewhat
irritable disquisition on the right spelling of his
second name, which so often incorrectly figured as
Iltitch in concert programmes. In the words of
his biographers, " he was too angry to be precious,"
and there was never any fumbling in his phrases,
no resort to euphemism in his censure or to effusive-
ness in his praise. He knew his mind, and spoke
it with perfect lucidity and unfaltering directness.
He early signalised himself by his whole-hearted
enthusiasm for the works of Richard Strauss and
Elgar, but he never disfigured his championship
of the new idols by any " brutal detraction "—to
quote his own phrase—of their contemporaries.

Of Johnstone's interesting personality and his
many and curious accomplishments a full and
sympathetic account will be found in the admirably

written Memoir—quite a masterpiece of its kind—which Messrs. Elton and Reece have prefixed to this collection of his writings. Indeed, the only criticisms we are inclined to offer are that in emphasising his services as a Bach propagandist they have, no doubt unintentionally, overlooked the efforts of his predecessors and contemporaries ; and further, that no mention is made of the keen sense of humour—all the more engaging in a man of an eminently serious bent—which now and then emerged in his criticisms. He was not a man of many friends ; but in congenial surroundings he could make himself delightful even to a chance acquaintance. Here, however, we are concerned less with the man than with his work as an educator and interpreter, and may close our notice by saying that few writers on music have exerted a more stimulating or salutary influence. Whether you agreed with him or not, he compelled you to listen to him by the sincerity of his views and the vividness of their presentation. His biographers complain, not without good reason, that far too little notice was taken of him in the London Press at the time of his death. The contents of this volume will certainly remove any excuse for the continuance of such neglect.

December 30, 1905.

X

CAMILLA LANDI

In his suggestive volume Mr. Ffrangçon Davies urges upon singers with eloquence and cogency the need of using their brains and cultivating their intelligences. The best voice in the world, without brains at the back of it, remains but an inefficient instrument of persuasion and interpretation. But this does not exhaust the list of desirable qualities. Temperament and charm—it is hard to draw a hard-and-fast line between the two, yet the distinction will, we think, be readily admitted—remain to be added to complete the equipment of that rare bird, the perfect singer. Such paragons have seldom emerged above the artistic horizon ; but now and again we encounter one who approximates more or less closely to the ideal, and if a plebiscite of enlightened judges were to be taken at the moment, it is more than probable that the name of Mlle. Camilla Landi would stand at the head of the poll. The English concert-going public has taken a considerable time in making up its mind as to her merits, partly because of her comparatively infrequent appearances, partly because her methods and choice of music are not always calculated to conciliate the English public. Some purists, for example, would doubtless still say that she was addicted to the *tremolo*, confounding that unquestioned vice with the legitimate pulsation of tone which is so effective in moments of emotional or dramatic intensity. Be this as it may, the attendance at her last recital, and the large number of musicians in the audience, revealed the agreeable fact that the circle of her admirers is no longer confined to a handful of cognoscenti, but embraces all sections of the musical world. This is an eminently satisfactory state of affairs, for Mlle. Landi is not only a great singer, but she has never displayed any special readiness to sing down to the level of her audience.

Her first appearance before a large London audience was in 1893, when she sang at an orchestral concert given by the late Sir Charles Hallé with his famous Manchester band ; and she then chose to be heard in Berlioz's " La Captive." The choice was characteristic, for though " La Captive " is the greatest of Berlioz's detached

songs, it must have been wholly unfamiliar to
ninety-nine out of a hundred of her hearers, and,
for the rest, is so steeped in an atmosphere of
exotic romance as to render its full appreciation
by a British audience almost impossible. Still,
some of those present must have read Berlioz's
Memoirs, in which he tells the story of its
composition—how Victor Hugo's *Orientales* was
lent him by a fellow-student at Subiaco when, as
the winner of the Prix de Rome, he was studying
at the Villa Medici ; how the book opened at
the poem in question, and he heard the music
immediately and scribbled it down, with the result
that the Director of the Villa a month afterwards
complained that wherever he went, " in the garden,
on the terrace or in the corridors, one hears people
singing, grunting or growling *le long du mur
sombre . . . le sabre du Spahi . . . Je ne suis pas
Tartare.*" Anyhow, Mlle. Landi triumphed, and
few of those who were present in St. James's Hall
thirteen years ago will ever forget the impression
created by her singing. Since that date few
seasons have elapsed in which she has not sung in
London, but her visits have never been so frequent
as to blunt the edge of appreciation. One year, it
is true, in an unexpected spirit of concession, she
appeared at the Ballad Concerts, but seemed quite
out of her element, and made little impression on

an audience accustomed to cruder methods and more direct appeals. But her reputation and her repertory have steadily increased, and of late years she has travelled widely on the Continent and won resounding success in Germany, perhaps for the very reason that she is so conspicuously endowed with the qualities in which German singers are so signally lacking. In intelligence, breadth, and dramatic intensity the best German singers have never been to seek ; but, as one of their own best critics, Moritz Hauptmann, said of a famous German prima donna, they have been at times inclined to sacrifice beauty to character, and the elegance and distinction of Mlle. Landi's singing, her perfect control of her resources, and her mastery of the niceties of technique would naturally appeal with additional force to those who are more accustomed to be impressed than fascinated by native vocalists. It is impossible in her case, again, to overlook the advantages derived from her origin, her training, and her experience. Of Italian origin, inheriting musical talent on both sides, she assimilated during her residence in Paris the best traditions of what is generally admitted to be the finest contemporary school of artistic singing. An admirable linguist, at home in four languages, she is thus enabled to sing nearly all the music that counts in the tongue for

which it was composed ; while her travels have
afforded her specially favourable opportunities for
enlarging the boundaries of her repertory, for if a
singer wishes, *e.g.*, to learn a Russian song, it can
be better learned in Russia than in London.
The career of the travelling virtuoso may be
difficult, or, indeed, impossible, to reconcile with
that of the creative composer, but it certainly
offers peculiar advantages to the interpreter, given
intelligence and the capacity of taking pains. The
singers who have counted have always remained
students, ready to assimilate new ideas without
forgetting Verdi's maxim, *torniamo all' antico* ; and
if only as a practical exemplification of this conception of self-culture, Mlle. Landi's programmes
are invariably stimulating and suggestive. At her
last recital the composers represented ranged from
Bach to settings of the latest effusions of the
French decadent Muse ; from Haydn to Max Reger,
compared with whom Richard Strauss is reported
to have declared himself to be a " thoroughgoing
classic." This catholicity of taste also found expression in the choice of songs by Handel and Gluck,
Brahms, Hugo Wolf, and Saint-Saëns. It would
be incorrect to say that the singer was equally
successful in all that she attempted. Mlle. Landi
is always artistic, but not invariably convincing.
Her taste is exquisite, but it is superior to her

judgment. She has all the virtues, but some of the limitations, of the French school, to which, after all, she is most closely related. Her voice sounds fuller and more beautiful when she is singing in French than in any other language, and this may account for the fact that after singing a song from Bach's cantata, "The Strife between Phoebus and Pan," in German, with an excellent accent, she chose to sing two of Brahms's *Lieder* with viola accompaniment, including the beautiful *Geistliches Wiegenlied*, to a French version. This, however, may be due to that waywardness which is so often the defect of a pronounced individuality. Thus we see that Mlle. Landi is announced to sing the *Dichterliebe* at her next concert. This, at best, is a *tour de force* which can only be partially justified by results, much as in the case of Madame Sarah Bernhardt's impersonation of Hamlet. Of one thing we feel pretty sure, that it would never have received the sanction of either Schumann or Heine, and we can only hope that it will not lead to such artistic reprisals as the singing of the *Frauenliebe und Leben* cycle by Dr. Wüllner, Mr. Plunket Greene, or Mr. David Bispham. This episode, however, is quite characteristic of Mlle. Landi, in whose attitude towards the public there always mingles a certain engaging element of defiance, the result, no doubt, of a serene and perfectly intelligible confidence in her ability to realise her intentions. " I am going to sing you this song," she seems to say to her audience, " not to please you or to fall in with conventional standards, but simply to show you how I think it ought to be sung " ; and the result, nine times out of ten, is so distinguished and delightful, so attractive alike to the ear and the mind, that the most fastidious hearer finds little or nothing to cavil at. For Mlle. Landi is quite capable of making even an educational Blue-book sound fascinating, if she took it into her head to recite it to music. She is a consummate *diseuse*, on whose lips the delirious maunderings of decadent poets—phrases like *la sonorité de mauve* and *les hallebardes de spleen*—assume an impressiveness and a charm that almost persuade rational people out of the conviction that they are listening to highly coloured nonsense. In her ability to glorify songs of flimsy texture and trivial significance by charm of voice, elegance of style, and easy mastery of technique Mlle. Landi recalls the exploits of de Soria—so happily described in du Maurier's *Trilby*—and of Madame Conneau. Those delightful singers, however, acting no doubt on Napoleon's maxim, *il faut se borner*, were only great in their limited grooves. Mlle. Landi, equally admirable in the serious literature and the *belles-lettres* of the art, is perhaps the only singer living who by the tones of her voice and her artistic temper reminds middle-aged amateurs of that incomparable artist, the late Madame Trebelli.

February 24, 1906.

XI

ANTOINETTE STERLING

Just as in the domain of letters there have been certain writers who have appealed with a special force to the members of their own calling—Gray, Stevenson, George Meredith, Pater, to choose a few names at random—so has it been in the realm of music with composers and their interpreters. But as might naturally be expected in the youngest of the arts, the gulf between the expert and the layman has here been wider than elsewhere, and the position of those who appealed to the uninstructed public has until recently been proportionately more exempt from criticism. The most conspicuous instances of what may be called illiterate musicians — i.e. those who achieved success and fame without ever having mastered more than the rudiments of their craft—have always been found in the ranks of singers. No violinist, for example, ever reached eminence with-

out being a good reader. The instrumentalist
has to go through the mill. But there have been
plenty of great singers who have not only dispensed
with all knowledge of theory, but to the end of
their days learned their music largely by ear, and
could never be trusted in an emergency to sing
the simplest air at sight. The famous Grisi was
a case in point, though in her case, as in that of
others, lack of science was made good by quick-
ness, industry, and an unusually retentive memory.
But the whole trend of modern music towards
complexity has rendered it increasingly difficult
for singers to take part in music of any real
significance without being trained musicians. The
greatest composers of the past—Bach and Beethoven, to mention no others — showed scant
consideration for vocalists ; but their uncompromising attitude had the result of confining
the appreciation of a great deal of their finest
music to scholars and students, and deferring its
general recognition until such time as the education
of singers was partially levelled up to that of
instrumentalists. There were brilliant exceptions,
it is true ; but they were frequently amateurs,
even in Germany, outside of which country the
long domination of the old Italian opera enabled
the *prima donna* and the *primo tenore* to attain a
maximum of success with a minimum expenditure

of intellectual effort. It was, we take it, the triumph of Wagner that dealt the death-blow to the illiterate singer, and rendered it henceforth impossible for a vocalist to achieve supreme distinction on the operatic boards without being a skilled musician. But in countries where opera is of secondary importance, amongst which England is the chief, the mere singer had still abundant opportunities left for achieving a wide popularity on the concert platform as an interpreter of music which makes but slight demands on musicianship. We use the past tense deliberately, because the progress of musical education and the improvement of musical taste, the great multiplication of orchestral concerts and the raising of the standard in regard to the choice of songs at recitals and chamber concerts, have of late years confined the activities of the " illiterate " singer within a much more restricted compass.

To say that the late Madame Antoinette Sterling, whose Memoir[1] has just been written by her son, belonged to this class would be an unduly harsh and ungenerous verdict on a woman of remarkable gifts and striking personality. But it is perhaps not too much to say that no singer is likely in the future to achieve such a position as

[1] *Antoinette Sterling, and other Celebrities: Stories and Impressions of Artistic Circles.* By M. Sterling MacKinlay, M.A. Oxon. With 16 Portraits and Various Facsimiles. London : Hutchinson and Co. [16s. net.]

she undoubtedly held with so limited a repertory or such disregard for the higher technical developments of the art. It cannot be said that this attitude was the result of imperfect training. In her youth she studied in Europe under three of the most famous teachers of the time, and on her return to America at the close of the "sixties," as her son reminds us, "almost her entire attention was devoted to classical music, and more especially to German songs." She was the first to introduce groups of *Lieder* at recitals in America, and delighted to sing Schumann's *Dichterliebe* and *Frauenliebe* cycles at her own concerts. A programme of one of these concerts given early in the "seventies," and reproduced in this volume on pp. 58-59, includes songs by Schubert, Schumann, Mendelssohn, Liszt, Rubinstein, and Beethoven's "Wonne der Wehmuth," which the present writer well remembers hearing her sing in London about the year 1878. At her *début* in England in November 1873 she chose an aria from Bach's Christmas Oratorio, and in those early years was occasionally heard at festivals, taking the contralto part at the first performance of Macfarren's *St. John the Baptist*. The cause of her subsequent abandonment of German *Lieder* and oratorio for English ballads, chiefly of the modern, and occasionally of the most insipid, brand, is not clearly indicated in the Memoir, but a certain amount of light is thrown on the subject by her biographer. Thus we are told that she was "exhorted by her friends to give up the *Lieder* and take to English songs interspersed with an occasional Italian aria, which the public did not object to so much." We gather that she resented this advice, or at any rate the recommendation, "if she must give the music of German composers, let her sing translations." But whatever were her feelings, she acted in accordance with the suggestion, and for the last twenty years of her career she devoted herself almost entirely to English ballads, notably those of Sir Arthur Sullivan, Dr. Cowen, and Messrs. "Stephen Adams" and J. L. Molloy. That she appreciated better music is evident, but her attachment to it was not of the uncompromising quality of the genuine devotee. Her instincts were hereditarily democratic, and she realised that the easier, simpler, and more obvious the melody, and the more conventional the sentiment of the words, the more swift and secure was the appeal to the emotions of the populace. Again, her style of singing was so individual that she found it hard to accommodate herself to the wishes of a conductor, no matter how eminent, and her attempts to sing with an orchestral accompaniment were seldom satisfactory. Indeed, as years went on her views as to time and expression reached such a pitch of individualism that, as her son confesses in a curious passage, accompanists sometimes found her very difficult to follow at the piano :—

They would perhaps ask for a rehearsal, and then after the song had been gone through one way, they would at the concert find it taken with quite a different tempo at various points. Above all things in her singing she placed the words first in importance. If the music and words were at variance in a song, there was never any hesitation as to what was to be done. Should the phrasing of the music interfere with *the true expression of the poem*, the music had to give way. Moreover, when the introduction to the song was over, she was very much against having more than a bar or two for the piano between the verses. Her feeling was that it distracted the thoughts of the listeners, and was apt to take away their interest from the story which she was telling. This tendency to delete any, to her mind, superfluous bars of music increased as time went on, and latterly the actual accompaniments to the songs in her répertoire were cut down to the smallest possible limits. Particularly was this the case with her Scotch songs. In these the verses would practically go straight on without a break, the symphonies between the verses being almost entirely eliminated. Still more drastic, if possible, was her treatment of the finish of a piece. A couple of bars, played very quickly, were the utmost she would permit to be sounded after the voice had ceased. Woe betide the composer who had rounded off the close of his composition with several bars of haunting melody for the piano. The chances were that they would be slashed out bodily, and a single chord inserted in their place. Musicians often sighed at the liberties which she took with their work, but as these had the effect of turning the songs into big popular successes, it is a question whether the ruffled feelings were not adequately re-compensed by the size of the cheques received on account of "royalties."

Her favourite dictum, we are told, was " More Heart and less Art." She did not discounte-nance serious study at the outset, but held that once command of the voice and the rules of artistic singing had been obtained, the singer should "go to Nature to cultivate heart, to find out how the rules which had been learned might be broken with impunity." Her views as to the future of the art of song are set forth with refreshing naïveté in the following passage :—

" I think there will be a reaction from the modern preoccupation and wild craving after technique, a return to simpler, more primitive conditions. I like more and more to sing without accompaniment. It makes me feel a greater freedom and amplitude, a completer possession of my own voice. A number of times I have passed thus into improvisation, the words and the music coming together and demanding utterance. It is the most wonderful, ecstatic sensation in the whole range of musical art. I have felt like one possessed, inspired !

Now *that* seems to me the real thing. That was the method of the old bards and poets. Thus Homer chanted his epics ; thus sang the Hebrew prophets, and thus have been born the Folksongs of great nations. The memory of it still survives in the Eisteddfods, where poets are crowned and songs still improvised."

Of Madame Sterling's relations with her various teachers—Manuel Garcia, Madame Mathilde Marchesi, and Madame Pauline Viardot-Garcia—several illuminating anecdotes are given in these pages. According to Madame Marchesi, the American contralto was "a dear girl, but a perfect little devil to teach." On the only occasion on which she sang to the accompaniment of Anton Rubinstein his comment was : "Sie haben nie geliebt." Her opinion of Brahms, of whom she saw a good deal when studying with Madame Viardot-Garcia at Baden-Baden, is given in the following characteristic reminiscence :—

"Herr Brahms would often come to see me, and sit down at the piano while I ran through some of his songs. He was very anxious for me to sing them, but I saw that they did not suit me at all, so had to refuse his request. One Lieder [*sic*] in particular was like a duet, being written very low in the first part, and very high in the second. What is more, I told him so."

What would one not give for Brahms's version of this interview ! The anecdote which her son gives in illustration of the unromantic temper of

Brahms is, we may add, rendered suspect by the opening words : " When Brahms came over to England." Brahms, to the great regret of his many English admirers, never visited these shores.

Mr. MacKinlay's Memoir of his mother, written in a spirit of true filial piety, yet with refreshing candour, is well worth reading by amateurs as well as professionals. Singers in particular may derive profit from these pages if only they recognise the dangers of attempting to carry into practice the anarchical and reactionary principles enunciated by, and acted on by, Madame Sterling. Her success cannot be regarded as establishing a precedent, because it was largely a triumph of personality, not of artistic method. She had great natural resources and advantages— a noble voice, a striking appearance, and an unperturbed yet unaggressive self-confidence. Though she devoted her talents latterly to ephemeral and inferior music, she glorified and redeemed much of its banality by her earnestness and simplicity. The few great ballads in her repertory she sang splendidly : no one can ever forget her singing of " Caller Herrin' " or " The Twa Corbies." Off the platform she was a generous, impulsive, warm-hearted woman, amiable in her eccentricities, and deeply and passionately interested in philanthropic work. But, for the reasons given above, we greatly doubt whether such an assemblage of qualities, even if they were once more to be united in a singer, would in the altered conditions of public taste secure similar recognition for their possessor.

April 21, 1906.

XII

ADELINA PATTI

" Oportet Pati," wrote Berlioz in punning dog-Latin, after making the acquaintance of the " melodious Hebe," the " young, beautiful, radiant, and celebrated artist who, at the age of twenty-two, had brought all the musical world of Europe and America to her feet " ; and in view of his generally ferocious views about *prime donne*, the sincerity of his admiration can hardly be doubted. More than forty years have elapsed since Berlioz paid his tribute, and now the announcement of " farewell" concerts affords an opportunity for reviewing the achievements of perhaps the most uniformly popular and successful of all the queens of song. With her it was never a case of *per aspera ad astra*. She was born with a golden tune in her throat, and as early as 1852, before she was nine years old, was touring with Ole Bull, the famous Norwegian violinist, in the

Southern and Western States, singing "Ah non giunge," Jenny Lind's "Echo Song," and other *bravura* songs with a brilliancy of execution and charm of voice that electrified her hearers. She was a full-blown *prima donna* at sixteen, and in 1861 made her memorable *début* in London. Launched forthwith on the flood-tide of success, she maintained her place in the van of Italian operatic singers for more than twenty years. In 1863 she was earning £1000 a month : in the mid "eighties," according to Mr. Sutherland Edwards, her fees had gone up to £500, £800, and (in America) to even £1000 a night. (On the relation of these figures to the general efficiency of operatic performances it is hardly necessary to insist. The economic aspect of Madame Patti's career would require a separate article to itself.) Abandoning the stage for the concert platform in the "eighties," she returned for a short while to the scene of her triumphs some ten years ago in almost unimpaired possession of her powers. Since then, though her appearances have been limited, she has never failed to draw huge audiences. Her career, in short, has been one long triumphal progress. As we have seen, she charmed the sardonic though susceptible Berlioz ; Rossini wrote and rewrote cadenzas for his incomparable Rosina. Enthusiastic opera-goers, always hovering on the verge of lunacy, outdid themselves in the extravagance of their admiration. On one occasion (in Spain, if we remember aright) a flock of canaries were unloosed in a theatre in her honour ; and the description of her palatial castle in Wales from the pen of the late Mr. Beatty-Kingston—with its lyrical rhapsodies on the generous diet provided in her servants' hall, including *vin ordinaire* on week-days and champagne on Sundays—touches the high-water mark of *diva*-worship. No singer since the world began has drunk such draughts of unmitigated eulogy, or reaped such a golden harvest by the exercise of her talents. She was the first *prima donna* to render necessary the enforcement of a special tariff on the nights when she sang at the Opera. And lastly, she was as consistent in her artistic aims as she was prosperous in their realisation. She came to her own in the palmy days of Italian opera, and has remained faithful to the Italian operatic school right through her long career. It is impossible to avoid regretting that a singer so richly endowed should have been so singularly unenterprising in the choice of music. Her repertory, with the glorious exception of Mozart, has been confined entirely to the stock operas. She has never " created " a new part of any importance, and she has never even essayed a

single Wagnerian rôle, though she sang two of
his songs ("Träume" and "Schmerzen") at an
Albert Hall concert a few years back. For this
abstention, however, there is a good deal to be
said in excuse. In the first place, as Napoleon
put it, *il faut se borner*, and whatever may be said
of the quality of the music she has occasionally
sung, her manner of singing it has seldom left any
loophole for adverse criticism. In other words,
she has never attempted what she could not
perform. There is a great deal of *bravura* music
which is only endurable when sung to perfection,
and Madame Patti contrived to make it not
merely endurable, but delightful. To dismiss
her as a mere "expensive warbler" is to ignore
the vivacity and charm which, when combined
with her perfect singing, rendered her impersonation of Zerlina, as of Rosina, altogether satisfying
to witness. On the other hand, one cannot by
any stretch of imagination *see* Madame Patti in
any Wagnerian rôle. Senta, Elsa, Elisabeth,
Sieglinde, Brünnhilde, Isolde, even Eva,—it is
enough to mention them to realise the impossi-
bility. You cannot *méditerraniser* Wagner, and
without some such process it would have been
hopeless to find a Wagnerian rôle that would fit
Madame Patti. But while we acquiesce in the
sound judgment which induced her to abstain

from the modern German music-drama, we cannot so easily forgive her for leaving the inexhaustible treasures of the German *Lied* unexplored and unexploited. To have expected her to attempt Brahms would have been exacting too much, but at least she might have carried her researches into Schubert further than the *Ständchen*, or have given Schumann a trial—even in Italian. Perhaps the best explanation of her artistic attitude, however, is to quote from an interview with her given in Mr. Sutherland Edwards's book, *The Prima Donna*. Asked what were her favourite operas, Madame Patti replied : " I could name many that I like, but if you mean the few I love most, they are *Lucia, Sonnambula, Traviata, Il Barbiere,* and *Romeo and Juliet*—the last especially, for it requires two first-class artists to sing it, and those two carry the entire opera." Which is after all hardly any advance on the *ma femme et cinq ou six poupées* of Catalani's husband.

It is, however, useless speculating over what might have happened if Madame Patti had not been predestined by parentage, temperament, physique, and environment to be the last, and perhaps the most wonderful, of the Italian *prime donne*. Even in the palmy days of Italian opera there were two orders of operatic artists,—those who, like Pauline Viardot-Garcia, Jenny Lind, Schröder-Devrient, and Ronconi, sought to superadd general culture to special equipment, who were prepared on occasion to sacrifice beauty of tone to intensity of characterisation, who never left off being students, and, to use Watts's phrase, regarded all art as a serious intellectual utterance. And there have been, on the other hand, the great singers like "the unique, the incomparable Banti" (who bequeathed her larynx to her native town), like Mario and Grisi and Madame Patti, superbly endowed by nature, who have moved on the lines of least resistance, whose influence on the evolution of the art has either been negative or positively reactionary, and who, having little to be remembered for but their voices, pass rapidly into the limbo of oblivion when once they retire from the active pursuit of their profession. It is otherwise with singers like Madame Viardot-Garcia, who, *duplices tendens ad sidera palmas*, was not only a great singer, but moved in the mid-stream of culture, and was intimately associated with some of the greatest literary figures of her time ; who supplied George Sand with the original of Consuelo ; who won the admiration of Heine and the lifelong friendship of Tourguenieff. Both orders of singers have the defects of their qualities, and nowadays we are beginning to suffer at times from the excessively psychological vocalist who is so

H

preoccupied with the emotional or intellectual content of the music as to sacrifice charm to intensity of expression. On the other hand, the exponents of the *bel canto* carried the *vox et praeterea nihil* principle to extremes. Madame Patti escaped coming under this condemnation because, in spite of her limitations, she was a first-rate comedian, and had a vivacity and *espièglerie* which enabled her to adorn whatever she touched. If not intellectual, she could never be termed unintelligent. Her impending withdrawal from public life inspires mingled emotions : gratitude for the pleasure she invariably furnished those who could afford to hear her, wonder at the miraculous prolongation of her powers, and regret that, as the most consistent representative of the " star " system, she has done more than any other singer in our generation to maintain opera in the position of an aristocratic or plutocratic preserve.

September 22, 1906.

XIII

JULIUS STOCKHAUSEN

THE great singer who passed away a few weeks ago at the age of eighty was little more than a name to the generation of British musicians— always excepting his pupils—which had grown up since his last public appearance in England more than thirty years ago, and this may account for the somewhat perfunctory nature of the notices of him which have appeared in the papers. Yet England as well as Germany has special reasons for holding Stockhausen's name in grateful remembrance, and pending the recognition which will doubtless be forthcoming from those better qualified for the task, it may be allowed us to sketch very briefly the nature of his services.

Stockhausen was a happy illustration of the value of a cosmopolitan training to the interpretative artist. Born in Alsace two years before the death of Schubert—with whose songs his name deserves to be eternally associated — he learned singing in Paris from Manuel Garcia, a Spaniard. This training, however, and his subsequent experience of the French lyric stage—he sang for two or three seasons at the Opéra Comique—were very far from denationalising him. There never was a more devoted or enthusiastic champion of German music. But his French training gave him *finesse*, suppleness, and urbanity, without impairing the seriousness of his aims. It also gave him a command of the *bravura* style, extended his repertory, and freed him from the danger of regarding art from a Particularist standpoint. His versatility, however, though aided by opportunity, was inborn. Inheriting his musical gifts from both parents, he was not only a singer, but a first-rate pianist, sight-reader, and transposer; he naturally gravitated towards the society of men and women of intellect and high artistic aims, such as Pauline Viardot-Garcia in France ; while in Germany he numbered amongst his most intimate friends Joachim, Madame Schumann, and Brahms. The great singers of that age as a rule lagged far behind the composers, but Stockhausen was not one of those who moved on lines of least resistance, and always kept fully abreast of the best contemporary art. From the outset he was a pioneer, and the peculiar nature of his

services to German art has been very happily
described by a German critic. Stockhausen was
the first, he says, to make the *Lied* of Schubert
and Schumann *konzertfähig*. The songs of
Schubert and Schumann had been reserved for
family use by enthusiastic amateurs, but Stockhausen was the first singer of note to bring them
within reach of the public by introducing them
habitually in concert programmes. To do this in
Germany was an innovation requiring enterprise
rather than courage. To do it in England forty
and fifty years ago was a piece of splendid audacity
which endeared Stockhausen to the small band of
Schubert and Schumann worshippers, but exposed
him to the hostility of the leading professional
critics of the day, headed by Davison and Chorley,
whose loyalty to Mendelssohn took the un-
fortunate form of depreciating and belittling his
contemporaries. Stockhausen, however, went on
his way undaunted. In England, as in Germany,
he was the first singer of note to introduce the
great song-cycles of Schubert and Schumann to the
concert-going public, and succeeded at length in
extorting from the reluctant Chorley (December
1870) the admission that in Schubert and
Beethoven he was unrivalled in accent and passion.
The great triad of song-writers — Schubert,
Schumann, and Brahms—are not even yet as

"concertworthy" in this country as they deserve to be, but at least no protest is now heard against their admission to any programme. In conquering the ignorance and prejudice which barred the way to their recognition Stockhausen did more in his day than any other European singer. The present generation of concert-singers reap the advantage of his disinterested efforts : it is to be hoped that they are duly grateful to their forerunner for smoothing their path, and will profit by his heroic example.

But while his claim to grateful recollection is most securely based on his work as a pioneer, Stockhausen in many other ways exerted a most salutary and stimulating influence. According to the old view of the function of the singer, it mattered little what the words were, or how they were uttered, so long as the vocalist produced a beautiful sound. To this view Stockhausen, both as singer and teacher, never failed to offer the most strenuous opposition. Slovenly enunciation was to him the worst of crimes, and in the matter of refinement of pronunciation he set an example which was all the more remarkable when his Alsatian origin is considered. Another admirable quality in Stockhausen was his loyalty to the intentions of the composer. He neither took liberties himself nor sanctioned them in others,

and on the occasion of one of his last visits to
this country threw up an engagement to sing in
Bach's *Passion according to St. Matthew* rather than
consent to the "cuts" and modifications introduced into his part by the conductor. His action
in the matter was thoroughly characteristic of his
artistic attitude throughout his life—an attitude
which, though it may not have conduced to the
amassing of a great fortune, testified to his
independence and disinterested devotion to the
highest ideals. At no stage of his career did
Stockhausen ever deviate from this uncompromising attitude. He never sang anything but the
best music, or sought to achieve popularity by
conciliating the public. It was just the same in
his teaching. He was too honest to make money
out of pupils who had neither talent nor aptitude,
and often gave offence by refusing to undertake
such uncongenial, though remunerative, work. A
story is told of two would-be pupils, one from
America and one from Oxford, who presented
themselves at the beginning of the term at Frank-
fort. The American was called up first and
offered as his *Probelied* Pinsuti's "Bedouin's Love
Song." Stockhausen retired into a far corner of
the room and listened in stony silence with a
Mephistophelean expression until the song was
over. He then came forward and said : "That

will do. You can go back to America." The turn of the Oxford man—half paralysed with nervousness—then came, and he presented Brahms's *Mainacht*. Stockhausen's verdict was as follows : "Very badly sung, and the pronunciation atrocious. You will take your first lesson on it—immediately." Even those who had zeal and intelligence, as well as natural gifts, found him at times an exacting and depressing master. His standard was too high for him to be content with anything but the best. But those who survived the ordeal had nothing but admiration and gratitude for their teacher, and many of the best *Lieder* and oratorio singers of the day were trained by him in the highest interpretative qualities.

No notice of Stockhausen, however imperfect, could fail to take account of his long, intimate, and peculiar relationship with Johannes Brahms. Their association began in 1856, the year of Schumann's death, and lasted without interruption till the close of Brahms's life. Even when Stockhausen was appointed conductor at Hamburg, a post which Brahms had peculiar claims to fill, and for which Joachim was a candidate, there was no disturbance of their cordial friendship. For fourteen years they were constantly associated in concert tours, on which Brahms habitually accompanied his colleague in the song-cycles of

Beethoven, Schumann, and Schubert, as well as
in his own compositions. The great *Magelone*
song-cycle was dedicated to Stockhausen, who
was the first to sing in public as well as in
private *Von ewiger Liebe*, *Mainacht*, and scores of
other immortal romances. He took the baritone
solo at the first performance of the *Deutsches
Requiem* in Germany, as well as the private
performance at the late Sir Henry Thompson's
house in London in 1871, when that masterpiece
was given for the first time in England, while at
the Popular Concerts and elsewhere he carried on
the Brahms propaganda on its vocal side with the
same enthusiasm and devotion that marked the
efforts of Joachim in the sphere of instrumental
chamber-music. There is a touching anecdote
given in Miss Florence May's admirable Life of
Brahms which tells how in 1884, when Stockhausen was trying over the song, *Mit vierzig
Jahren*, from the manuscript to the composer's
accompaniment, " he was so affected during its
performance that he could not at once proceed to
the end." The last meeting of the great composer
and (to quote Brahms's own words) " the best
musician amongst the singers " was at the funeral
of their old friend Madame Schumann in 1896.
This brief record of an artistic friendship, so rich
in its results and so unfaltering in its mutual

affection, may be closed by the passage in which Miss May describes their appearances at Hamburg and Altona in 1861, when Stockhausen was at the zenith of his powers :—

> At the first two concerts . . . the entire series of Schubert's *Schöne Müllerin* was given ; and at the last— who can imagine a more enthralling feast of sound than the performance of Beethoven's melting love songs, " To the Distant Beloved," the very thought of which brings tears to the eyes, sung by Stockhausen to the accompaniment of Brahms, followed by our composer's lovely second Serenade and this by Schumann's *Dichterliebe* ? Happy Hamburgers, happy Stockhausen, happy Brahms, to have shared such delights together ! Will their like ever come again ?

The mere singer has a precarious claim to remembrance, but the name of Stockhausen—the hierophant of Beethoven and Bach, of Schubert, Schumann, and Brahms—is indelibly inscribed in the golden book of German song.

October 27, 1906.

XIV

AUGUST MANNS

THOUGH Sir August Manns had withdrawn from the musical arena for several seasons, his interest in the art he had served so long and faithfully remained unimpaired to the end. Within the last year he had acted as external examiner of the orchestral class at one of our chief musical schools, and performed his duties not only conscientiously but with obvious enjoyment. He passed away on March 1st full of years, his old age was happy, and official recognition of his services was not wanting. Yet the present generation of concert-goers, who have come to regard symphony concerts as an integral part of the amenities of modern life, hardly realise the extent and value of the pioneer services rendered in this connection by Manns. What we now take for granted as part of the week's entertainment in Central London, amateurs now old or middle-aged could only secure in their earlier days by making a pilgrimage to Sydenham. There were, it is true, the Philharmonic Concerts, but they were less than half as numerous as the Saturday Concerts at the Crystal Palace, and decidedly less catholic in the framing of their programmes. Richter's advent belongs almost to a later generation ; and Manns laboured under several drawbacks as compared with his contemporary, Charles Hallé, whose famous Manchester concerts were started within two years of the Crystal Palace series. In the first place, Hallé had the support of the rich and cultivated German colony in Manchester ; secondly, there was the greater keenness of the middle and artisan classes of Lancashire and Yorkshire ; and thirdly, for the performance of choral works he had a practically unlimited supply of good voices. He also had the inestimable advantage of a splendid concert-hall, admirable in its acoustic properties, and capable of seating two thousand persons. Manns was hampered by the geographical drawback of a suburban position, by a train service which it would be rank flattery to describe as efficient, by a makeshift concert-hall, and by the fact that the Saturday Concerts were never a commercial success, however much they may have enhanced the prestige of the Crystal Palace. For the last ten or more years of their existence reports of their discontinuance were constantly being heard. On at least one occasion the public-spirited conductor actually paid out of his own pocket for the extra rehearsals necessary to secure an efficient performance of a very difficult and complicated modern composition. It was that spirit of devotion, coupled with a fiery zeal and a masterful personality, that enabled Manns to keep the concerts going for more than forty years. And if he was fortunate in his temperament and equipment, he was not less so in having George Grove, for many years secretary to the Crystal Palace, as his colleague, backer, and programme-writer. Grove's greater versatility and his distinction in the world of letters naturally appealed to a wider audience, but he certainly never attempted to appropriate any of the credit due to his colleague.

Manns was already sixty when the present writer first saw him conduct, but the Saturday Concerts in the mid " eighties " showed little, if any, signs of decadence. The band—the usual permanent orchestra of the Crystal Palace—enlarged for the Saturday Concerts to more than twice its numbers, was slightly smaller than Hallé's band in Manchester, and, as we have already said, the acoustic properties of the concert-room were far inferior to those of the Free-Trade Hall. The quality of the orchestra, however, was excellent, and the very best London instrumental players were always well represented at its leading desks. At the time we speak of, it was especially strong in the wood-wind. Wells, the principal flute, was an excellent player, and his colleague rejoiced in the ideal name of Tootill. The first clarinet was Clinton, a fine performer ; Mr. Malsch, who succeeded another admirable artist, M. Dubrucq, was then what he happily is still, an oboe player of classical excellence, notable alike for beauty of tone and purity of phrasing ; and the bassoons were led by the inimitable Wotton the elder, a notable figure at these concerts from his genially patriarchal appearance. It was his happy gift to be able to produce the finest effects from his instrument with the minimum expenditure of effort, and his playing of the wonderful bassoon passage in the last movement of the Choral Symphony was an ever-recurring delight to those who were lucky enough to hear it. The horns and trombones were excellent, and the latter always rose to the opportunities given them in Schubert's C major Symphony. Nor should we fail to mention J. A. Smith, the drummer, a dexterous performer, who used to elicit a beautifully round and well-tuned tone from his timpani. There were many other excellent players and good artists amongst the strings, some of them happily still in the active pursuit of their calling, and the balance and tone of the band left little room for complaint except in one particular. From whatever cause, cornets were (except on special occasions) employed instead of valve trumpets, with results which never failed to disconcert, and even disgust, the ears of purists. Why Manns exhibited this heretical and Philistine preference for the most ignoble of all instruments we have never been able to make out, unless it was that he held that the superior precision of the cornet compensated for its inherent vulgarity. But it is ungenerous to dwell further on the only serious flaw in the organisation of an orchestra associated for upwards of forty years with the interpretation of the best music in accordance with the best traditions. The repertory of the Crystal Palace Concerts, a full account of which is to be found in the pamphlet published a dozen or more years back, is a really splendid record of the consistent pursuit of high ideals in the face of considerable difficulties. It was the happy union of Manns and Grove, the expert and the amateur, both of them enthusiasts, which rendered the achievement possible, and drew Saturday after Saturday a contingent of London music-lovers to swell the numbers of the Sydenham audience. The concert-room had no architectural beauties, but on Saturdays it had many personal features of interest, not the least remarkable being the presence and the rapt attention of the blind students from the Normal College. The best place for hearing was the gallery at the back of the hall, in the back row of which Grove for many years was the centre of a group of his special musical associates and friends.

As a conductor, Manns was a gallant and picturesque figure, with his velvet coat, his snowy hair, his waxed moustaches, keen features, and alert gestures. As a young man he had been the bandmaster of a crack Prussian regiment, and he retained his martial bearing to the close of his long life. He had not the Olympian calm of Richter ; the sweep of his beat was generally restricted and its motion fidgety, though it was remarkable to note how successfully he adapted his methods to the requirement of the huge band and chorus at the Handel Festivals. But those who have played under him declare that what appeared to be tricks of manner had their meaning and value. Certainly he must have known exactly what he wanted, or he would never have got such admirable results out of his men. As for his "readings," we have no hesitation in saying that Schubert was never played with greater sympathy or poetry, or in a manner better designed to make the audience realise the point of Schumann's remark that Schubert made his instruments sound like human voices. The annual performance of the great C major Symphony was a red-letter day for many seasons at the Crystal Palace, and nowhere have we heard its "heavenly length" sound more celestial. Grove used to tell, with deep satisfaction, how one of his friends, a successful business man, who combined a love of music with a passion for the chase, once gave up a day's hunting to hear the C major, and we are sure the sacrifice was well repaid. Manns was also a great conductor of Schumann, Beethoven, and Mendelssohn ; and if in his earlier days his sympathy with Wagner was imperfect, and his readings at variance with tradition, his admiration grew steadily with advancing years. He retained his spirit of adventure to the last, and was never put off by anything because it was new or difficult or unpopular. The spirit with which he championed Schubert and Schumann in the "fifties" and "sixties" impelled him to pioneer the cause of Brahms in the "seventies" and "eighties," and to tackle Richard Strauss at the very end of his career. And all along he was a true and constant friend to British composers. The encouragement that he lent Sullivan at the outset of his career he extended to many others. Indeed, it would be hard to mention a single native orchestral composer of established repute who did not get his first or an early hearing from Manns, and it is therefore peculiarly appropriate that the appeal for subscriptions to a memorial in his honour which recently appeared in these columns should have emanated from the Society of British Composers. It is premature to discuss the precise form which the memorial should take, but we may at least express the hope that it will include some visible means of keeping his memory green at the Crystal Palace, within whose walls, if we except the concerts in Scotland which he conducted for a number of seasons beginning in the year 1879, he laboured continuously in the cause of his art for nearly fifty years.

March 30, 1907.

XV

CHARLES SANTLEY

THE late Lord Bowen, in an address delivered before the Working Men's College in 1893, illustrated the uncritical spirit of the age in an often-quoted passage in which he observed that "we pursue successful men and men to their downsitting and uprising : we enjoy descriptions of their household furniture. . . . We write long biographies of nobody, and we celebrate the centenaries of nothing." Lord Bowen's criticism is certainly not less needed now than when it was uttered fourteen years ago, and there are few subjects in regard to which it is more appropriate than the worship of popular singers and actors. Happily, there are bright exceptions, and the recent celebration of the fiftieth anniversary of Mr. Charles Santley's entrance on the calling which he still adorns was very far from being an exercise in unnecessary laudation. Indeed, to put it in this negative way is a niggardly and churlish expression of the truth. Here, for a wonder, was a public tribute to a "servant of the public" which did not exceed the merits of the recipient. The occasion was well chosen, and the interest of the celebration was enhanced by the fact that the central figure was not merely a passive spectator, but an active participant in the concert organised in his honour.

Popularity in the world of music is not synonymous with the possession of the highest artistic qualities. The agreeable feature about Mr. Santley's popularity is that it is entirely due to causes which redound to his credit. If we were asked what was the quality in Mr. Santley's singing which more than anything else had endeared him to the British public, we should be inclined to say that it was manliness. Neither in dress nor in appearance nor in manner was there ever anything about him that savoured of affectation or effeminacy. He never relied on the "capillary attraction" of the pianist; indeed, you could never have told from his bearing that he was a musician at all. He was simply contented to look like an ordinary, unaffected, burly Englishman, with a certain *noli me tangere* air about him, as of one who would stand no nonsense and would be a good man in a tight place.

Mr. Santley, in short, never experienced the temptation, which has assailed so many of his colleagues, "to belong to other nations" either in name or deportment. He just remained an Englishman all through, and we have no doubt that his good sense and sincerity in this regard have contributed not a little to his popularity. We do not wish to imply that he stood alone in this patriotic resolve, but that he embodied the best national qualities more thoroughly and successfully than any of his contemporaries. But if Mr. Santley stood for four-square British manliness, his solidity was tempered and inspired by fire, energy, *élan*. "The roast beef of Old England" occasionally enters rather too deeply into the soul of British singers, but the last thing that could be said of Mr. Santley was that he was stolid or beefy. Admirable in music which called for a passionate or pathetic intensity— witness his singing of "Is not His Word like a Fire?" and "It is Enough" in *Elijah*—he was equally successful in expressing the spirit of comedy or genial humour. How delightfully he used to sing "Time was when Love and I were Acquainted"; how incomparable he was (and is) in "O Ruddier than the Cherry," in "The Leather Bottel," "Simon the Cellarer," and "Father O'Flynn"! The last-named song, it may be added, reminds us of the fact that Mr. Santley is about the only English singer who can sing an Irish song without offending Hibernian susceptibilities by parodying or misrepresenting the brogue.

But the qualities which we have mentioned, admirable and valuable though they were as legitimately appealing to the sympathies of the public, were greatly reinforced by his more purely musical equipment. The weakest point in most British singers and players is their sense of rhythm. Now in Mr. Santley the sense of rhythm was exceptionally fine and sensitive, and lent a peculiar magic to his singing. This was shown not only in songs of an essentially rhythmic character—*e.g.* "O Ruddier than the Cherry"— but in his declamation, his delivery of recitative, and his realisation of the organic cohesion of a musical phrase. His long and arduous apprenticeship in the best Italian school of *bel canto*, alike as a student under Nava and as an operatic singer on the boards both in Italy and in England, gave him a complete control of the *bravura* as well as the *cantabile* styles, and his singing of florid passages and Handelian divisions was always delightfully clean and finished. Another great advantage that he possessed in comparison with most British singers of his generation was his command of languages. Mr. Edward Lloyd,

admirable singer, musician, and artist, never
ventured on either French or German, and was
rarely heard in Italian. These languages, so
indispensable to an interpreter of the best
music, had no terrors for Mr. Santley, who,
as we have seen, added to them a proficiency,
so rare in the benighted Sassenach, in the Irish
brogue. Brahms used to say of Stockhausen
that he was the best musician of all the singers.
Adapting this appreciation, we may safely say
that Mr. Santley was the best musician among
British male singers of his generation. His
interesting volume of autobiographical reminiscences, published in 1892, is entitled *Student
and Singer*, and the claim involved in the title
is fully justified by his career, in which he made it
his aim, musically speaking, to realise the ambition
of Solon, *quotidie aliquid addiscentem senem fieri.*

Mr. Santley's reminiscences are worth attentive
study, not merely as a record of a life of honourable achievement, but as a revelation of a strong
if somewhat prejudiced individuality. It is
refreshing to learn that, of all the great singers
of his time, he regards Pauline Viardot-Garcia
and Ronconi as the Mount Everest and Aconcagua of the mountain-peaks of song. It will
be a surprise to not a few readers to hear that
all the triumphs which he won on the concert

platform and as an oratorio singer failed to compensate him for the abandonment of the operatic stage. His scepticism as to the educational value of musical academies and colleges is more pronounced than convincing. In regard to his taste in music it must be admitted that he has shown a certain disinclination to tread the new paths. His repertory was large, but it had conspicuous gaps. Thus, in spite of his command of German, he left the inexhaustible treasury of German *Lieder* unexplored, confining his attention to a few popular masterpieces. It cannot be maintained that he gave much encouragement to native composers of high aims. In a word, while keeping well abreast of sound popular taste, he did little pioneer work in enlarging the horizon of the average concert-goer. Yet, with all deductions, he has rendered signal services to the art of song. His methods were above reproach. His natural gifts had been assiduously cultivated, and were exercised with a happy blending of intelligence and emotional force. He always gave of his best ; whatever he did, he did with his might. The late Hans von Bülow declared that a tenor was a disease. Mr. Santley has proved that a baritone is all the better for being a man.

May 25, 1907.

XVI

STERNDALE BENNETT

BIOGRAPHIES of living musicians who are still in mid-career have become so common of late years that it is worth noting that we have had to wait thirty - two years for an authoritative Life of Sterndale Bennett. This delay is thoroughly in keeping with the character of one of the most modest and self-effacing of musicians, and it has been completely justified by results. The task has been done once and for all with a discretion and delicacy worthy of the subject, and with a filial piety that is never disfigured by hero-worship, by the composer's son.[1] The memoir is at once concise, adequate, and—as far as could be expected in the circumstances—critical. No attempt is made to claim for Bennett a place among the great masters, but his right to be

---

[1] *The Life of William Sterndale Bennett.* By his Son, J. R. Sterndale Bennett, M.A. Cambridge : at the University Press. [12s. 6d. net.]

regarded, within the limits prescribed by his temperament and his environment, as a consummate musician and a composer of high aims and distinguished achievement is temperately preferred and convincingly supported.

When we speak of the limits prescribed by his temperament, we do not for a moment wish to imply that Bennett was not admirably equipped for the service of Art. He had many of the highest qualities of the artistic temperament, but they were neutralised by traits which rendered him more lovable than conspicuous. His caution and self-criticism were extreme. He thought less of himself than his admirers did, and he habitually considered the convenience of others. He had none of the exuberance, the egoism, or the intolerance of genius. The notion that his talents entitled him to depend on the generosity of patrons or admirers never entered into his head. He had not only the artistic conscience which rendered it impossible for him to write down to the level of the gross public, but that other and larger conscience which enabled him to accept cheerfully any drudgery, so long as it was honourable, which ensured his own independence. His attitude in regard to money matters was disinterested to the verge of quixotry. Many people, if asked to name their terms,

proceed on the assumption that it is good policy
to ask for more than they expect to get.   Bennett
went to the opposite extreme, and though he may
have often suffered from his modest estimate of
his own value, it is on record that on one occasion
at least he was given more than he asked for.
The bargaining faculty was in him absolutely
non-existent.   When, at the height of his fame,
he was approached by one of the great music-
publishers, who proposed that he might name
his own terms if he would wholly devote himself
to composition, he " at once changed the subject,"
and " next morning, when one of his family who
had been present the night before referred to the
matter, he said, apparently with some effort,
' Nothing shall induce me to place myself in
the hands of men of business.' "   Again, when
a serious financial crisis occurred at the Royal
Academy of Music, shortly after his appointment
as Principal, and the Directors of themselves were
powerless to avert its doom, Bennett called the
Professors together and found them ready to
follow his lead by offering their services for the
summer term, without regard to remuneration,
if the Directors would consent to postpone the
closing of the Academy from March to July
1868—a proposal which saved the situation just
as similar action on the part of Dr. Cotton and

his devoted assistant-masters saved the situation in the early days of Marlborough. The result of Bennett's self-denying ordinance is best given in his son's words :—

The years following his appointment at the Academy—where he had anticipated no excitement or disturbance of his affairs—not only brought a burden of responsibility in connection with its management, but also a great change in his private circumstances. His habit had been, after his wife's death, to add up at the end of each year the income derived from teaching. This reached its maximum in the year preceding his election to the Principalship. It then began to decrease, but there was to be a payment from the Academy as a set-off. After he resigned his stipend as Principal, and ceased to place any fixed limit on the time spent in performing his duties, there was at once a great shrinkage of his income. At the end of 1869, after making his calculation, he added, as was his wont, his few words of thanks to the Almighty ; but the figures were in front of him, and he must have noticed how serious matters were becoming. He seems, however, to have wished to banish from his mind the sacrifice he was making ; for he never added up his income again. The cheques which he received from the Academy, in return for all the work he did there, were drawn, term after term, for six-and-a-half guineas. This sum must have represented some reduced fees for the teaching of composition. The other Professors, after voluntarily allowing their fees to be taxed for a term or two in 1868, had then been paid in full, but Bennett must have declined to receive, or perhaps, as Chairman, to award himself the higher fee. Balancing what he received against what he lost through decrease of other work, the writer has carefully calculated that during the eight years from the time of his election to the Principalship in 1866 to the time when he was again assigned a salary in 1874, his position at the Academy cost him an annual average sum equivalent to twenty-seven per cent on the income he was making when he accepted the appointment.

In this context, and as a final instance of his unselfishness, we may note that on the day before he was struck down by his last illness—only eight days before his death—he declined the offer of a friend to drive him to the Crystal Palace, where his Symphony in G minor was to be played, on the score of another engagement. " It was his wont to finish his week's labour by giving a free lesson to three girls from the Clergy Orphan School, the house of which lay hard by his own dwelling-place in St. John's Wood. The lesson thus given on Saturday, January 23rd, 1875, proved to be the last act in his vocation and ministry," and was alluded to by Dean Stanley, from the pulpit of Westminster Abbey, as a fitting close to his life's work. This strong sense of duty, it should be added, was allied to a fatherly concern for the health of his students, in illustration of which a charming story was told by a writer in *Fraser's Magazine* for July 1875. " He found a very small boy crying over the intricacies of chromatic chords and enharmonic modulations. 'Ah,' said he, 'I see what you want, my little fellow, it is pudding!' and he took him straight to his own house, where he was regaled for a fortnight, and perhaps got a little assistance in his musical difficulties."

No doubt there are some critics who will be prepared to assert that Bennett was too good, or at any rate too well-balanced, a man to be a great musician. He never "ate his bread with tears," though if he did he never would have talked about it. He had his disappointments and felt them keenly, for he was a sensitive if reserved man. But his life was, on the whole, well-rounded and happy ; he enjoyed the respect as well as the affection of his friends, he was singularly fortunate in his marriage and his home, and simply and solely on his merits he achieved a very considerable reputation on the Continent. Schumann and Mendelssohn welcomed him as an equal, and he was the first and only English musician who was ever invited to undertake the conductorship of the famous Gewandhaus Concerts at Leipzig. Yet all this appreciation never for a moment shook his loyalty to his native land or tempted him to denationalise himself. The influence exerted on him by Mendelssohn—the recent reaction against whom has undoubtedly affected Bennett's reputation—was considerable, and in view of their personal relations and a certain affinity of mind it would have been surprising had it been otherwise. But Bennett was no slavish imitator ; the core of his work was his own, and his great exemplar was not Mendelssohn, but Mozart. His music was neither sublime nor poignant ; the stream of his inspiration had not the depths or the foaming cataracts of a mighty river, but in its limpid and refreshing purity it reflected the good and gentle spirit from which it sprang.

There are many other points in Bennett's industrious but uneventful career that we have left untouched : his visits to Germany ; his friendships ; his estrangement from Costa, who remained implacable to the last ; his pioneer work in popularising the great works of J. S. Bach. There is also the honourable record of his official association with the Philharmonic Society, the Leeds Festival, and the University of Cambridge. But if we have dwelt more on his character than his accomplishments, the book must be held responsible. The abiding impression that one gains from its perusal is that of a man who was finer than his music, gracious and beautiful though it was. The memoir is appropriately issued by the Press of the University which honoured itself by

electing him Professor of Music, and is enriched
by several excellent portraits and illustrations.
The photograph taken when he was about thirty-
five, and reproduced at p. 209, is even happier
than Millais's fine portrait in recalling the
grave intellectual beauty and distinction of his
countenance.

December 21, 1907.

XVII

MANUEL GARCIA

MANUEL GARCIA the younger, who was born
in 1805 and died in 1906, had so much to
recommend him beyond his longevity that we
cannot congratulate Mr. Mackinlay on the choice
of his title—*Garcia the Centenarian.*[1] True, he
was the only musician of note who attained to
that patriarchal age, and of him, as of the old
negro woman in Walt Whitman's " Ethiopia
Saluting the Colours," it could well have been
said, " How strange the things you see and have
seen." He was in Spain during the whole of
the Peninsular War, and in Naples when Murat
was executed. Journeying to America in 1825,
he saw Joseph Bonaparte, the ex-King of Spain,
in exile. Paris was his headquarters from 1828
to 1848, where he witnessed both Revolutions,

---

[1] *Garcia the Centenarian and his Times.* By M. Sterling Mackinlay.
London : W. Blackwood and Sons. [15s. net.]

129   K

and for the last fifty-eight years of his life he lived in England. He was born before Mendelssohn or Schumann, and outlived the first by nearly sixty, and the second by fifty, years. He received lessons from Ansani, who knew, and was old enough to have been the pupil of, Porpora ; and in 1876 he was invited by Wagner to train the singers for the opening performances at Bayreuth. Finally, he attended and took the liveliest interest in the celebrations in honour of his hundredth birthday in 1905. But though profoundly interesting as a link with the past, and as bridging the gap between Porpora and Wagner, Garcia had far greater and more enduring titles to recollection than his prodigious longevity. He will be remembered, not as Garcia the centenarian, but as Garcia the inventor of the laryngoscope ; Garcia the author of the *Traité de l'art du chant* ; Garcia the elder brother of the two most interesting and gifted female singers of the century—Malibran and Pauline Viardot-Garcia.

Musical genius seldom remains on the same plane for two generations, and Manuel Garcia the elder has long been eclipsed by his more famous children. But the record of his life proves him to have been a man of astonishing versatility and resource, equally distinguished as singer, teacher, composer, and impresario. He created the rôle of Almaviva in the *Barbiere* ; sang with great success in Spain, France, Italy, and England ; took the first Italian opera company to America in 1825 ; composed some forty operas, in many cases writing the words as well as the music. The most amazing instance of his resourcefulness is connected with his visit to Mexico, where, discovering that nearly all the music of the company's repertory had been left behind or lost, he reproduced the entire scores of *Don Giovanni, Otello,* and *Il Barbiere* from memory, and then set to work to compose eight new operas for his company ! This Admirable Crichton—who was also, it appears, a competent scene-painter—had the temper as well as the energy of a demon. When Malibran declared that she could not learn a rôle in two days, he is reported to have said : " You *will* do it, my daughter ; and if you fail in any way, I shall *really* strike you with my dagger when I am supposed to kill you on the stage." On the other hand, as a set-off against the numerous stories of his tyranny, and even cruelty, to his children, we have the testimony of Madame Viardot : " How often have I heard my sister Maria remark, ' Si mon père n'avait pas été si sévère avec moi, je n'aurais rien fait de bon ; j'étais paresseuse et indocile.' As for myself, I never saw my father lose his patience with me while he taught me the solfège, music and singing." Manuel the elder died in 1832 at the age of fifty-seven, and the meteoric Malibran only survived him four years, throwing away her life in a mad fit of emulation rather than yield to a rival and disappoint the public. It is more than seventy years since her tragic death at Manchester, and there can be very few persons living who heard her sing ; but fate has been kinder to her than to most of her contemporaries, and for the excellent reason that she combined with great natural gifts extraordinary personal charm, vivacity, and intelligence. Unlike the great majority of *prime donne,* she was a first-rate musician. The charming reminiscences of M. Ernest Legouvé, on which Mr. Mackinlay might have drawn far more freely, prove her to have been an exceptionally brilliant and witty talker. The glamour of her irregular beauty and the magic of her voice are immortalised in the verse of de Musset ; but the true secret of her continuing fame is that she had not only a charming face and an exceptional larynx, but a most engaging and distinguished mind, and a certain intrepidity of temperament which prompted her to do chivalrous as well as reckless things.

Pauline Viardot-Garcia, though inferior in the quality of fascination to her elder sister, eclipsed her in dramatic power and all-round mastery of her art. Like Malibran, she was a first-rate musician, studied composition and the pianoforte under the best masters and to excellent purpose, and from the very first appealed to the leading writers and artists as well as musicians of her time. She is generally believed to have been the proto-type of George Sand's *Consuelo*, and moved in the mid-stream of culture when the Romantic movement was at its height, numbering amongst her admirers and friends Heine, de Musset, Berlioz, Chopin, and Liszt. She was that *rara avis*, a *prima donna* who kept abreast of the times, and lent encouragement to pioneers in the new paths. She was probably the first singer of her class to appreciate Brahms, who was a welcome visitor at her villa at Baden-Baden, and Schumann dedicated to her his beautiful *Liederkreis*. Sir Charles Santley in his reminiscences deliberately places her and Ronconi at the head of all the operatic singers he ever heard in his long career. Lastly, it may be noted that the remarkable and delicate sympathy with which Tourguenieff always wrote of music and musicians may fairly be attri-buted to her lifelong friendship with the great Russian novelist.

The fame of Manuel Garcia the younger rests on a different basis. Like his sisters, he was carefully grounded in the technique of the art ; like them, he was trained to be a singer, and for a short space appeared on the boards with credit, if not with special distinction. But his voice, never a powerful organ, suffered severely from the strain imposed on it during his visit to America as a member of his father's company, and by the time he was twenty-five he realised that the avenue to success was closed to him as a public singer. For a while he contemplated entering the Navy, and it appears that he actually served in the commissariat department of the French expedition to Algiers in 1830. By the end of that year, however, he had decided to devote himself in real earnest to the career of teaching, and, with a thoroughness more characteristic of a Teuton than a Spaniard, undertook a prolonged course of medical studies with a view to mastering the physiology of the larynx. The result triumphantly justified this elaborate scheme of self-preparation. Established as a singing-master early in the " thirties," he trained Jenny Lind in the years 1841-42, published his famous *Traité de l'art du chant* in 1847, and migrated to London after the Revolution of 1848. His invention of the laryngoscope, which Huxley described as a new ally against disease and a most valuable addition to that series of instruments which have revolutionised the practice of medicine, dates from the year 1854. In 1857 he gave lessons to Santley, who has called him the King of Masters, and was still teaching more than forty years later, Mr. Mackinlay, the author of this memoir, having been his pupil from 1895 to 1900. The secret of his longevity could not be better explained than in his own happy phrase : "Je suis trop occupé pour avoir le temps de mourir."

Mr. Mackinlay brings to his task a sincere enthusiasm for his subject. He gives us an interesting account of Garcia's method as a teacher, and illustrates his modesty, courtesy, patience, and humour by some characteristic anecdotes. He has also unearthed some curious information bearing on the visit of the Garcias to America in 1825 from New York journals of the time. Here, unfortunately, commendation must end. His style is slipshod, undistinguished, and disfigured by facetious comments and gross solecisms. He uses the dreadful word "rendition," and habitually alludes to Garcia as the "maestro." His narrative is cumbered with a great deal of wholly irrelevant padding, both in the way of text and illustrations, which include full-length photographs of the present King and Queen of Spain (to whom the book is dedicated), of

Madame Melba (who was not Garcia's pupil at all), and of Mr. Hermann Klein. He always speaks of Malibran as a contralto, which is a most misleading statement. Her voice *was* a contralto, but she combined with it a soprano register and achieved her greatest successes in soprano rôles. The curious omissions in the narrative are doubtless to be accounted for by the fact that in the Preface acknowledgment is made of the assistance only of Garcia's friends and pupils. To sum up, the new matter contributed by Mr. Mackinlay might have furnished forth a magazine article, but affords no excuse for the publication of a volume of three hundred and thirty pages.

April 18, 1908.

XVIII

JACQUES BLUMENTHAL

The notices of M. Blumenthal, who died on May 17th, 1908, with the exception of an appreciative estimate which appeared in the *Daily Telegraph* of May 20th, have been both perfunctory and inadequate. It is true that he was not a commanding figure in the musical world. A generation has grown up since he retired from the active pursuit of his profession whether as teacher or performer, and his songs, once widely popular in the concert-room and the drawing-room, though marked by a fervour and grace rarely found in the literature of the *salon*, have long been superseded by compositions for the most part greatly inferior in workmanship and sentiment. But without preferring any undue claims on behalf of his creative talent, it may fairly be contended that for many years he filled an almost unique position in the musical world—that of a patron who had been a professional—with such tact, geniality, and generosity that his removal causes a gap which no living musician seems likely to fill.

Before dealing more fully with this later phase of his life, some obvious omissions in the notices of his career may be briefly remedied. Mention has been made of the thoroughness of his musical schooling at Vienna and Paris, but little or nothing seems to have been said of his pianoforte-playing, which was of a very finished and delicate quality. He came to this country in 1848 as a pianist, and used to perform regularly at the concerts of the Musical Union under the management of John Ella. "He and Otto Goldschmidt," writes an old friend of his, himself a fastidious critic, "were boys together in Hamburg, and in their young days had been rival *virtuosi*. Blumenthal's touch was equal, if not superior, to that of any other pianist I ever heard, and his readings of Beethoven and Chopin, stamped with his own individuality, showed in every detail the patient study and thought he had given to them."

M. Blumenthal's fine musical equipment and engaging personality soon secured for him a large and lucrative *clientèle*, and for more than twenty years he was in great request as a pianoforte teacher, while his songs—notably "The Requital" and

"The Message"—endeared him to amateurs in a day when the glories of Schubert, Schumann, and Brahms were still something of a sealed book. But while his reputation with the public as a composer rests on the songs mentioned above, most of which were composed in his early or middle life, during the last twenty years or so he wrote only to please himself, and produced a number of lyrics little known to the public, some of which were published under the title of *Intimate Songs* and are marked by qualities of a high order.

M. Blumenthal practically retired from the profession in 1868, after making a singularly happy marriage, and for the remainder of his life, released from the drudgery of teaching, he was able to devote himself to the study of his art and the encouragement of artists. There never was a more inveterate concert-goer when any important or significant music was to be heard, for, though grounded in the classics, he took the deepest interest in the development of the modern school, and his admiration for Wagner was combined with an enthusiastic love of the works of Brahms. But M. Blumenthal's devotion to music was no selfish pre-occupation. He had a real genius for friendship : he was a most gracious host, and no one who had the privilege of being invited to his birthday-parties in old days is likely to forget them. Almost every musician of note—singers and instrumentalists—took part in these entertainments, and the assemblage of artists, men of letters, statesmen, and other celebrities lent these gatherings a peculiar lustre. One of the special features of these parties was the performance of Brahms's wonderful *a cappella* part-songs—heard in many cases for the first time in this country— by a small choir of about twenty singers, including, among others, Mrs. Hutchinson, Miss Hilda Wilson, Miss Lena Little, Miss Agnes Janson, Miss Carlotta Elliot, Mrs. Robert Lyttelton (Miss Santley), Miss Friedländer, the Misses Robertson, Mr. Shakespeare, and Mr. David Bispham, all of whom delighted in doing homage to their friend. De Soria was a frequent attraction at M. Blumenthal's parties, and, allowing for a certain amount of characteristic exaggeration, there is no better picture of that remarkable performer, or of the company assembled under M. Blumenthal's hospitable roof at Hyde Park Gate, than that given by Mr. du Maurier in *Trilby* :—

Glorioli—the biggest, handsomest, and most distinguished Jew that ever was—one of the Sephardim (one of the Seraphim !)—hailed from Spain, where he was junior partner in the great firm of Moralés, Peralés, Gonzalés and Glorioli, wine merchants, Malaga.   He travelled for his firm ; his wine was good, and he sold much of it in England. But his voice would bring him far more gold in the month he spent here ; for his wines have been equalled—if it be not libellous to say so—but there was no voice like his anywhere in the world, and no more finished singer. . . . He looked at the beautiful ladies, and ogled and smiled ; and from his scarcely-parted, moist, thick bearded lips, which he always licked before singing, there issued the most ravishing sounds that have ever been heard from throat of man or woman or boy ! He could sing both high and low and soft and loud, and the frivolous were bewitched, as was only to be expected ; but even the earnestest of all, caught, surprised, rapt, astounded, shaken, tickled, teased, harrowed, tortured, tantalised, aggravated, seduced, demoralised, degraded, corrupted into mere naturalness, forgot to dissemble their delight. . . . Thus the night wore itself away The Prinzessen, Comtessen, and Serene English Altessen (and other ladies of less exalted rank) departed home in cabs and carriages ; and hostess and daughters went to bed. Late sitters of the ruder sex supped again, and smoked and chatted and listened to comic songs and recitations by celebrated actors.

The entertainment described by du Maurier took place at the house of " Sir Louis Cornelys," who is almost certainly meant for Leighton. None the less, it may serve to recall better than any words of ours the spirit and the comprehensive character of those parties at Hyde Park Gate where De Soria or Madame Conneau warbled their delectable ditties, and Lionel Benson's picked choir gave Brahms's *Stand das Mädchen*, *Vineta*, and other incomparable specimens of unaccompanied part-music ; where Simonetti fiddled, and Miss Cheetham sang American coon-songs, and Arthur Cecil preached his mock-sermon on " Pat-a-cake, Pat-a-cake, baker's man." The programmes were eclectic, and may occasionally have offended purists ; but you were sure of hearing either fine music or music finely performed. In a word, there was always an educative influence at work, and, given the character of the audience and the proportion of people present who were not really musical, it was impossible not to recognise the judicious opportunism of the host. But after all, these entertainments, delightful as they were, only illustrated one side of M. Blumenthal's character —his social gift and his faculty for enlivening the leisure hours of his friends. Closer acquaintance revealed in him a man who took an intelligent interest in letters and politics, and, above all, one whose own early experiences made him generously sensitive to the claims of aspiring talent. He had himself known the difficulties which confront young and friendless artists, and this knowledge gave a peculiar zest to his benevolence. He took the deepest interest in the career of young musicians of promise, did all he could to help them to obtain engagements, and encouraged them with sound advice and substantial assistance. The number of his kind acts was legion ; the tale of his secret benefactions endless. It was not, perhaps, a strenuous life, but it was far from being an idle or unprofitable one. He was a diligent student of his art to the end of his long life, he watched its latest developments with a keen but not unsympathetic eye, and he has left a name that will long be associated with happy memories of his graceful and generous services as host, patron, and friend.

June 20, 1908.

XIX

MENDELSSOHN'S CENTENARY

OF all the remarkable men who were born in that
annus mirabilis 1809, Mendelssohn has probably
undergone the greatest vicissitudes of posthumous
popularity. Berlioz, unappreciated in his lifetime,
said that he should be well content if he could
live to be a hundred and twenty ; as a matter of
fact, if he had said eighty or ninety he would have
been nearer the mark, for already his fame, apart
from his influence on the evolution of orchestral
music, is somewhat on the down-grade, judged by
the test of performances. Mendelssohn, on the
other hand, early achieved popularity, and this
recognition went on growing for two or three
decades after his death. His relations with this
country were altogether remarkable. Not only
did he visit our shores ten times in his short life,
but he drew the inspiration for some of his finest
orchestral work from Scots lore and landscape, and

more than one of his most important compositions were produced in England. He met almost every one worth knowing in London, and the testimony to his charm from people so widely different as Thackeray and Mrs. Grote may be taken as conclusive evidence of his personal magnetism. He was a *persona grata* at Court, a favourite in society, impressed the intellectuals and won the applause of the great musical middle class. Since the days of Handel no foreign musician had twined himself more closely round the fibres of the average Englishman. The popularity of the " Songs without Words " was prodigious, and it affected musical taste in England so deeply that the Mendelssohn worshippers, more Royalist than the King, regarded it as an act of duty to disparage the music of any newcomer—notably Schumann— who ventured to imperil the supremacy of their idol. This was extremely unfair to both sides, but perhaps Mendelssohn has suffered most in the long run from the indiscretions of his admirers. The systematic overpraise of his music, and the habit of overestimating his slighter compositions, led gradually to a reaction in which his really great achievements have been indiscriminately confounded with his weaker work. This is all the harder when one remembers the

L

generosity and loyalty of Mendelssohn to his
contemporaries and predecessors. How charming
was his tribute to Chopin when he spoke of a
Prelude which he would like to go on playing for
ever, especially because by no possibility could he
ever have composed it himself. And how finely
he rebuked the players at the Philharmonic when
they laughed at the triplet figure in the Finale of
Schubert's C major Symphony, telling them that
if they would not listen to Schubert, he would
withdraw his own new overture. The part he
played in the revival of Bach's music is alone
enough to win him immortal gratitude.

But while Mendelssohn's fame suffered from
the "sixties" onward from legitimate competition as the genius of Schubert, Schumann, and
Brahms gained wider recognition in the concert-
room, and the tremendous influence of Wagner
made itself felt on the stage, he gradually became
the special aversion of those who base their claim
to enlightenment on the extent of their divergence
from the opinion of the majority. No doubt
there was a good deal of sincere reaction against
the unfailing urbanity of Mendelssohn's music—
the lack of poignancy, regret, passion, and
abandonment. But along with justifiable criticism
there was mixed up a great deal of unwarrantable
disparagement. This hostility was chiefly shown

amongst the extreme Wagnerites — though Wagner himself, as Mr. Dannreuther reminds us, had a lively appreciation of Mendelssohn's work, and in particular of his remarkable gifts as a musical landscape painter — and it gradually became so acute in certain circles that to confess to an admiration of Mendelssohn exposed one to the risk of being written down as Early Victorian, *bourgeois*, and altogether "out of the movement." This attitude has found copious expression during the last ten years in the Press and in books devoted to musical criticism, and the reasons for which Mendelssohn has been relegated to the category of the mediocre afford a most instructive commentary on the doctrine of "art for art's sake" and the cant of talking against cant. Mendelssohn, it is urged, cannot be regarded as a great composer because he came of wealthy parents, never "ate his bread with tears," and was not "by suffering made strong." He was born with a silver spoon in his mouth, and had his path smoothed from the very outset by devoted relations and influential patrons. Again, he was carefully and regularly trained, and, as the head of a conservatorium, has been exposed to the deadly charge of being an academic. Then he had none of the irregularity, angularity, or colossal egotism associated with daemonic genius. It was his misfortune—as a claimant to immortality—that he was a perfect gentleman without a redeeming vice. He was irreproachable in all his domestic relations—whether as son, husband, and father—he was singularly happy in his married life, and, so far as we are aware, never lost a friend. All the kind and gracious acts on which his biographers insist in evidence of his moral excellence, integrity, lovableness, and charm are treated as so many damning proofs of his shortcomings when tried by the test of heroic antinomianism. His methodical habits, his beautifully regular handwriting, his courtesy and consideration for others, his fondness for society, his neatness,—all these traits only serve to aggravate the charge against him that he was at once too uniformly prosperous, too cheerful, and too good a citizen to be a great artist. Even his good looks, or perhaps we should say his peculiar type of good looks, are a source of complaint, and one of his detractors gracefully describes his portraits as representing a "simpering noodle." As for his all-round musical equipment, his remarkable performances as an organist and pianist, and his skill as a draughtsman, linguist, dancer,—these, according to such critics, are only evidences of a superficial versatility irreconcilable with the true concentration of genius.

There remains his music, and the centenary

celebrations of the past month happily make it clear that, setting aside some grotesque ebullitions of ill-conditioned animosity, the violence of reaction and detraction has given place to an attitude of discriminating recognition. The sifting process of time has already done its work ; but still there is a considerable number of his works the freshness and vitality of which repetition is unable to impair—notably the three beautiful seascapes, the Scotch and Italian symphonies, and the exhilarating *Midsummer Night's Dream* music. When Mendelssohn was at his best, he maintained an even perfection to which few of the immortals have attained, unlike some of the belauded moderns whose greatest achievements, by the admission of their most faithful admirers, oscillate between the sublime and the monstrous. As Dr. Ernest Walker says in the *Manchester Guardian*, in what is probably the best appreciation of Mendelssohn that has appeared in the English Press, there is no music in existence that expresses so flawlessly " the moods of one who has put away childish things but is not yet a full-grown man—the buoyant freshness and frankness, the healthy delight in nature, the first stirrings of sincere emotion which has as yet had no time to be deep . . . and assuredly such an achievement deserves immortality." The peculiarity of

Mendelssohn's development was acutely summed up in Bülow's saying that he "began by being a genius and ended by being a talent," but that he was perfect in both phases. The wisest comments on his limitations are to be found in the concluding words of Grove's biography. After contending that he had high genius, Grove continues :—

But his genius had not been subjected to those fiery trials which seem necessary to ensure its abiding possession of the depths of the human heart. "My music," says Schubert, "is the product of my genius and my misery ; and that which I have written in my greatest distress is that which the world seems to like best." Now Mendelssohn was never more than temporarily unhappy. He did not know distress as he knew happiness. Perhaps there was even something in the constitution of his mind which forbade his harbouring it, or being permanently affected by it. He was so practical, that as a matter of duty he would have thrown it off. In this as in most other things he was always under control. At any rate he was never tried by poverty, or disappointment, or ill-health, or a morbid temper, or neglect, or the perfidy of friends, or any of the other great ills which crowded so thickly around Beethoven, Schubert, or Schumann. Who can wish that he had been ? that that bright, pure, aspiring spirit should have been dulled by distress or torn with agony ? It might have lent a deeper undertone to his songs, or have enabled his adagios to draw tears where now they only give a saddened pleasure. But let us take the man as we have him. Surely there is enough of conflict and violence in life and in art. When we want to be made unhappy we can turn to others. It is well in these agitated modern days to be able to point to one perfectly balanced nature, in whose life, whose letters, and whose music alike, all is at once manly and refined, clever and pure, brilliant and solid. For the enjoyment of such shining heights of goodness we may well forgo for once the depths of misery and sorrow.

The laconic eulogy of the Latin epitaph, *neminem tristem fecit*, is peculiarly appropriate to this musical Prince Charming, who fascinated all whom he ever met. Rubinstein spoke of his work as the swan-song of classicism ; but the phrase is more attractive than true, since Mendelssohn's best work was always suffused with the glowing tints of romance.

Anniversary celebrations are sadly overdone nowadays. But the Mendelssohn centenary has not been without its value, if only as affording an occasion, in the words of Dr. Walker, to call a halt to the unfounded and unjust depreciation of to-day :—

Much of his work we must renounce. . . . But, beyond the Mendelssohn whose appeal to us is fettered and dulled by his failure to express the ultimate things, there stands the eager youth who looks out with bright eyes upon the world, and, behold, all is very good. Many a young composer of to-day, who seems while still in his teens to stagger like a musical Atlas under a world of sorrow and sin, would be all the better for more knowledge of the great Mendelssohn. He would learn how the natural expression of his time of life can be given musical shape as a permanent artistic treasure . . . he would learn supreme clearness of expression, supreme polish of style.

In a word, Mendelssohn's finest works not only can be heard with pleasure, but studied with profit. Dr. Walker's praise is all the more valuable in view of the severity with which he has exposed the weaknesses and mannerisms of Mendelssohn. But with due reserves, he would evidently re-echo the punning salutation of the friend who quoted *donec eris Felix*—the Felix Mendelssohn of the *Hebrides—multos numerabis amicos.*

February 20, 1909.

XX

MELBA

THE *prima donna*, as portrayed in earlier memoirs
—*e.g.* the reminiscences of Mapleson and other
impresarios or conductors—was an eccentric rather
than edifying type of humanity. Her wardrobe
recalled that of Queen Elizabeth. She was habitually accompanied by a miscellaneous menagerie,
in which as a rule parrots figured largely, and
she lived principally on bonbons. Her greediness
for sweets—and applause—was only equalled by
her jealousy, and if she was inclined to malinger,
the impresario's trump card was to threaten to
" bill " a hated rival. Berlioz spoke of her as a
monster, with the reservation that she was often
a very attractive monster ; Handel had a summary
method of dealing with a recalcitrant *diva* ; and
Wagner went his own way with a sovereign
disregard for her vagaries ; but most composers
have either accepted her as a necessary evil, or
yielded to her arbitrary requirements.

But does this capricious, spoiled child of fortune, half nightingale, half peacock, still exist ? Certainly not, if we are to believe Miss Murphy, the industrious biographer of the most world-renowned of living queens of song still on the stage.[1] The picture given by her of Madame Melba entirely explodes the old traditional view. The life which the new *prima donna* leads is no longer one of luxurious self - indulgence tempered with violent vocal effort. It is a continuously strenuous life in which the singer reconciles her allegiance to art with the claims of diplomacy, philanthropy, and patriotism. She rises, if not with the lark, at any rate in time for breakfast soon after eight, and spends two hours on her correspondence before fulfilling the other engagements of the day. These are multifarious, and by no means all connected with music. The new *prima donna* finds time to cultivate her " mentality." She does not despise fiction, but her favourite author is not Miss Corelli ; it is Balzac. She is a devout student of Shakespeare and Omar Khayyám, and is specially attracted by biographical and historical works. Nor can the claims of society be forgone, for the modern *diva*, in virtue of her many-sided

[1] *Melba : a Biography.* By Agnes C. Murphy. London : Chatto and Windus. [16s. net.]

equipment, is a *persona grata* in the most select coteries. Withal she is thoroughly domestic, and observes an almost Spartan simplicity in her diet. On the lyric stage her acknowledged pre-eminence does not prevent her from accepting subsidiary rôles to achieve an artistic *ensemble*. She " stoops to conquer " by playing Michaela in *Carmen* or the Queen in *The Huguenots*. Secure in her supremacy, she is incapable of jealousy. Her common-sense is never demoralised by eulogy, and even when " the dazzling virtuosity and personal sonorousness " of her " sweetly timbred voice " arouse audiences to an alarming state of enthusiasm, she never betrays any undue exultation in her triumphs. Naturally these heights of self-control are attained by slow degrees, and the early stages of the *prima donna's* career are not free from disappointments and rebuffs. Madame Melba was not considered good enough for inclusion in the Savoy Opera company in 1886, and though her *début* in *Rigoletto* at the Monnaie in October 1887 was a great success, she " cried almost incessantly for a whole week " because a musical critic discovered signs of evident inexperience in her subsequent appearance in the *Traviata*. She was received so coldly in London in her first season that she cancelled her engagement and returned to the Continent. At the Scala she had to overcome the prejudice of the public, and the appreciation of her talents in New York was of gradual growth.

Miss Murphy approaches her task in a spirit of high earnestness that is vastly impressive. There is an old story of an excellent officer who had one peculiar failing. Whenever he began to talk of the aristocracy his jaw dropped, and he became quite inarticulate. Miss Murphy, though dealing reverentially with such august topics, is never inarticulate, even when describing how Madame Melba was "accompanied to the [Ulster] Hall [in Belfast] by the Duke and Duchess of Abercorn, the Marchioness of Hamilton, the Ladies Gladys and Alexandra Hamilton, the Marchioness of Dufferin, Lady Hermione Blackwood, and Lord Frederick Hamilton." Madame Melba is probably the only living *prima donna* who has been kissed on both cheeks by a reigning Sovereign ; but Miss Murphy narrates this incident without any undue emotion, in fact quite in the spirit of the Christian Scientist who, relating the experiences of a brother-believer, observed : " He has raised six persons from the dead, but he isn't in the least stuck up about it." And certainly Madame Melba's experiences and exploits have been enough to unhinge the mental balance of most singers. At a farewell performance at St. Petersburg in 1891 "a band of music-loving youths belonging to the Russian aristocracy, like so many Raleighs spread their coats on the snow-covered footpath for her to walk on, and indulged in all sorts of other complimentary excesses." Only once in her career—in Holland in 1899—was her artistic success not endorsed by the Sovereign of the country in which she was performing. The tributes of famous musicians and composers to the superhuman and divine beauty of her voice may be passed over as natural ebullitions of the artistic temperament ; but Madame Melba was not merely called "Madame Stradivarius" by Joachim ; Cecil Rhodes pronounced her to be "a great singer, a great woman, guided by a prodigious individuality." When she entered the banquet-hall of a New York hotel on the arm of Archbishop Corrigan "a more stately pair it would be difficult to imagine. It might be suspected that the selection of her gown for the day had been made with an extra thought as to the colour possibilities of the occasion, for her delicate mauve toilette was in happiest harmony with the purple on Dr. Corrigan's clerical attire." And yet the Archbishop, on p. 141, is quoted as observing that Madame Melba had attained her pre-eminence "despite a persistent disregard for those nuances of diplomacy which I have always understood to be essential to the structure of operatic fame." This want of clerical insight, however, is nothing to that of the vicar of Stoke Poges, who when Madame Melba, attracted by her interest in Gray's poetry, had been playing and singing in his church, asked : " And who is Madame Melba ? " But such rebuffs have been few and far between of late years, and they have been long submerged by the floods of unbounded enthusiasm on which Madame Melba has been swept from triumph to triumph in the last fifteen years of her career. Her return to Australia in 1902 partook of the nature of a Royal progress, Governors, Mayors, and leading public men " associating themselves with the people's unrestrained ardour." Up to this time the highest fee ever paid to any singer for a single performance was £2000, but Madame Melba established a " financial record for the whole world " at her third concert, when she received the net sum of £2350 for her services. Miss Murphy's comments on this achievement are worth reproducing. After noting that the previous highest remuneration had been paid to Jenny Lind by Barnum, she continues :—

When Melba appeared in Sydney, the advertising tactics which Barnum and his early contemporaries had

so impudently favoured, and which it was assumed must
have been personally distasteful to the reserved Swedish
nightingale, had become hopelessly effete, and the business arrangements for the Australian singer's concerts
were carried out on formal and conservative lines of
unassailable dignity.

Perhaps the most dramatic incident in this
wonderful campaign was the demonstration at
Auckland, when the Maori chiefs paid homage
to Madame Melba, assured her of their allegiance
and love, and, hailing her as one of their queens,
presented her *inter alia* with an ancient nose flute,
made from the thighbone of a war captive, and
a small whalebone club. Demonstrations in
England in "honourment" of Madame Melba
—we borrow this word from one of the choicest
exercises in eulogy in these pages—have been
sadly lacking in these picturesque features ; but
it must have been some consolation to her to be
assured on the authority of an old resident, *à
propos* of her welcome at Plymouth in 1906, that
"the only time to compare with it was when
Gladstone visited Plymouth, and even that did
not equal the present occasion." Fed on what
Sir Walter Scott called "the pap of praise" for
twenty years, from the days when the *Etoile Belge*
"boldly placed the young Antipodean with ' the
profile of an Empress' in the same category with

Patti and Nilsson," Madame Melba has, we
gather, been preserved from *megalomania* by what
she herself calls "her level Scottish head." It is
also reassuring to learn that, "in spite of everything, Melba still retains a trace of the rigid
Presbyterianism in which she was reared."

The artistic lessons to be learned from this
record can be summed up in a few sentences.
Madame Melba had great natural gifts to start
with, but they were fortified by ambition, industry,
and persistence. She owes quite as much to force
of will as to temperament. Above all, she has
consistently gauged her powers at their true value
and never essayed more than she could perform.
Independently of its subject, however, the book
throws a good deal of light on the psychology of
musical hero - worship. Personally we have a
distaste for these "lauds of the living," but in
this case they are animated by a perfect sincerity
and redeemed by a most engagingly unconscious
humour.

October 30, 1909.

XXI

AUGUST J. JAEGER

THE announcement that it has been decided to hold a memorial concert to the late Mr. August J. Jaeger is most welcome to those who held the man in affection and appreciated the single-hearted and unselfish devotion with which he served the art he loved so well. No one ever got to know him without admiring his simple, generous nature, but the circle of his friends was never large. Even in the world of music Mr. Jaeger was by no means widely known. He was neither a composer nor a performer, and though he wrote a good deal in the *Musical Times* and was responsible for the analyses of most of Sir Edward Elgar's principal compositions, his work was largely anonymous, and this fact, coupled with his natural modesty and his delicate health, withdrew him from public notice. The valuable service he rendered Sir George Grove in revising his *Beethoven and his Nine Symphonies* was unaccountably left unacknowledged, for it was not in Grove to be ungrateful, and as a matter of fact he had a cordial admiration for Jaeger. Anyhow, the only notable recognition that Jaeger ever received in his lifetime was in Elgar's "Enigma" variations—which are supposed to reflect in music the personalities of several of his friends—where he appears under the alias of "Nimrod." No acknowledgment, however, could have been devised more delicately calculated to please his taste than this veiled association with his favourite modern composer. But if the rank-and-file of musicians knew little about him, everybody who was anybody in the musical world knew of Jaeger of Novellos as a musical enthusiast who could always be counted on to press the claims of the younger men to a hearing.

His life, which ended in early middle age in May 1909, was unmarked by any striking incident. Coming to London with his family from Düsseldorf—a city musically associated with the romantic Schumann and the pedantic Tausch—in the year 1878, he found employment in a map-publishing firm in the Strand in the early "eighties." But in those days he was already *fanatico per la musica*. The present writer met him first somewhere about the year 1885, when the Novello Oratorio Choir was formed under the conductorship of Sir Alexander Mackenzie, and, sitting next him among the tenors, soon struck up a firm friendship on the strength of a common enthusiasm for the "blond Johannes." Those were the days of the old Richter Choir, an organisation of amateurs largely recruited from the German colony, and mobilised from time to time to take part in performances of the Ninth Symphony. The average age of the choir must have been somewhat venerable, and the quality of tone emitted was often excruciating. Jaeger had no pretensions to be regarded as a singer, and used to compare his voice to a tenor trombone at full blast. But he sang with every fibre of his being when the music appealed to him, and the choir made up in goodwill what it lacked in charm. Mr. Frantzen was a first-rate chorus trainer, and Dr. Richter generally professed himself satisfied with the results at the final rehearsal. Jaeger was not in his element in the map-publishing business, though his uncongenial labours were lightened by the companionship of a lifelong friend, and he gladly availed himself of the offer of employment in the firm of Novellos, to whom he had been recommended by a musical acquaintance. His connexion with Novellos lasted practically for the rest of his life, for he retired only eighteen months before his death, and then solely because of the precarious state of his health. The association was mutually advantageous in a high degree. Jaeger on his side was glad of regular work which, even in its most "drudgical" aspect, was at least bound up with the art which interested him more than anything else, and during the last ten years of his life brought him into touch with a number of distinguished composers and musicians. When their works were passing through the press Jaeger's intelligence and sympathy rendered him an invaluable intermediary, and he enjoyed special facilities for attending festivals and concerts as the representative of his firm. On the other hand, his employers were singularly fortunate in securing the services of a man who was not only zealous, industrious, and efficient, but also a tremendous enthusiast, keenly sensitive to new developments, and a *persona gratissima* with the leaders of the musical world. Of the taint of commercialism there was not a trace in his character. He may have overestimated the talent of some of his idols, but at least he never extolled mediocrity or inanity. It is pleasant to know that Jaeger was appreciated as well as respected by the directors of his firm. During the long absences enforced by broken health, they treated him with a consideration and generosity which the present writer has more than once heard him gratefully acknowledge. For many years he struggled bravely against the ravages of "the captain-general of Death," as an old writer called consumption, until in 1908 he found himself no longer able to stand the strain of office work, and was reluctantly obliged to retire on a pension. These latter days were often sadly clouded by physical weakness. There were times when, as he put it, he was a thorough-going *Schwarzseher* ; when he envied those "who had so much work to do and were strong enough to stand the strain" ; when all that he could hope for was that music might raise him from the Inferno of hopelessness to "some gentle, stimulating Purgatory." But these black moods did not affect the sweetness of his disposition, and there were brighter days when he took long walks with his children, or managed to get to a Queen's Hall Symphony Concert. "Elgar's Symphony," he wrote a year ago, "has been a perfect godsend to me, for it has made me forget for a few happy hours that I am a doomed man." He was happy in his friends, happier still in his home life, and when his summons came he met it with an uncomplaining fortitude. "He loved his life, though not of death afraid," and the last wish that he expressed to his devoted wife was that she should write to his friends and bid them all good-bye for him.

The services that Jaeger rendered to many of the British composers of to-day cannot be easily over-estimated. For these services were not confined to a liberal interpretation of his official duties and responsibilities as the representative of a great publishing firm. He was an indefatigable propagandist and proselytiser. All that he wrote and said was animated by a heartfelt sincerity, and the only thing that disappointed him in his friends was when they failed to share his enthusiasms. His attitude was not judicial. Music either left him cold or filled him with ecstasy. But he always contended that the newcomer should have the benefit of the doubt until he was self-condemned. "It is only fair," he once wrote of a much-discussed modern work, "to extend to the composer that goodwill with which all amateurs *must* approach the greatest works of the classics (including our beloved Brahms) if they wish to enjoy their music. They take the quality of the classics for granted and *go to enjoy them*. A modern composer is *abgeschlachtet* [butchered] after one hearing." Yet though perhaps over-prone to praise, he was by no means uncritical. Writing again of the same work, he says :—
"Well, the work will have to go through the crucible of foreign opinion, where no patriotic enthusiasm affects the public verdict. I consider

the enthusiasm of last week exaggerated, certainly greatly affected by a display of patriotic pride in the composer. No foreign audience, American or European, will display a quarter of that frenzy. In fact I shouldn't be surprised to read of fiascos in Germany." If he spoke more of the moderns, it was because he felt that they were in more immediate need of encouragement, and that he gave them without stint. Yet when it came to a downright comparison, he would temper his lauds of the living with such frank admissions as : "He's not a Wagner. He's not a Brahms." But his foreign upbringing in no way biased him against the land of his adoption. Indeed, latterly he spoke with regret of the vitiation of musical taste in Germany, and the enslavement of modern composers to that over-exacting mistress—the orchestra.

Jaeger's letters were like the man—sincere, outspoken, impulsive. They show the pathetic, patient fight with disease, but they also reveal an enthusiasm as unflagging as "G.'s" at its biggest —another really great amateur. "I think Jaeger's secret," writes one of his closest friends, himself one of the most distinguished of our younger composers, "was his unfailing ear for the emotional signs in music. From that point of view alone, he could register how much vitality there was in a new work.   His defects in judgment arose from the same cause.   He believed in a piece if it made him feel like tears.   But he did not only bid for emotion.   He demanded noble effort and sanity, and sometimes came to hate that which had once moved him, but subsequently showed its over-emotion.   His help to young composers was marvellous.   If he gave us over-praise, he tempered it with much candid criticism."

Men so charged with emotion are not often practical, but, by a happy anomaly, Jaeger did not allow his romance to interfere with routine. Musicians are often terrible egoists, but Jaeger was an eminently unselfish enthusiast.   Despondent about himself, he was full of hope for others, and spent himself in smoothing their path to fame.

December 25, 1909.

XXII

PAULINE VIARDOT-GARCIA

ALFRED DE MUSSET, in the elegiac stanzas on Malibran written in 1836, descants melodiously on the transitoriness of the singer's fame :—

> le peintre et le poëte
> Laissent, en expirant, d'immortels héritiers ;
> Jamais l'affreuse nuit ne les prend tout entiers :
>
> .   .   .   .   .   .
>
> Recevant d'âge en âge une nouvelle vie,
> Ainsi s'en vont à Dieu les gloires d'autrefois ;
> Ainsi le vaste écho de la voix du génie
> Devient du genre humain l'universelle voix.
> Et de toi, morte hier, de toi, pauvre Marie,
> Au fond d'une chapelle il nous reste une croix !
> Une croix ! et l'oubli, la nuit et le silence !

The great singers of the past, with very few exceptions, have served to illustrate the truth of his lament. "The unique, the incomparable Banti," as Lord Mount-Edgcumbe called her, probably the greatest prima donna of the eighteenth

169

century, is now a veritable *nominis umbra*, and the redoubtable Catalani, the pioneer of the " star " system, only survives in one or two anecdotes. The case of Malibran, who died tragically at twenty-eight, was sad enough, but there was a magic about her which has defied the doom prophesied by the poet. She had a fascinating personality, and she was not merely a singer ; she was a first-rate musician and a witty and delightful woman, whose whimsical talk is still preserved for us in the reminiscences of the late M. Legouvé, while her amazing gifts of mimicry are chronicled in those of Moscheles. Now much the same qualities which won immortality for the radiant Malibran descended in an even richer abundance —as Malibran herself admitted—to her younger sister Pauline, who passed away in May 1910. Born in 1821—the year of Napoleon's death—she accompanied her parents to New York in 1825, and was with them when on their return journey from Mexico they were robbed of all their earnings, and Manuel Garcia had to sing for the delectation of his captors. In the next dozen years she travelled and studied to such good purpose that in 1838, when she made her *début* in Paris, she was mistress of five languages—Spanish, Italian, German, French, and English—an admirable pianist, and a clever draughtswoman. She was

a pupil of Liszt, and studied counterpoint under
Reicha,—fancy a prima donna in pre-Wagnerian
days studying counterpoint !   Her first appearance
in Paris was at the house of the Belgian Minister.
The next was at a matinée given by Madame de
Musset, at which she sang *Felice Donzella* by
Dessauer, show airs by de Bériot and Costa, as
well as *boléros et ariettes*.   Alfred de Musset was
enchanted by her singing and not less impressed by
her intelligence.   She talked " like an artist—and
a Princess."   His brother Paul describes how he
came back saying : " La charmante chose que le
génie !   Qu'on est heureux de vivre dans un
temps où il en existe encore et de le voir de près !"
The likeness to Malibran was so remarkable that
he called her a *revenant*,[1] and when Mlle. Garcia
gave a public concert at the Théâtre de la
Renaissance, he hailed the new star in a special
article in the *Revue des Deux Mondes* for January
1839.   Alfred de Musset is careful to state that
he was no musician ; but he had an unerring
instinct for quality, and his appreciation of " the
sister of Ninette and the daughter of Don Juan "

[1] In 1837 or thereabouts, according to de Musset, a young English lady
came to take a lesson from Lablache (who was lodging in the same house in
London with Mlle. Garcia and her mother) in the cavatina from *Norma*.
Lablache proceeded to tell her how Malibran sang it, and just as his pupil
was about to begin, a voice was heard from the next room singing the
identical air.   The pupil thought she recognised Malibran's voice, was overcome with fright, and fainted !

is a masterpiece of felicitous eulogy. Pauline Garcia was not beautiful, but he notes her extraordinarily expressive features, which changed not only with each song, but each phrase that she sang. " Elle possède, en un mot, le grand secret des artistes ; avant d'exprimer, elle sent.   Ce n'est pas sa voix qu'elle écoute, c'est son cœur."   He notices also the absence of effort and consciousness about her singing.   Whatever the music, " elle se livre à l'inspiration avec cette simplicité pleine d'aisance qui donne à tout un air de grandeur. Bien qu'elle ait fait de longues études, et que cette facilité cache une science profonde, il semble qu'elle soit comme les gens de qualité qui savent tout sans avoir jamais rien appris."   The article describes how on the day of Mlle. Garcia's concert de Musset had seen Rachel—another *débutante* of 1838—in a cabriolet, and was irresistibly impelled to compare these two girls, the one so extraordinarily accomplished, the other who knew no more than how to read, yet united by the common dower of genius.   Though they had never met they were none the less sisters, and he appeals to them, in prose, and finally in verse, to fulfil their true destiny and bring about that return to truth of which Art was then sorely in need :—

> Discutons nos travers, nos rêves et nos goûts,
> Comparons à loisir le moderne et l'antique,

Et ferraillons sous ces drapeaux jaloux ;
Quand nous serons au bout de notre rhétorique,
Deux enfants nés d'hier en sauront plus que nous.

O jeunes cœurs remplis d'antique poésie,
Soyez les bienvenus, enfants aimés des dieux !
Vous avez le même âge et le même génie.
La douce clarté soit bénie
Que vous ramenez dans nos yeux !

. . . . . .

Obéissez sans crainte au dieu qui vous inspire.
Ignorez, s'il se peut, que nous parlons de vous.
Ces plaintes, ces accords, ces pleurs, ce frais sourire,
Tous vos trésors, donnez-les-nous :
Chantez, enfants, laissez-nous dire.

Alfred de Musset's enthusiasm for these *deux nobles enfants*, as he called them, was no passing fancy, but founded on genuine admiration, and when Mlle. Garcia made her operatic *début* at the Théâtre Italien in Rossini's *Otello* next year, he devoted a second article in the *Revue des Deux Mondes* to the event. Meantime she had already appeared in the same opera in London in the spring. Writing to Madame de Musset, she described how the audience had wished her to repeat *Che smania* and the "Willow" song, but that she had refused to interrupt the dramatic continuity of the opera—an early but characteristic proof of her artistic conscience which greatly delighted de Musset.

The history of Pauline Garcia's subsequent relations with the Parisian public justified the misgivings expressed by de Musset in his second article. He doubted whether she would appeal to the stalls and boxes, and his doubts were well founded. Paul de Musset in the Life of his brother notes that the fashionable public failed to endorse the acclamations of genius and taste. Malibran's sister ·sang in her own way and at the prompting of her own heart. She would have none of the vulgar cut-and-dried passports to applause which were alone recognised at the Théâtre Italien. She followed a path diametrically opposed to that of routine, and despised the hackneyed " effects " which the *habitués* looked forward to at certain places in her rôles. On the other hand, her strokes of genius passed unperceived. In a word, she was original. " You had to understand her, and people did not understand her." So it came about that, after singing with a steadily diminishing success in the *Barbiere, Otello,* and *Cenerentola,* she decided to seek her fortune elsewhere, and went abroad, to the bitter regret of de Musset, who had regarded her as one of the hierophants of the new era. That she should be neglected and forgotten in two years was one of the many bitter drops in the cup of general disillusionment which prompted him to say at the age of thirty-two that he had lived too long. Mlle. Garcia, already Madame Viardot, went to Russia, Germany, Italy, Spain, and England, and Paris was given up to " twenty years of shrieking, bad taste, and complete decadence, until one fine evening pure art, unaffected singing, and dramatic music were again revealed at the Théâtre Lyrique. The sister of Malibran had reappeared in Gluck's *Orphée*."

We have dwelt at length on this episode of Madame Viardot-Garcia's life because it shows that in youth as in old age she displayed an unconventionality which endeared her to the elect, but perplexed the lovers of routine. " We shall always find," wrote Berlioz, " a fair number of female singers, popular from their brilliant singing of brilliant trifles, and odious to the great masters because utterly incapable of properly interpreting them." Berlioz in his wrath said that such singers were monsters ; but Madame Viardot's performance in *Orpheus* not only satisfied but enthralled that exacting and fastidious critic. By birth a Spaniard, she became a great international figure in the Republic of Art. Wherever she went the " intellectuals " and artists rendered her homage. We have read the tribute of de Musset, a Frenchman of genius, and Théophile Gautier was hardly less enthusiastic. It is generally admitted that George

Sand's *Consuelo* was a free portrait of Pauline Viardot-Garcia, and Michelet acknowledges her goodness of heart in the following rhapsodical passage : " Le jour où le monde plus sage rendra le sacerdoce aux femmes, commes elles l'eurent dans l'antiquité, qui s'étonnerait de voir marcher à la tête des pompes nationales la bonne, la charitable, la sainte Garcia-Viardot ? " Her most intimate friend was the great Russian novelist Tourguenieff, a supreme literary artist. Schumann dedicated his *Liederkreis* to her, and Brahms composed a choral serenade in honour of her birthday, when she was living at Baden-Baden in the " sixties," and conducted it outside her villa in the Lichtenthaler Allée early in the morning. The mention of Brahms reminds one of another abnormal trait in Madame Viardot— abnormal, that is, in a prima donna. She was not only abreast of her time, but positively ahead of it. Brand-new music never frightened her, but was sure of a sympathetic hearing. From the days when as a child of ten she used to try over Schubert's songs with Nourrit down to the end of her career, she consistently befriended and encouraged young composers. Long after her retirement from the stage she took part in the first public performance, at Jena, of Brahms's Alto Rhapsody, and in 1871 sang some of his

duets with Stockhausen in London.   Santley in
his   reminiscences — *Student   and   Singer* — after
speaking of the great artists who towered over
the rest, places her above all other female
singers.   She and Ronconi were the Mount
Everest and Aconcagua of his musical mountain-
range.   "No woman in my day has ever
approached her as a dramatic singer ; she was
perfect, as far as it is possible to attain perfection,
both as vocalist and actress."   It only remains to
be added that Madame Viardot was excluded
from the pages of the *Biographie universelle des
musiciens* of Fétis until the publication of the
supplement edited by M. Arthur Pougin in 1878,
and then she is described as a *cantatrice française*,
presumably because she was born in Paris.   As a
matter of fact, she was a Spanish singer, trained
in the Italian school, and married to a Frenchman, who by preference made her home in
Germany until she was obliged to leave after the
war of 1870-71.

May 28, 1910.

N

XXIII

CLARA NOVELLO

CLARA NOVELLO, whose Reminiscences [1] have all
the charm that belongs to a record never intended
for publication, was a great early and mid-
Victorian musical heroine. She was, indeed,
linked to that age in many ways : by her likeness
to Queen Victoria—humorously noticed by Lord
William Russell, our Ambassador at Berlin in the
" thirties," and perpetuated in the beautiful portrait
by her brother Edward which forms the frontispiece
to the volume—as well as by her preferences and
her limitations. In many respects, and in spite
of her mixed descent—her father was half English
and half Italian, and her mother half German and
half Irish—she was typically English. Her
calmness and composure, her stoicism, her honesty,
and her entire freedom from egotism, conceit, or

---

[1] *Clara Novello's Reminiscences.* Compiled by her Daughter, Contessa
Valeria Gigliucci. With a Memoir by Arthur D. Coleridge. London :
Edward Arnold. [10s. 6d. net.]

affectation, lent her an enviable distinction amongst the capricious tribe of *prime donne*. Nothing is so remarkable in these memoirs—given her eminence and achievements—as the absence of all mention of her triumphs. The testimonies to her greatness as an artist are almost without exception added by her daughter or Mr. Coleridge, and the chief interest of her own contribution resides in the light it throws on the personal history of the time and on her own delightful personality. Of the vanity and self-assertion only too common in great female singers she was singularly free. Her fame was untainted by notoriety ; indeed, as Mr. Coleridge says, "she bore a character beyond reproach ; it silenced any whisper of envy or detraction." Her attitude towards her contemporaries and rivals, though critical, was in the main generous and appreciative. But she could not stand pose, eccentricity, or ingratitude even in the greatest musicians. This wholesome sanity, however, though admirable in itself, perhaps militated against her success as a dramatic singer, and her greatest triumphs were achieved in oratorio. Her singing was like herself, pure, unaffected, and informed by a noble simplicity of manner. As Schumann said of her early performances at Leipzig, she was most in her element with Handel, "amid whose works she has grown up and become great." He also dwelt on the beauty of her voice, " every tone as sharply defined as the tones of a keyed instrument," and her evident desire not to seek prominence for herself but for the composer and his work only. Mendelssohn was equally enthusiastic about her purity of intonation and " thoroughbred musical feeling." But, curiously enough, there is no written testimony about Clara Novello that will endure longer than that of the utterly unmusical Charles Lamb. His affectionate references to her and her father are too well known to be quoted ; but these Reminiscences contain a passage relating to Clara Novello's early days at Shacklewell Green which shows how deeply she appreciated his notice :—

" How I loved dear Charles Lamb ! I once hid—to avoid the ignominy of going to bed—in the upright (cabinet) pianoforte, which in its lowest part had a sort of tiny cupboard. In this I fell asleep, awakening only when the party was supping. My appearance from beneath the pianoforte was hailed with surprise by all, and with anger from my mother ; but Charles Lamb not only took me under his protection, but obtained that henceforth I should never again be sent to bed *when he came*, but— glory and delight !—always sit up to supper. Later, in Frith Street days, my father made me sing to him one day ; but he stopped me, saying, ' Clara, don't make that d——d noise ! ' for which, I think, I loved him as much as for all the rest."

Clara Novello, who was born in 1818, was one of the many children of Vincent Novello, a fine organist and industrious composer, who numbered amongst his intimates Keats, Shelley, Leigh Hunt, and Charles Lamb. One of his daughters became the wife and collaborator of Cowden Clarke; his son Edward, who died young, showed remarkable promise as an artist; another son, J. A. Novello, was the founder of the famous publishing firm and pioneer in the movement for the circulation of cheap music. Clara, the fourth daughter, early showed pronounced musical aptitude, and after studying at York and in Paris made her mark as a public singer in 1834, when she took part in the Handel Festival in Westminster Abbey along with Malibran, Grisi, Tamburini, Braham, and other stars. Then followed tours in England and Scotland and on the Continent, where she was welcomed at Leipzig by Mendelssohn and Schumann. But her precocity was allied with a remarkable desire for improvement, and in 1839, already famous as a concert-singer of the first rank, she went to Italy to study seriously for the operatic stage under Micheroux. In this course of preparation Rossini acted as her mentor and friend, and, indeed, took a benevolent interest in her entire career, which she gratefully acknowledges. In 1843 she married Count Gigliucci, left the profession, and settled down to a domestic life on her husband's estate. The troubles of 1848, however, led to the practical confiscation of his property, and she resumed her profession, singing in opera in Italy, Spain, and Portugal, and in oratorio, where she achieved her greatest success, at all the English Festivals and choral concerts until 1860, when she finally retired, while her powers were still in their prime. Her husband, who, though a devout Roman Catholic, strongly opposed the political claims of the Papacy, was an ardent supporter of the *Risorgimento*, and was ultimately restored to his estates and honours and created a Senator. Retirement from the stage and concert-platform brought no repinings or boredom to his wife, who took the deepest interest in politics, shared with him the responsibilities of his position as a landowner, kept up her correspondence with her friends, and was cheered by frequent intercourse with her relations, several of whom settled in Italy. Count Gigliucci died in 1893, and his wife survived him for fifteen years. The unbroken happiness of their fifty years of married life is finely summed up in the lines from the favourite song of her favourite composer, inscribed after their names on her tomb in Rome : " In sweetest harmony they lived " (*Saul*, Handel). The picture of Clara Novello in her old age has many charming touches, none more characteristic of her unselfishness and forbearance than the following :—

Good, general conversation she considered one of the highest intellectual enjoyments, and it was therefore a keen loss and sorrow to her when her hearing grew a little hard and debarred her from it.   Unlike most people troubled with that infirmity, she was never known to ask for a repetition of what caused merriment around her. " It is a great bore to have to repeat to a deaf person," she would say.   " I see you are enjoying yourselves, which makes me very happy, and I daresay you will tell me about it later."

In her long life Clara Novello met a very great number of famous men and women, and her estimates of them, conveyed in a few sentences, often quaintly expressed, but always vivid and incisive, are seldom at fault.   She gives us a striking sketch of Liszt, mobbed by infatuated admirers, " eccentric by system," yet capable of exquisite kindness.   Mendelssohn was to her " dear Felix."   Chopin she worshipped as a girl of sixteen in Paris, where she often met him at his mother's house : " He would only play, he said, if *la petite* Clara would recite ' Peter Piper picked, etc.'   How proud I felt ! . . . I remember waltzing to his and Thalberg's playing —*excusez du peu !* "   Then we have illuminating sidelights on the Court life of Berlin, St. Petersburg, and Venice, anecdotes of the caprice and fascination of the incomparable Malibran, the nobility of Pasta, and the somewhat *farouche* attitude of Jenny Lind towards her sister-artists. Of Clara Novello's wit we have spoken in general terms ; we may end this notice with a characteristic example.   Dickens once embarrassed her by asking which of his female characters she preferred ; but with a lucky inspiration she promptly replied : " Oh, the highest in rank ranks first : the Marchioness, of course."

January 28, 1911.

XXIV

THE CULT OF THE "LIED"

THE welcome reappearance of Herr Raimund von zur Mühlen, who once more gave welcome proof this week of his signal powers as an interpreter of the songs of Schumann and Schubert, serves to remind us how modern a growth in this country is the cult of the romantic *Lied*, and how deep is the debt we owe to those rare artists who, instead of singing down to their public, have steadfastly striven to educate the popular taste up to their own level. It is difficult to apportion the merit of this work of education, since a great deal was done by the efforts of amateurs like the late Sir George Grove, who with an unerring instinct recognised the supreme beauty of Schubert's and Schumann's music, and in the face of indifference, or even open obloquy, availed themselves of their opportunities to spread the light. Much credit also is due to the enterprise of the German publishers who placed collected editions of these songs within the reach of the most modest purse. But we may take it that Stockhausen was the first great singer who constituted himself a sort of travelling hierophant of the modern romantic lyric. It is a melancholy fact that he had been singing Schubert for the best part of twenty years in Germany before he found that his songs would be listened to with patience in this country. On the occasion of his earlier visits in 1849 and 1851 we are told by Sir George Grove that " taste in England was not then sufficiently advanced " to call for the *Lieder* of Schubert, still less for those of Schumann, whose music even in the " sixties " was regarded as only less anarchical than that of Wagner. It was not till 1870, when he had passed the zenith of his powers, that he began his campaign in England in earnest, and revealed to those who were fortunate enough to hear him the beauties, as yet unfamiliar or only imperfectly appreciated, of the immortal songs of Schubert and Schumann. Later on as a singer, and still more as a teacher, he rendered a similar service to the third of the great triad of German song-writers, Brahms. From that date onward with little intermission the cult of the *Lied*— using the term to denote the highest artistic

expression of the lyrical impulse — has never
lacked adequate interpreters amongst us. It is
invidious to particularise where so many have
distinguished themselves by their devotion to
the highest ideals, but one cannot overlook the
services rendered by Mr. Henschel and Herr
von zur Mühlen—whose appearances date back
to the early " eighties "—or, coming down to the
last decade, by Mr. Bispham and Mr. Plunket
Greene. The fact that German singers were
pioneers in the good work of introducing the
songs and song-cycles of Schumann and Schubert,
Franz, Löwe, and Brahms, to English audiences
is natural enough. What is harder to understand is the long neglect meted out to the first
two of these composers by our leading native
singers of both sexes. Mr. Sims Reeves, great
singer and consummate artist though he was,
confined himself almost exclusively to oratorio,
Italian opera, and English ballads ; and on the
few occasions when he introduced a new song
in the last thirty years of his career, it was nearly
always a royalty ballad of the most insipid description. The only great detached German song
that he habitually sang was " Adelaida." Mr.
Santley was undoubtedly more enterprising at one
time, and occasionally used to sing the " Erl-
King " and " The Wanderer," just as Mr. Edward

Lloyd used to sing Schubert's Serenade (in English) ; but none of these singers, to our knowledge, ever sang one of Schubert's or Schumann's song-cycles, and for practical purposes left German *Lieder* severely alone. The same remark applies to the best operatic *prime donne* who have made their home in England. The only German *Lied*, for instance, that the present writer can remember having heard one famous operatic soprano sing was Brahms's *Wiegenlied*, with an interpolated high note in the last verse. If, however, one reflects a little on the conditions, surroundings, and equipment of these singers, this abstention is by no means so difficult to account for. First of the deterrent influences must be reckoned the wide-ranging domination of the oratorio tradition. For the musical million in England music until comparatively recently meant oratorio, just as for the upper ten thousand it meant Italian opera. To this must be added the fact that the recognised leading exponents of public opinion in the Press until the last three decades of the last century assumed an attitude of uncompromising hostility towards the modern romantic spirit in music in whatever form it manifested itself. Thirdly, it must be borne in mind that by virtue alike of training and temperament the British singers of the last generation were not ideal interpreters of the *Lied*. The sentiment of it was too *intime*, too emotional, too unconventional, to suit their robust and well-balanced natures. Even at the present moment educated persons are to be found who object to the faithful and sensitive interpretations of such songs, as being too intense, too " psychological," to accord with the reserve of the national character. They pardon it in a foreigner, but deprecate it in a native. Last and most effective reason of all was the imperfect linguistic equipment of the singers of the past generation. The English are, as a race, indifferent linguists—we are speaking now not of scholarship and book knowledge, but of the fineness of ear and flexibility of tongue on which accuracy of accent and delicacy of inflection depend—and the normal equipment of a public singer in this regard was, up to comparatively recently, limited to English, Italian, and occasionally a little French. Of the elder generation, Mr. Santley was by far the most versatile and the best equipped in this respect ; but even he, as we have pointed out, confined his German repertory, certainly during the last twenty years, to at the outside half a dozen German songs. Madame Albani, as a French-Canadian trained in Italy, enjoyed advantages which rendered her an exception ; but on the

concert platform she was rarely heard in German.
But Mr. Edward Lloyd, beyond a rare excursion
into Italian, never sang except in his native tongue,
though it is only fair to say that we believe this
abstention was not due to any aggressive insularity,
but to a conscientious disinclination to do what
he was convinced he could not do well. This
attitude is not only intelligible, but honourable ;
but none the less it involves a serious restriction
of the repertory of an artistic singer. There is
a good deal of music—notably in the domain of
Italian opera—where the language in which it is
sung, so long as it is euphonious, is a matter of
the purest indifference. But when it comes to
the conjunction of Schumann with Heine, or
Schubert with Goethe, the omission of the words
to which the song was originally composed is
like a performance of *Romeo and Juliet* with the
part of Juliet left out.

Whatever may be said as to the quality of
voice and method of "production" of the
younger generation of singers, there can be no
doubt whatever of their superior linguistic attainments, and, as a natural corollary, the wider
range of their repertory. Sometimes, indeed,
of late years there has been a danger of singers
running to the opposite extreme, and making a
parade of their polyglot attainments. But, in the

main, the results, from an artistic point of view, have been most advantageous and stimulating. One can have nothing but respect for artists who deliberately set themselves to complete their education by foreign residence and study. This movement has naturally and inevitably tended to secure for the great German song-writers in England that appreciation and recognition which they had already won in Germany, and we cannot help thinking that this appreciation has reacted on the quality of the songs written by our leading native composers. The history of the evolution of the art of music has in its earlier stages so often seemed to illustrate the retarding effect exercised by singers on composers that it is pleasant to be able to recognise that in the case of the romantic *Lied* interpreters have, on the whole, loyally striven to spread the light.

February 27, 1904.

XXV

AMERICAN MUSICAL CRITICISM

THE debt of modern music to America, though it may be hard to set down in terms of solid achievement, is none the less worthy of recognition. She has not yet produced a musical Sargent or Whitman or Henry James, though critics are not wanting to claim for Mr. Macdowell a place amongst the immortals both as symphonist and song-writer ; but the stimulating atmosphere of American life has already made its influence felt in a variety of ways on the cultivation of the art. The rapidity of progress which has marked the material development of the United States finds an analogy in the musical education of the cultivated classes. The tyranny of Italian opera lasted in England for more than a century and a half, while in America the history of its rise and decline—the first troupe visited America in 1825 —is contained within a period of sixty years. No doubt the exceptionally large number of German immigrants has had a good deal to say to this; and to this day the leading members of the profession in America are, with few exceptions, Germans, or of German extraction. It is otherwise in the domain of vocal music, where American singers, and especially female singers, have for some time past occupied a distinguished position on the concert platform and the lyric stage. Music now plays as large a part in the social life of the leisured Americans as it does with us, and in point of equipment and efficiency of performance there is little to choose between the great American cities and those of Europe. Such results are not attained except in congenial surroundings, and it speaks well for Boston that, though the performers are all Europeans, the famous Kneisel Quartet should have been organised and reached so high a pitch of excellence in an American city. A pessimistic critic once called America the grave of art, but musicians, whether resident or visitors, will not endorse this gloomy dictum.

What we are chiefly concerned to insist on at the present moment is that if in the domain of music America has hitherto been assimilative rather than creative, she has already begun to stamp the impress of her individuality on the alien

o

elements incorporated in her system. Of the curious episode of Dvorák's sojourn in New York we have already spoken elsewhere. But instances might be multiplied of the transmutation or modification of racial characteristics in the crucible of American life. A strange story, in illustration of this process, was recently told the present writer by an artist who, in the course of a visit to America last year, encountered an Italian singing master who had migrated to an American city from London a good many years ago. The inducement was that, owing to the higher remuneration, he could earn enough in nine months to spend the remainder of the year in agreeable indolence in Italy. The results justified the move, and for a while he was able to arrange his life on this plan, to his entire satisfaction. Unfortunately, he gradually became infected with the "accursed industry" of the Americans, with the result that he could never enjoy his holiday because of the longing to get back to work, and has now given up the annual visit to his native land. If such a transformation can take place in a man already in the prime of life, how much more may be expected after the stock has been transplanted for a generation or two?

The case of the indolent Southerner converted in spite of himself into a "hustler" exhibits the

metamorphic influence of the American environment on the Latin race in a picturesque, and even
pathetic, light. But its effect on the Teutonic
temperament is none the less striking. Here we
may take our concrete instances from the realm of
musical criticism, where three of the best-known
writers and journalists are Germans or German-
Americans—Mr. Krehbiel, Mr. Finck, and Mr.
Huneker. In the case of the first-named, his
critical attitude and style do not exhibit any notable
lapse from the orthodox, and his readiness *stare
super antiquas vias* has been happily exemplified
by his honourable association with the completion
of Thayer's monumental Life of Beethoven.
Thayer, it may be noted in passing, was an
example of the converse process—of an American
who by long residence in Europe became more
Teuton than the Teutons in his indomitable
industry. But in Mr. Finck the process of
emancipation from conventional standards and
Teutonic traditions has gone to the length of his
extolling Chopin at the expense of Beethoven,
who, in Mr. Finck's opinion, was a most unsatisfactory composer for the piano ; of consistent
depreciation of Brahms ; and of claiming for
Mr. Macdowell a place alongside of Schubert and
Schumann as a song-writer. In Mr. Huneker,
whose *Overtones : a Book of Temperaments*

(Isbister and Co., 6s.) lies before us, we are carried several stages further along the "new paths" of musical criticism. The book is dedicated to Richard Strauss, "an anarch of art," and the honorific significance of the title is expounded at length in one of the chapters, in which Mr. Huneker sets himself to show that all great composers have been anarchs, from Bach to Strauss himself. But Mr. Huneker is not only one of those writers who permit themselves the luxury of a great deal of self-contradiction, but his definition of an anarch proves that he means little more than an insurgent individualist. As he puts it, "anarchy often expresses itself in rebellion against conventional art forms, the only kind of anarchy that interests me." Just as he credits Richard Strauss with the invention of a new musical speech, so Mr. Huneker has adopted a new form of criticism, in which, generally speaking, superlatives are employed in place of positives, the obvious is shunned like the plague, and incontestable truths are stated in violent terms. When, however, we learn to discount this habitual vehemence of expression, there is much in his volume with which the normal reader can find himself in cordial sympathy. Mr. Huneker is extremely catholic in his tastes, and his enthusiasm for the "flaming individualists" is combined with a generous appreciation of Verdi and Boïto, and above all of Brahms, whom it is the fashion amongst so many of his emancipated colleagues to decry, but to whom Mr. Huneker devotes what is perhaps the most illuminating piece of criticism in the book. After discussing Wagner as the last of the great romantics, Mr. Huneker continues :—

A curious return to soberer ideals of form was led by Johannes Brahms. I may add that this leadership was unsought, indeed was hardly apprehended, by the composer. A more unpromising figure for a musical Messiah would have been difficult to find. Wagner, a brilliant, disputatious, magnetic man, waged a personal propaganda ; Brahms, far from being the sympathetic, cultured man of the world that Wagner was, lived quietly and thought highly. His were Wordsworthian ideals ; he abhorred the world, the flesh, and the devil,—this last person being incarnate for him in the marriage of music with the drama. Yet his music is alive to-day ; alive with a promise and a potency that well-nigh urge me to fatidical utterance, so sane is it, so noble in contrast, so richly fruitful in treatment. A sympathetic writer he is, and also a man who deals largely in the humanities of his art. Learned beyond the dreams of Wagner, Brahms buried his counterpoint in roses, set it to blooming in the Old-World gardens of Germany ; decked his science with the sweet, mad tunes of Hungary, withal remaining a Teuton, and one in the direct line of Bach, Beethoven, and Schubert. And yet Brahms dreams of pure white stair-cases that scale the infinite. A dazzling, dry light floods his mind at times, and you hear the rustling of wings,—

wings of great, terrifying monsters, hippogriffs of horrid mien ; hieroglyphic faces, faces with stony stare, menace your imagination. He can bring down within the compass of the octave moods that are outside the pale of mortals. He is a magician, often spectral ; yet his songs have the homely lyric fervour and concision of Robert Burns. A groper after the untoward, I have been amazed at certain bars in his F sharp minor sonata, and was stirred by the moonlight tranquillity in the slow movement of the F minor sonata. He is often dull, muddy-pated, obscure, and maddeningly slow. Then lovely music wells out of the mist ; you are enchanted, and cry, " Brahms, master, anoint again with thy precious chrism our thirsty eyelids ! " Brahms is an inexorable form maker. His four symphonies, his three piano sonatas, the choral works and chamber music—are they not all living testimony to his admirable management of masses ? He is not a great colorist. For him the pigments of Makart, Wagner, and Théophile Gautier are unsought. Like Puvis de Chavannes, he is a Primitive. Simple, flat tints, primary and cool, are superimposed upon an enormous rhythmic versatility and a strenuous-ness of ideation. Ideas—noble, profundity-embracing ideas—he has. They are not in the smart, epigrammatic, flashing style of your little man. He disdains racial allusions. He is a planetary Teuton. You seek in vain for the geographical hints that chain Grieg to the map of Norway. Brahms's melodies are world-typical, not cabined and confined to his native soil. This largeness of utterance, lack of polish, and a disregard for the politeness of his art do not endear him to the unthinking. Yet, what a master miniaturist he is in his little piano pieces, his intermezzi ! There he catches the tender sigh of childhood, or the faint intimate flutterings of the heart stirred by desire.   Feminine he is as is no woman ; virile, as few men.   The sinister fury, the mocking, drastic fury of his first rhapsodies,—true Brahmsodies,— how they pierce to the core the pessimism of our age ! He reminds me more of Browning than does Schumann. The full-pulsed humanity, the dramatic—yes, Brahms is sometimes dramatic, not theatric—modes of analysis, the relentless tracking to their ultimate lair of motives, are Browning's ; but the composer never loses his grip on the actualities of structure.   A great sea is his music, and it sings about the base of that mighty mount we call Beethoven.   Brahms takes us to subterrene depths ; Beethoven is for the heights.   Strong lungs are needed in the company of these giants.

Though Richard Strauss is something of an obsession with Mr. Huneker—he observes in one passage : " I have written so much of Strauss that it is beginning to be a fascination, as is the parrot in Flaubert's *Un Cœur Simple*, and this is not well "—this hero-worship is tempered by a great many damaging admissions.   He owns that Strauss as a symphonist is to seek in melodic invention : that his pianoforte music is often crabbed.   "The noble art of simplicity he lacks " ; and again, with one of those plainly worded observations all the more effective by reason of their contrast with the writer's habitual extravagance, he happily remarks : " Often [in *Ein Heldenleben*] we cannot hear the music for the score." Finally, he admits that "unity is sometimes absent, and also the power that makes for righteousness, which we find in Beethoven's music." It is certainly a far cry from *Fidelio* to *Feuersnot*, and Mr. Huneker naïvely confesses that he is "puzzled" by the "absolute departure" of the Straussian dispensation "from the ethic of Christianity." On the other hand, when Mr. Huneker indulges in eulogy of his hero he leaves nothing to be desired in the strenuousness of his panegyric. Nor need we greatly wonder at the fascination exerted by Strauss on the American or Americanised temperament, which he attracts alike by the prodigious machinery and mammoth dimensions of his scores, by his record-breaking achievements in sonority, and by that cerebral quality in his work—a quality which one would expect to find in the music of the Martians as conceived by Mr. Wells—which must appeal with peculiar force to a people who attach the highest value to the fearsome but suggestive epithet "brainy."

We have only to add, in conclusion, that however much one may dissent from Mr. Huneker's views, there is no gainsaying the force and picturesqueness with which he expresses them. No modern musical critic has shown greater ingenuity in the attempt to correlate the literary and musical tendencies of the nineteenth century.

The analysis of Mr. Henry James's method and style, as viewed from this standpoint, is really illuminative ; and admirers of the omniscient genius of Balzac will not fail to be struck by the extraordinary prevision of the musical decadence of our days which Mr. Huneker proves him to have displayed in *Gambara* and *Massimilla Doni*.

June 18, 1904.

XXVI

THE VIENNESE PERIOD [1]

It involves no disparagement to Mr. Hadow's able and erudite collaborators in the great *Oxford History of Music* to say that the fifth volume, for which he is responsible, is likely to appeal to a wider circle of readers than any of its predecessors. This result is largely due to the nature of his theme, which Mr. Hadow describes as "The Viennese Period," and which embraces the contributions to the evolution of the Art of Music made by Gluck, Haydn, Mozart, Beethoven, and Schubert. But if Mr. Hadow has been fortunate in the period allotted him, he has not proved unworthy of the trust. It is an exacting as well as an inspiring subject, and he has shown himself finely equipped both by temperament and education for his arduous task. He has reverence, enthusiasm,

[1] *The Oxford History of Music.* Vol. V. "The Viennese Period." By W. H. Hadow. Oxford : at the Clarendon Press. [15s. net.]

and sympathy.   His style is easy, yet distinguished ; enriched with felicitous literary allusions
and pointed epigrams, yet never degenerating into
preciosity.   How excellent, for example, is the
characterisation of Spohr's attitude : " His whole
conception of the art is soft and voluptuous, his
Heaven is a Garden of Atlantis, and even his
Judgment - day is iridescent " ;   or the happy
phrase on Beethoven's Mass in D : " It does not,
like Mozart's *Requiem*, defy criticism, but simply
ignores it."

We do not know whether Mr. Hadow is
original in the choice of his title, " The Viennese
Period," but the epithet is as satisfying and
suggestive as could have been devised.   The
genius of place is a potent factor in the history
of art, and nowhere has its influence been more
strikingly manifested than in the case of the
Austrian capital.   There must have been something compelling in the atmosphere, something
inspiring in the environment, which drew so many
of the great masters to make Vienna their home.
For of those mentioned above only Schubert was
a true Viennese born, and the greatest of them
all came from furthest afield.   Nor was Vienna
always an *Alma Mater* to her children.   She
treated Gluck like a stepmother, she let Mozart
go down to a pauper's grave, and Schubert die

without the chance of hearing his greatest works. The Opera House was a battlefield of chicanery and intrigue, as was shown time and again in the cases of Gluck and Mozart.

If, however, Vienna was far from being the composer's paradise in the eighteenth century, and if her musical annals are stained by grievous instances of ingratitude and inappreciation, a variety of causes conspired to render her atmosphere more congenial and stimulating to creative effort than that of any other capital. Most of these causes are set forth in Mr. Hadow's illuminating pages, and may be summarised and, in a measure, supplemented here. To begin with, there was the traditional affability of the Viennese, that easy-going *bonhomie* and love of the amenities which, in spite of all rebuffs and disappointments, must have appealed peculiarly to the temperament of Mozart.[1]   Another peculiar feature of Vienna, which tended to promote a certain fusion of classes, was its lack of distinctively poorer quarters. The nobility lived inside the city, not in the environs, and "the same tall mansions sheltered wealth, competence, and poverty under one roof."

[1] Mr. Hadow quotes with approval M. Chouquet's happy epithet of " Sophoclean " as applied to the perfection of Mozart's work.   The εὐκολία of Sophocles which Aristophanes noted as rendering him invulnerable to parody was another point in common.

This state of affairs is vividly illustrated by the case of Haydn. On the third *étage* of the old Michaeler-Haus in the Kohlmarkt, where he took up his quarters on being dismissed from the choir school of St. Stephen's, lived Metastasio, his first patron in Vienna, while the lower part of the house was the town residence of Prince Paul Esterhazy, who twelve years later appointed him to his office at Eisenstadt. The mention of Metastasio reminds us to note, as another powerful factor in the diffusion of musical culture in Vienna, that contact with Italy, politically and geographically, had placed the resources of the peninsula within reach of the Austrian musicians. It is true that these influences were largely concerned with the training of executive talent, and the promotion of technical dexterity, vocal and instrumental; but the importance of this training from the point of view of the composer is not to be gainsaid. It was, as Mr. Hadow points out in an interesting passage, a case of *Graecia capta ferum victorem cepit* over again :—

Italy was not then, as now, a single undivided kingdom, but was partitioned among many princes, foreign as well as native. Naples and Sicily belonged to Spain : a great part of Northern Italy was under Austrian rule ; and in this way was opened a certain freedom of intercourse which enabled the captive land to take captive her conquerors. At the Viennese court the Italian language was more readily spoken than the German : Francis I., the husband of Maria Theresa, was Duke of Tuscany, and for some generations his family held the title with all that it implied. The large Slav population of Austria was fertile in musicians, many of whom had Italian blood in their veins, and most of whom softened their harsh patronymics with Italian syllables and terminations. Even Haydn at first wrote his Christian name Giuseppe, and the list may be extended through Tartini, Giornovichi, and several others. Had this been only deference to a passing fashion, still the fashion itself would have been significant, and as a matter of fact it was far more than this. The bond was strengthened by all the ties of intermarriage, of contiguity, of common government, and Salieri and Paisiello felt as much at home in Vienna as Scarlatti and Farinelli at Madrid. In the second place this intercourse was further maintained by operatic companies who poured from Italy in a continuous stream, and carried their voices, their language, and their method to every palace where there was a patron and to every city where there was a theatre.

Next we have to notice the peculiarly favourable conditions under which the system of patronage was developed in Austria. " In every capital from Madrid to St. Petersburg there were court-appointments of varying dignity and position : in most countries aristocracy followed the royal practice and established a private orchestra as an essential part of its retinue." This, be it marked in passing, was at a time when the corresponding classes in England were occupied mainly in politics or fox-hunting. The contrast struck that acute observer Arthur Young, who remarks, *à propos* of the Duc d'Aguillon's private orchestra, "this elegant and agreeable luxury, which falls within the compass of a very large fortune, is known in every country of Europe except England." Young wrote in 1787, but English millionaires and American multi-millionaires of to-day are still conspicuous for their failure to resort to this blameless method of expending their surplus wealth. But while the maintenance of musicians by munificent patrons was common in all European countries in the middle of the eighteenth century, it was in Austria that the custom was chiefly prevalent ; " partly, it would seem, from a doctrine of *noblesse oblige*, partly from a genuine love of music which ran through every rank and grade of society." Royal personages frequently took part in performances in their private theatre, and "almost all the great Viennese families—Lichten-stein, Lobkowitz, Auersperg, and many others—displayed the same generosity, the same artistic appreciation." The relation between patron and *protégé* was not without humiliating aspects. Even at its best, as in the case of Haydn and Prince Esterhazy, the musician was clad in a servant's livery, and was paid with a servant's wages. But

if the system was fraught with evil as well as good
—the tyranny of the Archbishop of Salzburg
must be set against the enlightened generosity of
the Esterhazys—it afforded opportunities to at
least two of the greatest masters of the eighteenth
century—Haydn and Gluck—without which they
might never have made their memorable contributions to the development of symphonic and
dramatic music.

Mr. Hadow's survey closes with the third
decade of the nineteenth century, but in the main
Vienna has remained true to the noble and
enlightened traditions which honourably distinguished her among the musical centres of Europe
in the period under discussion. Berlioz, writing
in the "forties," though he laments the incredible
ignorance of Gluck's operas displayed by the
Viennese, waxes enthusiastic over their passion
for music. Incidentally, he pays a handsome
tribute to Strauss, the founder of the dynasty of
the Viennese Waltz-Kings, for the influence he
has exerted over musical feeling throughout
Europe by the introduction of cross-rhythms in
waltzes. Sir George Grove never wearied in
extolling the liberality and enterprise of Viennese
amateurs and publishers, of which he had such
ample experience in his visit in 1867. The record
of the famous Society of the Friends of Music

deserves to be written in letters of gold in the annals of the art. Vienna was the home of the greatest violin school of the nineteenth century ; it is still the seat of the greatest pianoforte school ; it was the home of Brahms in the days of his maturity, and of Hans Richter, another of the Olympians, until he migrated to our shores.

We have only touched on one aspect of Mr. Hadow's deeply interesting and suggestive volume, full justice to which cannot possibly be rendered in a single article. We can only add that, while he deals fully with such technical details as the development and elaboration of the sonata and symphony forms, his appreciations of the great masters and his descriptions of their environment will be read with enjoyment and delight by all lovers of music, whether scientifically trained or not. Not even Sir George Grove, devout and faithful worshipper of Beethoven and Schubert as he was, has written with more eloquent or infectious enthusiasm of the greatest of symphonists and the most inspired of song-writers.

December 24, 1904.

XXVII

SONORITY

A MUSICAL correspondent, in the course of a
pleasant account of the recent Bonn Festival,
speaks of the contrast between the tones of the
ancient instruments—quinton, clavecin, and so
forth—and those of a modern grand pianoforte,
not without a certain implied disparagement of
the former. That the contrast exists, and that
the great majority of people honestly prefer the
sound of the new instruments, cannot be denied ;
but there are other aspects of the question on
which it is by no means so easy to pronounce
an unhesitating opinion. " M. S." is evidently
convinced that we are gainers by the development
of the mechanism of modern instruments, with
their increased volume of tone ; but the view is
not universally held. Writing as far back as
1887, in his survey of music in the Victorian
epoch Sir Walter Parratt observed that " this

aggrandisement of the organ, so to speak, has not been an unmixed good. Increased power has been obtained in many cases at the expense of sweetness of tone, and the tendency has been to make the instrument a caricature of the orchestra" —a remark which, within certain limits, is equally applicable to some of the grand pianofortes of to-day. And what is true of individual instruments is not less true of instruments in combination. In a suggestive article on "Wagner and Wagnerism" in the *Nineteenth Century* for March 1883 the late Mr. Edmund Gurney maintained that our ears were being debauched by the sonority of the modern orchestra; that what we gained in colour and excitement and emotional stimulation we lost in form and clarity and classic restraint. While admitting that "the blaze of sonority may cover fulness as well as emptiness," he speaks of the intoxicating effect of the mere "natural tone of a superb orchestra," and condemns as the chief bane of contemporary music "the displacement of coherent form by incoherent colour." That this was not a mere expression of individual opinion has been sufficiently proved by the subsequent emergence in different quarters of various reactionary movements against the dominion of sonority and complexity— notably the cult of the harpsichord and other delicate old-world instruments, not only amongst amateurs but professionals.

Now of the various problems suggested by " M. S." not the least interesting is this : how far persons whose musical experiences are dominated by the full modern orchestra and the modern grand piano are capable of enjoying or appreciating music which was written for the smaller band and the less powerful instruments of a bygone age. The analogy of literature is not altogether complete. There it is easier to range from Meredith to Milton, or from M. Anatole France to Homer, because music has travelled further in three hundred than literature in three thousand years, and, further, because in the appreciation of a literary as opposed to a musical masterpiece the physical factor, the direct appeal to the senses, is eliminated. The fact that music, for the average music-lover, has to be materialised and translated into audible sound makes it all the harder for those who have become habituated to the puissant sonority of the orchestra as wielded by Wagner or Tchaikovsky or Strauss to accommodate their ears to the more frugal methods of the old masters. In other words, it is far harder to lead the Simpler Life in music than in letters because the senses are directly engaged, and the senses are so readily subdued by that which works immediately upon them as to be always in danger of enslavement.

Another point on which Mr. Gurney laid stress in the article from which we have already quoted is that music, by being so much in the hands of the performers, runs a peculiar risk from that very fact. As he puts it, "all skilful performance of difficult things, and accurate thridding of labyrinthine things and collaboration in the production of overpowering things, are exciting outlets of energy; and in these respects connoisseurs who appreciate technical difficulties and can see how the thing is made are more or less one with the performers." The intelligent and susceptible amateur is insensibly led on to the attitude which may be summed up as *amo quia difficillimum*, and this sympathetic relation undoubtedly tends to promote and stimulate that feverish activity which is the characteristic of so much modern music—music of which it has been truly said that it impresses "not so much by its depth of thought and feeling as by the force and fury of its expression." Constant and prolonged indulgence in music of this type is bound to affect the hearer and impair his enjoyment of the simpler forms, so that it is by no means an uncommon thing nowadays to encounter people who have submerged themselves so deeply in musical modernity that to their ears everything written before Wagner sounds " thin." Indeed, the attitude of the music-lover has altered so much in the last two decades that one is almost tempted to doubt whether our ears are the same as those of our fathers. Physiologically, no doubt, it would be impossible to maintain such a view. It takes more than twenty or thirty or two hundred years for the structure of a human organ to be substantially modified. None the less, for practical purposes the ears of the average music-lover may well be said to have changed. Things that sounded harsh and discordant sound so no longer. The same people who began by finding Wagner hideous now find him beautiful. The process by which a hearer finds genuine delight in that which originally repelled or disconcerted him, in so far as it extends his area of appreciation, is not to be condemned, but encouraged. But if it limits that area, produces a distaste for that which the hearer knows to be good, and develops an ever-increasing and insatiable thirst for novelty, excitement, sonority, and complexity, the gain is outweighed by the loss. To put it in a more concrete form, there are a good many music-lovers to-day who, if asked to state in an album of confessions " Whom do you consider to be the greatest composer ? " might put down Bach or

Beethoven, but if the question were worded
" What is the composition which you would make
the greatest effort to go and hear ? " would
probably single out some such work as Tchaikovsky's Fifth Symphony or Strauss's *Heldenleben*.
Familiarity with the old has bred, not exactly
contempt, but something like tedium. Their
attitude is rather akin to the *meliora probo
deteriora sequor* of the classic saw : it is not that
they respect the ancients less, but that they find
the moderns more exciting.

It would be difficult, even if it were justifiable,
to prescribe a remedy for undisciplined indulgence
in music of this " sumptuous and sonorous " kind.
After all, the number of those who can afford
to indulge in this luxury is limited, and most
music-lovers complain that they hear too little
rather than too much music. Even amongst
those who are highly favoured in this respect
signs of a reaction are occasionally to be noticed,
and just as one hears of people who read Walter
Scott to wash away the taste of modern fiction, so
one encounters connoisseurs who find in the
crystal purity of Mozart and Haydn refreshment
and change after a too prolonged immersion in
the turbid waves of modernity. To specialise in
any one school is to lose a great deal of enjoyment.
For the average music-lover the aim should be

to preserve a balance between the old and the new as far as the arrangement of concert programmes will allow him. The ideal condition is of course that of the highly trained expert who can dispense with the perturbing influence of performances and performers, and read his music like a book from a score in his study. This is the only way of hearing music of which one can never have too much, for where this enviable capacity is fully developed, every instrument in the mental orchestra is of the best quality and sounds perfectly in tune.

June 17, 1905.

XXVIII

TWO BOOKS ON BRAHMS

I

WHATEVER may be said of the claim of the English to be considered a musical people, the record of their relations with the great German masters, from Handel onwards, may be contemplated with satisfaction, if not with complacency. England adopted Handel, lent munificent encouragement to both Beethoven and Haydn, and became almost the second home of Mendelssohn. The cult of Schubert and Schumann, though slow in taking root, has nowhere been tended with greater fervour or enthusiasm ; and the course of the last thirty years has witnessed the growth of an appreciation for the genius of Brahms at least as genuine and sincere as that excited by his forerunners. To trace the genesis and progress of this appreciation would be an interesting task. If the credit is to be referred to one person more than another, that one person would be Dr. Joachim, who was from the first indefatigable in familiarising the British concert-going public with the chamber-music of his friend and contemporary.   But the seed fell on fruitful if limited soil.   Though the Press, with few honourable exceptions, adopted an attitude of cold reserve or active depreciation—the phrase "smelling of the lamp" must have been worn threadbare in its application to Brahms—the faithful disciples of Schumann and Schubert, naturally predisposed in his favour by the testimony of the former, hailed the newcomer as adding fresh glory to the German *Lied* long before the *Deutsches Requiem* and the Symphonies proved him to be of the authentic lineage of Bach and Beethoven.   George Grove was from the first an enthusiastic Brahmsian, and the Cambridge University Musical Society under Stanford was an early centre of the new cult, which in the last twenty years has owed so much to the interpretative genius of Richter.   Nor must one overlook the admirable services rendered by a host of devoted amateurs—using the term in the best and highest sense of the word—who found an ever-increasing delight in the study and performance of Brahms's songs, part-songs, and chamber-music. There was a time, no doubt, when the genuine

Brahmsians suffered not a little from association with pseudo-devotees on the one hand, whose adherence was due simply to the desire to be " in the movement," and intolerant enthusiasts on the other, whose excessive earnestness savoured of a consciousness of intellectual superiority, not to say priggishness.   It was doubtless one of these uncompromising Brahmsians who, some fifteen years ago, hissed the performance of a waltz by Johann Strauss at an orchestral concert, in ignorance of Brahms's close friendship with, and enthusiastic admiration for the genius of, the " Waltz King."   Brahms, in short, suffered from the fanaticism of some of his admirers, much as Browning, perhaps his closest analogue in the domain of literature, suffered from the eccentricities of Browningites.   But that phase in the history of the appreciation of his genius has, we believe, passed away.   There is no longer any pose in the admiration of Brahms, for it is no longer a short cut to a reputation for musical enlightenment to pretend to enjoy him.   Again, the example of Dr. Richter, to mention only one conspicuous instance, equally renowned for his devotion to Brahms and Wagner, has read a salutary lesson to those uncompromising votaries who think it impossible to testify their allegiance to one master without professing hostility to all his contemporaries. If any further lesson be needed, it is to be found in the attitude of Brahms himself, who was entirely void of musical intolerance, detested comparisons, and never once, by word or action, countenanced those supporters who sought to pit him against Wagner, for whose commanding genius he had the deepest respect. In fine, the controversial epoch in regard to Brahms has come to an end. If we are not all Brahmsians nowadays, at any rate admiration of his works has long since ceased to be the property of a musical coterie or sect ; it has long since exceeded the limited proportions of a cult. Brahms worshippers are to be found, in the phrase of an eccentric orator, "from the Queen who sits upon her throne to the labourer who sits upon his cottage." Nowhere in this country is his chamber-music more attentively listened to than at the free concerts given at the South Place Institute to a working-class audience. And if you once learn to appreciate him there is never any waning of the attachment. Some composers inspire love at first sight, which may or may not develop into an abiding affection. Others inspire progressive dislike. Others, again, awaken interest, which, if it does develop, grows into the deepest devotion. In this class Hans von Bülow's favourite trio of "B's"—Bach, Beethoven, and Brahms—are con-

spicuous.   Let no one, however, be discouraged
because he finds more of the *res severa* than the
verum gaudium in his first contact with Brahms.
It took von Bülow himself more than twenty years
before he finally made up his mind that Brahms
was not a *maestrinello*, but a giant.

Miss Florence May's deeply interesting Life,[1]
the latest and one of the happiest proofs of the
attachment of Brahms's English disciples, throws
a great deal of new light on his career and
character, and goes a long way towards explaining
the secret of the attraction and repulsion he exerts
on different minds.   She brings out to an extent
hitherto unrealised by many of those who know
his music well how severe were his early struggles,
how protracted the period that elapsed before he
was in a position to abandon the drudgery of
teaching, to emancipate himself from the anxieties
of public performance, and devote himself exclusively to composition.   It is true that at the very
outset of his career he was welcomed with enthusiastic admiration by Schumann.   But the famous
"New Paths" article excited quite as much antagon-
ism as sympathy.   Schumann's predictions had not
always been fulfilled, and many experts regarded
as extravagant and premature eulogy what was

---

[1] *The Life of Johannes Brahms.*   By Florence May.   2 vols.   London :
Edward Arnold.   [21s. net.]

really—in view of Brahms's limited achievements at the time—an act of clairvoyance. For the moment it hampered his advance by exciting hostility in certain quarters, and if Brahms had been less well balanced, less richly endowed with the saving grace of self-criticism, Schumann's momentous panegyric might easily have unhinged him. As matters stood, it merely acted as an incentive and encouragement. Instead of believing himself to be already deserving of this tribute, he resolved to prove himself worthy of it, and thus, "enduring his felicity with fortitude," took his place among the elect few who instinctively realise the responsibilities as well as the delights of receiving praise from the praiseworthy. Brahms's gratitude to Schumann was deep and abiding, and the account of his relations with the composer and his widow which Miss May has given us in her engaging volumes cannot be read without emotion. Yet she is far from allowing her admiration for the musician to blind her to his shortcomings as a man. These shortcomings were largely the defects of his qualities,—his dislike of pretence, insincerity, and ceremony ; his hatred of interviews, lionisers, and, in a word, his refusal to furnish "copy" to enterprising journalists. It is probably true, as one of his intimates put it, that his manners were those of a

frolicsome child ; but they were at times very bad
—his unconsciousness of having given offence is
certainly no excuse for his appalling tactlessness
during his visit to Denmark after the war of
1864. But when all reserves have been made,
the picture given of Brahms in these pages—a
picture based largely on the first-hand testimony
of those who knew him best at successive stages
of his career—is one which will afford singularly
little disillusionment to those who may have
hitherto only known the man through his music.
It is the picture of a devoted son, a faithful if at
times exacting friend, who thought more of his
art than of himself, shunned the cockpit of controversy, and lived a life of dignified and strenuous
seclusion. Miss Florence May's qualifications
for her task are amply proved by the thoroughness of its execution ; but one may mention here
that, besides being an accomplished musician, she
had the good fortune to be Brahms's pupil in the
" seventies," and kept up friendly relations with
him for the remainder of his life. Her attitude
towards him is one of a sincere and affectionate
admiration ; but her enthusiasm never degenerates
into idolatry, and she has laid all who venerate
his memory and recognise his genius under a
deep obligation by her industry, her sound
judgment, and her excellent taste. The book

would have been improved by a bibliography ; but it has a good index, useful appendices, and is enriched by several admirable portraits, notably the beautiful profile likeness of Brahms at the age of twenty.

October 28, 1905.

II

Mr. Fuller Maitland, in his new and suggestive study of Brahms,[1] tells an anecdote which is curiously illustrative of the altered attitude of the British public towards Brahms. Any time from forty to twenty years ago it was a common occurrence for a musical critic to have to correct the printer's substitution of "Braham" for "Brahms." Now the whirligig of time has brought in its revenge, and if one has to speak of Braham, the printer is apt to rename the illustrious tenor Brahms. This anecdote, which the present writer can confirm from his own experience, has no bearing on the intrinsic merit of Brahms's compositions : it only serves to show that a name which formerly enjoyed only a limited repute has now achieved a much wider

---

[1] *Brahms.* By J. A. Fuller Maitland. With 12 illustrations. London : Methuen and Co. [7s. 6d. net.]

familiarity, and it incidentally throws an interesting sidelight on the transitory fame of singers. The growth of the appreciation of Brahms's music can be illustrated in a variety of other ways, significant or entertaining, and nothing is more remarkable about it than its gradual progress. Brahms never was, and never will be, a fashionable composer. No *prima donna*, except Pauline Viardot, was ever deeply interested in his music. No composer has ever made fewer concessions to amateurishness or been at less pains to conciliate the public. The adequate performance even of his songs entailed an amount of musicianship which was naturally resented by the pioneers of the royalty ballad industry. All the forces of incompetence were mobilised against a composer who made such intolerable demands on efficiency, intelligence, and self-surrender, for there is no peacock music in Brahms. And yet in spite of all these drawbacks his reputation advanced, slowly but irresistibly, without either set-back or *furore*. The limited circle of musicians genuinely interested in chamber music soon recognised in him a master who had permanently enriched the repertory of the quartet-player, and they have never wavered or faltered in their allegiance. The austere splendour of the *Requiem* and the *Schicksalslied* has never failed to move hearts

Q

once responsive to their magic, just as they have never failed to evoke the homage of obloquy from those who only feel music in their nerve-centres or their head. Manns and Richter and Hallé were assiduous in familiarising the frequenters of their concerts with the symphonies and overtures, the Haydn variations and the concertos for pianoforte and violin. The glories of the motets and part-songs for mixed choir were revealed to amateurs of *a cappella* singing by madrigal societies, and a few native artists, emboldened by the example of Stockhausen and later of Henschel, carried on the work of popularising Brahms's songs. And every one in this movement, whether conductor, instrumentalist, or singer, never altered or varied in his devotion to Brahms, except on the *crescendo* side. Once a Brahmsian always a Brahmsian is a maxim of modern musical culture. And it expresses a truth which need excite no surprise. There is no composer who can stand the test of repetition more triumphantly, who reveals more beauties at each successive hearing than Brahms. And there is none who inspires in his admirers a more sovereign contempt for the futility of his detractors.

This attitude, perfectly intelligible, but at times extremely irritating to the unsympathetic, probably accounts for the imputation of priggishness and intellectual arrogance under which the adherents of Brahms have laboured in the past. But this much must be allowed them : that very few people have insincerely professed to be admirers of Brahms, for the excellent reason that no obvious advantage—no reputation for audacity or emancipation or wickedness—was to be gained therefrom. Now that the battle has been won, and Brahms has passed into the list of established reputations, the violence with which he is assailed by half-baked, eccentric, or neurotic critics is positively diverting. There was one writer whose favourite epithet for the *Deutsches Requiem* was " cowardly." Heaven alone knows why. Mr. Bernard Shaw, while occasionally admitting that he had immense science, has always been one of the most consistent depreciators of Brahms. The *Requiem* used to be a red rag to him ; he once went out of his way to deny any merit to the *Fest- und Gedenksprüche* ; and at the present day there is still quite a large number of people, alleged to be educated, who would sooner die than own to even a sneaking liking for what Mr. Shaw has condemned. The Straussians and post-Straussians are, for the most part, extremely hostile to Brahms, all the more so, perhaps, in view of the fact that in the early stages of Strauss's development the influence of Brahms is distinctly traceable. Again, extremes meet, and the *Daily Mail* has recently said in so many words that Brahms will not do. Last of all, Mr. George Sampson, writing in the *Daily Chronicle*, has pronounced Brahms to be "a bastard Beethoven." The fidelity with which Mr. Sampson clings to the hereditary weapon of his clan is indeed touching.

The literature dealing with Brahms, though not a tithe of that devoted to Wagner, has grown steadily since his death, and now receives a valuable addition in Mr. Fuller Maitland's volume. It is written with a full and intimate knowledge of Brahms's music, the structure and content of which are analysed with acuteness as well as sympathy. It is also written by an avowed enthusiast who glories in his enthusiasm; but this fact, while it detracts from the critical value of the book, lends it a fervour not to be found in more judicial writers. After all, who was ever converted by musical criticism whose opinion was worth having? Besides, no genuine Brahmsian wants to convert people like Mr. Shaw, who are the most dangerous and compromising of allies. The hostility of those who dislike Brahms is one of the surest guarantees of his immortality.

March 25, 1911.

XXIX

TCHAIKOVSKY AND HIS
BENEFACTRESS

Lives of great musicians are not always interesting
to the general reader. The exacting nature of
their artistic allegiance narrows their interests,
and the constant resort to technical terminology
on the part of their biographers repels the layman.
They remind one, *parvis componere magna*, of Sam
Gerridge, who looked at life through a gas-pipe.
Again, Gibbon's phrase that solitude is the school
for genius is peculiarly true of great composers,
who, if they are to compass any enduring achievement, must lead in the main sedentary and
secluded lives. Bach and Schubert, two of the
supremely great creative musicians, never saw the
sea, and Brahms, to whose works, far more than
to those of Mendelssohn, Rubinstein's description,
"the swan song of classicism," may be applied,
led a life in which the adventurous element was

purely that of the mind and wholly detached from the arena of action. With Tchaikovsky—whose Life,[1] monumental even in the skilful condensation given us by Mrs. Newmarch of the colossal memorial erected by the fraternal piety of M. Modeste Tchaikovsky, now lies before us—the case is entirely different. Though appealing primarily to the musical reader, this huge volume is not only intensely interesting as the revelation of a remarkable personality, but its pages are charged with romantic interest of that strange quality peculiar to the works of the great Russian novelists. The central and governing episode of Tchaikovsky's life — his relations with the generous, eccentric widow who came to his rescue at the nadir of his fortunes and gave him a free life, relieved from the anxiety of earning his daily bread by uncongenial drudgery — is perhaps the most extraordinary incident in the entire annals of artistic patronage. In a novel by an English writer such an episode would have been denounced as extravagantly and grotesquely improbable. In its proper, and, let us add, Slavonic, context, though amazing, it fits in appropriately enough. For, judged by the standards of Western Europe, the Slav might belong

[1] *The Life and Letters of Peter Ilich Tchaikovsky.* By Modeste Tchaikovsky. Edited from the Russian, with an Introduction, by Rosa Newmarch. London : John Lane. [21s. net.]

to another planet, so perplexing is the nexus between cause and effect in his life, with such lightning speed does action follow upon impulse. After forty years of residence in the Far East, one of the sanest of observers has declared himself unable to fathom the mystery of the Japanese character. The triumph of the unexpected in this recital of Tchaikovsky's life, to say nothing of the events now being enacted in Russia, indicates the need of a similar reserve in attempting to master the enigma of the Slavonic spirit.

Peter Ilich Tchaikovsky, who was born in 1840, was the son of an Inspector of Mines, an official who held lucrative appointments in the provinces, but ultimately fell on evil days. There were no traces of musical talent in any of his ancestry, and he himself was introduced to the art through the medium of a musical-box. Like most contemporary Russian composers, he adopted the musical career as a second thought, after being educated in the School of Jurisprudence and serving for a short time as an official in the Ministry of Justice. As a very young man he affected dandyism and frequented " smart " society, but his brief experience only engendered a lifelong hatred of the tyranny and senselessness of fashion. Combining for a while musical studies with official duties, he soon decided to abandon the latter, a

step which he took with the approval, if not at
the direct instigation, of his father — another
instance of the unexpected.   His friendly relations
with the Rubinsteins secured him a post at the
Moscow Conservatoire, then under the direction
of Nicholas Rubinstein, where he remained for
many years.   Morbidly sensitive, painfully conscious of the limitations of his equipment, and
wounded by the absence of any general recognition
of his powers as a composer, the hostile criticisms
of the Press, and the disconcerting candour of his
colleagues, Tchaikovsky during this period found
his only real solace in the society of his married
sister and her family and of his two younger
brothers, whom he cherished with a truly paternal
affection.   It was at this stage of his life that
the *dea ex machina* intervened in the person of
Nadejda Filaretovna von Meck, a rich widow
with eleven children, a great lover of the arts in
general, and of Tchaikovsky's music in particular.
She had known the pinch of poverty herself,
having for half her married life lived on an
income of £150 a year, and, like her *protégé*,
detested society.   Relations were established by
letter through a common friend, and by letter
were maintained till the end.   Madame von Meck
made Tchaikovsky an allowance of six thousand
roubles—£600—a year ; she constantly placed

her country-houses at his disposal ; above all, she enabled him, at the most critical period of his life, when the disastrous failure of his sudden marriage had unhinged his mind, to find the best anodyne for his sorrows in the untrammelled pursuit of his art. She did all this, and she did more. In the words of Tchaikovsky's biographer—

The peculiar characteristic of the close and touching friendship between Nadejda von Meck and Tchaikovsky was the fact that they never saw each other except in a crowd—an accidental glimpse at a concert or theatre. When they accidentally came face to face they passed as total strangers. To the end of their days they never exchanged a word, scarcely even a casual greeting. Their whole intercourse was confined to a brisk correspondence.

This peculiar relationship, which lasted for nearly fourteen years, was entered into and maintained at Madame von Meck's express wish. The motives which induced Tchaikovsky's benefactress to adopt this curious attitude were partly revealed in her letters, and may be partly divined from their general tone. His music made her life "easier and pleasanter to live," and she was moved to express her gratitude in a fashion at once tangible and helpful ; but she shrank from meeting him, because her admiration "might seem ridiculous to you ; and my admiration is something so precious that I do not care to have it laughed at." Again, she says : "There was a time when I earnestly desired your personal acquaintance ; but now I feel the more you fascinate me, the more I shrink from knowing you. It seems to me I could not then talk to you as I do now." Tchaikovsky himself entered into her feelings with complete appreciation :—

The fact that we both suffer from the same malady would alone suffice to draw us together. This malady is misanthropy ; but a peculiar form of misanthropy, which certainly does not spring from hatred or contempt of mankind. People who suffer from this complaint do not fear the evil which others may bring them, so much as the disillusionment, that craving for the ideal which follows upon every intimacy. There was a time when I was so possessed by this fear of my fellow-creatures that I stood on the verge of madness. The circumstances of my life were such that I could not possibly escape and hide myself. I had to fight it out myself, and God alone knows what the conflict cost me ! . . . I was saved by work—work which was at the same time my delight. . . . From all you have said, you will understand I am not at all surprised that, although you love my music, you do not care to know the composer. You are afraid lest you should miss in my personality all with which your ideal imagination has endowed me. You are right. I feel that on closer acquaintance you would not find that harmony between me and my music of which you have dreamt.

This was written a few months before Tchaikovsky, in the hope of emulating the domestic happiness achieved by his sister, hastily plunged into matrimony, and experienced the bitterest disillusionment of his life. There was no scandal ; it was simply a case of radical incompatibility of temperaments, and the catastrophe was all the more humiliating in that Tchaikovsky recognised that he was chiefly to blame for undertaking responsibilities which he had not the courage or the force to fulfil. It was at this crisis, which for a space completely upset his mental balance, that Madame von Meck's invisible friendship stood him in the greatest stead. Her financial assistance enabled him to return to the work he loved as soon as he was physically fit for it. Her letters brought him the balm of complete under-standing, while her resolute abstention from all personal contact removed their friendship from the breath of scandal. If, as Tchaikovsky put it, she felt that to meet him might shatter her ideal, she may well have also realised that the danger was two-edged and that a widow with eleven children was not likely to inspire him with romantic devotion. That she was a woman of great force of character and considerable intel-lectual attainments is clear from the few letters from her pen which are printed in this memoir. And if she was eccentric, there was a great deal of method in her eccentricity. There are few harder things in this world than to persuade a proud and self-respecting man to accept pecuniary assistance without giving what the world considers an adequate return for it, and it is extremely improbable that Tchaikovsky would ever have consented to become Madame von Meck's pensioner except on the strange terms on which she insisted. Anyhow, they enabled her to achieve her end to her own satisfaction, and to the great ultimate profit of the world of musicians and music-lovers. The scheme worked like a charm, and to the period of nearly fourteen years during which it lasted belong the ripest and most brilliant fruits of his genius—the Fourth and Fifth Symphonies, *Eugene Oniegin*, the "1812" Overture, the Suite in C, the Symphonic poem *Manfred*, the operas *The Maid of Orleans*, *Les Caprices d'Oxane*, etc.

Tchaikovsky's favourite symphony, the Fourth, was dedicated to Madame von Meck—he alludes to it as "our symphony"—and throughout the whole of their intimacy he wrote to "his incomparable friend" with the utmost freedom and affection. Their final estrangement was perhaps the saddest of the many inexplicable or unnecessary tragedies of Tchaikovsky's career. Madame von Meck, having reason to believe that she was on the verge of bankruptcy, wrote to him to announce that she could no longer afford to make him an allowance. Tchaikovsky's reply, while he did not pretend to deny that it would make a great difference to him, was that of a chivalrous gentleman. But on his learning that her fears were illusory, he was beset with the suspicion that the financial motive was only a pretext for breaking a tie which had become irksome to her, and this suspicion was quickened into conviction when his letters, in which he endeavoured to resume the old familiar relations, remained unanswered. As a matter of fact, Madame von Meck's nerves and health had given way, and it is more than probable that her capacity for altruistic enthusiasm was destroyed by her preoccupation about herself. The rupture became complete, and they died unreconciled within a few months of each other, Madame von Meck's name, uttered in "indignant or reproachful tones," being the last heard from Tchaikovsky's lips in the delirium that preceded his death. The irony of the situation was that as long as he was in her debt he was never galled by a sense of obligation, but that as soon as the pension ceased he became conscious of the burden. It is impossible to avoid comparing the relations between Tchaikovsky and Madame von Meck with those which existed between Wagner and Madame

Wesendonck. In both cases the women emerge with credit,—the one for her eccentric wisdom, the other for her loyalty. On the other hand, the attitude of Tchaikovsky as a man was incomparably more dignified and honourable than that of the composer of *Tristan*. But, as a perusal of these pages abundantly proves, Tchaikovsky—a true *Heautontimorumenos* if ever one existed—in spite of his highly strung and morbidly sensitive nature, had in him a great fund of nobility, generosity, and considerateness. His criticisms of literature show a profound and sincere appreciation for all that was pure, wholesome, and of good report. He was a great lover of Dickens, but was revolted by the lubricity of the modern French realists. Apart from some curious, but perfectly honest, likes and dislikes, his musical judgment was essentially sound. He held Beethoven in awe, finding in him much of the *terribilità* of Michael Angelo ; he adored the serene beauty of Mozart, he recognised the spirituality of Schumann, and he entertained a deep respect for Brahms the artist and the man, though repelled by the austerity of his music. We have left ourselves no space to dwell on a host of other attractive and engrossing features in this remarkable book, which will undoubtedly enhance the admiration with which Tchaikovsky has long been

regarded in this country, and must content ourselves with congratulating Mrs. Newmarch on the
zeal and intelligence with which she has accomplished her task. Of the delicacy, the candour,
and the affection shown by M. Modeste Tchaikovsky it is impossible to speak two highly.
The most unobtrusive of biographers, he has yet
made it perfectly clear why he was so beloved by
his illustrious and unhappy brother.

November 25, 1905.

XXX

LONDON'S CONCERT-HALLS

Dismissing the establishment of national or municipal opera as a project which for the moment hardly falls within the sphere of practical musical politics, the need of a really satisfactory central concert - hall for London is generally admitted, and may be not unprofitably discussed. "A *new* concert-hall ! " it will at once be objected ; "why, we have dozens of them already ! " And so we have ; but a dispassionate survey of their qualities, geographical, acoustic, and otherwise, should convince all but the most indifferent that we are not only a long way off perfection, but in some respects actually worse off than some provincial cities. To begin with, the large halls available for concerts in many of the principal provincial cities and towns form part of the Corporation buildings, and consequently are not hampered by the heavy rents which have to be paid in the case of the best London concert-halls. London, within the memory of man, has never had so good a concert-hall as the Free-Trade Hall in Manchester ; and, now that St. James's Hall has been sacrificed to the Juggernaut car of gastronomy, we have no hall which combines decorative and acoustic properties so satisfactorily as the Philharmonic Hall in Liverpool. It will be said, again, that we are doing injustice to the great qualities of the Albert and Queen's Halls. The former, we readily admit, is admirable for concerts of massed brass bands, or performances of works with angelic choirs, or fanfares of trumpets ; but alike from the point of view of the soloist and the orchestral conductor, it is so unsatisfactory that under a Republic it would probably be at once converted into a free hippodrome, in which music would be relegated to the ancillary function of accompanying chariot races, " daring bare-backed acts," and other engaging feats of fancy horseman-ship. All musicians owe a great deal to the Queen's Hall, but it has seriously fallen short of the expectations which its imposing proportions aroused. It is not, like the Albert Hall, so big as to present a desolate appearance when only half full : it holds enough people to enable an impresario to " get home " even when he engages the most expensive star pianist, or to render it

R

possible for a choral work with full orchestra and solo quartet to be given without serious loss—supposing that the public are in the mood to go and hear it. It is good, though not first-rate, for the performance of symphonic music by a large orchestra, and it is more than good enough for ballad concerts. But as a set-off, the immense width of the platform impairs the concentration of sound, and neither for vocal nor instrumental recitals can it be pronounced altogether satisfactory. This drawback is all the more serious since, in spite of the large increase in the number of orchestral concerts, the great majority of musical entertainments take the form of recitals, or are devoted to the performance of chamber music. To meet this want the existing supply of halls leaves nothing to be desired in respect of numbers. In Central London alone there are, apart from town halls, half a dozen small or medium-sized concert-rooms, some of them excellently equipped for the purpose. Yet here, again, it cannot be contended that any of them entirely meets the situation created by the demolition of the ill-ventilated St. James's Hall, which was the only hall in London designed effectively "a double debt to pay," being at once large enough for orchestral music, and not too big for chamber concerts. Subterranean echoes from the Moore and Burgess Minstrels, wafts of irrelevant odours from the adjoining restaurant, the clattering of carts on the cobble-stones in the yard at the back, and the persistent minstrelsy, during the tea-cake season, of the Vine Street muffin-man,—all these and other drawbacks impaired the equanimity of the *habitués* of St. James's Hall. But when all deductions were made, it was a first-rate room for sound, and its disappearance has left a gap which still remains to be filled. Besides, the best of the small halls now available are, as their name frankly indicates, of the nature of "tied houses." We use the term in no offensive sense, for the method is perfectly legitimate, and offers in some ways unquestionable advantages to the performers. None the less, we hold that any limitations which restrict concert-givers in the choice of *matériel*, or, as occasionally happens, of *personnel*, are irreconcilable with the conditions which should govern the management of the ideal concert-hall ; and the self-denying ordinance adopted by the managers of the Broadwood concerts, though commercially it represents a counsel of perfection, would, if we ever have a municipal concert-hall in London, necessarily form one of the guiding rules under which such a building should be let for performances. Subject to the enforcement of such regulations as are needed to secure public safety, to protect public morals, and to guarantee the payment of the fee for hiring the room, a concert-giver should be perfectly free to engage whom he pleases, and to be exempt from any dictation in the choice of instruments.

If, then, London has not got the concert-hall that it needs, what are we to say of the chances that this want will be supplied ?   So far as private enterprise is concerned, the outlook is the reverse of hopeful.   There seems to be no difficulty whatever in securing capital for the erection of new theatres, new hotels, and new restaurants. We hear a great deal about the cult of the simple life, and the adoption of various regimens at once eupeptic and economical ; yet wherever in Central London old buildings are demolished, it is generally to make room for some new temple dedicated to the pleasures of the table, and the transformation of the old War Office into the Hotel Heliogabalus [1] is, we suppose, only a question of time.   According to the new scheme [2] adopted this week by the London County Council, the syndicate to which the Aldwych site is to be let propose to include a concert-hall among the various buildings on which they undertake to expend a minimum sum of £500,000 ;

[1] Now the site of the Automobile Club.
[2] The site still remains vacant, July 1911.

but the chief features of the scheme are clearly to be exhibition buildings, and the inevitable theatre and restaurant. In any case, it may be assumed that when the Chairman of the Improvements Committee stated that "the concert-hall would be treated as an ordinary music-hall," he unconsciously foreshadowed the nature of the entertainment to be given in the building. The site predetermines the character of the performance. It is one of the peculiarities of London that certain areas are dedicated to certain purposes, and a concert-hall in the heart of theatreland is as much out of place as a club in Bayswater, a mission hall in Park Lane, or a ducal mansion in the Harrow Road.

Whether or no we are to look to the London County Council for assistance in providing musical London with the concert-hall that it needs, the Aldwych scheme may be ruled out as at best a negligible contribution to the solving of the problem. The attitude of the Council towards music, as shown by their liberal expenditure on bands in the public parks, is of good augury. They have done a good deal in the way of what may be called the primary musical education of the masses. Are they prepared to supplement this by the provision or facilities for their higher or secondary education?

In view of their existing and extensive commit-
ments, and of their manifest intention at the
earliest possible date to substitute for their present
premises a new and necessarily costly Council
Chamber of their own, they are hardly likely to
launch out upon any further building scheme
unless there is an assured prospect of its turning
out a profitable investment. The acquisition of a
suitable site is the great difficulty. Geographical
conditions, as we have already indicated, are of
prime importance. The hall must be central, it
must be as far as possible isolated, and it must be
placed so as not to aggravate the existing conges-
tion of traffic. And if such a site be available,
how are the Council, as trustees for the ratepayers,
to be convinced that in devoting it to music they
are not turning a valuable asset into an instrument
of further extravagance ? That is a matter on
which we have not the knowledge to pronounce
an opinion, though possibly the balance-sheet of
such an institution as the *Gewandhaus* at Leipsic
might throw valuable light on the subject.
Perhaps the scheme of the County Council's own
Chamber might include a public hall suitable for
the purpose ; or perhaps, when the present craze
for restaurant life has abated, and there is a swing
of the pendulum in the direction of domestic life,
one of the superfluous monster hotels may be

converted from the service of appetite to that of art. We may note in conclusion that although it was recently decided in the City of London Court that a concert-hall is not a necessary for an "infant," it cannot be indefinitely dispensed with by the largest city in the world.

March 24, 1906.

XXXI

THE GENTLEMAN IN MUSIC

In a recently published volume of musical essays by Mr. E. A. Baughan[1] will be found an interesting paper on " The Gentleman in Music." To prevent misunderstanding, Mr. Baughan is at pains to state with the utmost particularity the exact meaning he attaches to the word. For the purpose of his article a gentleman must be of good family—" not necessarily rich or noble, but gentle "—have had a public-school and University education, and be comfortably off. His brothers and relations must be in the liberal or learned professions, or the higher walks of commerce,— none of them brilliant, but all well-educated, well-mannered, and trained to live laborious days and to all kinds of self-denial. Formerly they would have had nothing to do with art, but nowadays

---

[1] *Music and Musicians.* By E. A. Baughan. London : John Lane. [5s. net.]

" the gentleman class is making its way more and more in music, as professors, composers, pianists, and even singers." Mr. Baughan cheerfully admits that in the abstract it is a good thing for the art to be taken seriously enough for men of education to enter it, and that the profession has been socially improved by the accession of gentlemen to its ranks. None the less is he of opinion that the gentleman by birth and training is the last man who should be a musician. The grounds on which he reaches this decision are manifold. To begin with, the ideals of our public schools, uniformity and stoicism, are incompatible with the free expression of the emotions, while the ideal of University life, the apotheosis of the intellect—it is most refreshing to hear how far we have travelled from the time when undergraduates were described as " young barbarians *all* at play "—though it makes for sanity and clear thinking, is uncreative and inexpansive. Our gentlemen musicians are not free from austerity and intellectual pose. They adore Bach, but they do their best to strip him of his humanity. They worship Brahms, but perversely exaggerate the importance of the dry and intellectual side of his genius. As performers these University musicians carry this suppression of emotion to excess, make war on sentiment, and

interpret everything sanely and coolly. Worse
still, they are hampered by "a curious effeminacy
of thought and outlook," a "strange fastidiousness
which manifests itself in a love of all old music,
especially if it is little-known music." Their
enthusiasm is ladylike : they distrust emotionalism,
abhor singers who have made reputations, and
greatly prefer artists, no matter how much they
sing out of tune, provided they are of gentle birth
and good education. Mr. Baughan does not
condemn general intelligence in a musician ; what
he insists on is that the culture he requires is not
the culture of any of our Universities, which are
"peculiarly Philistine," and turn out men who
are "singularly wanting in artistic appreciation."
The real desiderata of the musician are then
enumerated. "He ought to know most of what
has been done in literature, especially modern
literature : he should have a knowledge of the
plastic arts . . . and have . . . a fair and working knowledge of modern languages. . . . Above
all, he must live, and I deny that any man has
really lived whose circumstances have been
comfortable from childhood." If it should be
contended that after all the University musician
is a negligible factor in our musical life, Mr.
Baughan is ready with his reply. "This *dilettante*
attitude of mind is the curse of our England.

You will find it everywhere—in the Army and in politics ; and . . . those who are behind the scenes know full well what a power this new type of musician is gradually becoming in the country." He has good intentions, a real love of music, in many cases will work hard for the realisation of his ideals, and is free from insularity, "but he is essentially of his class and training, and both are inimical to music." Mr. Baughan is not concerned with the question of whether this is good for the country or not ; he is convinced that it is bad for music. "The great fault of British music and British performers has been a certain coldness and want of emotion, and those very defects are precisely the merits for which our universities strive. They specialize in the national character, but the very parts in which they specialize are those which can have no traffic with music."

We do not profess to be "behind the scenes," but if any one is anxious to take up the cudgels on behalf of the class so vigorously impeached by Mr. Baughan, it would be impossible to find better materials for their defence than in the pages of this volume. The admissions which accompany the indictment are in themselves considerable,— education ; a capacity for taking the art seriously ; ardent admiration for Bach and Brahms ; a catholic appreciation of all schools as opposed to "the parochial spirit that continually cries for British music for the British people." But they are greatly reinforced by the fact that the very limitations — coolness, sanity, restraint — which Mr. Baughan here condemns as inimical to the progress of the art are precisely those which he never wearies of extolling in his other chapters. The essay which immediately precedes that under review is headed "The Art of Restraint," and in it we find such sentences as : "modern music-making suffers much from exaggerated emotional-ism, which defeats its aim by losing plasticity of expression in the desire to be too expressive " ; "naturalness of expression is only obtained by control " ; "if we learnt to look on music as a language we should soon resent the hard rantings of many of our singers and pianists." A little later on we encounter a paper on "The Hooligan in Music," in which we read : "In all pianoforte recitals and orchestral concerts, and, to a lesser degree, in all vocal recitals, there now seems to me an element of unbridled violence, of Hooliganism in music." And again : "The worst of it is, the modern piano pugilist has been the cause of the death of the amateur pianist." In another chapter we read (p. 60), *à propos* of the difference between Beethoven and Tchaikov-sky : "The secret of great expression in literature and music is that all is *not* expressed fully. There is always a reserve." Further, Mr. Baughan condemns unbridled emotion in the auditor as well as in the performer. Personally, he has never felt asphyxiated by the emotional appeal of music, and he defends his attitude on the ground that the emotion of all art is artistic make-believe. " It does not, and should not, arouse the precise emotion which the same thing in real life arouses, and it is only inferior art that attempts to do so, either psychologically or objectively. The emotion of the great composers is intellectualised before it reaches us." Hence there is at least something to be said in favour of the University musician who, according to the writer, modified the human side of Brahms until it was intellectualised. But it is when Mr. Baughan comes to deal with the leading representatives of modern music on its creative side that his unconscious testimony to the forces that make for sanity and restraint is most striking. Here, for example, is his deliberate verdict on Richard Strauss at the close of a chapter entitled " The Parting of the Ways " :—

One must look to Richard Strauss as the exponent of the music of the future. His works have form—it is absurd to say they have not ; but though it is a form which does bear some kind of relationship to the older forms, it is almost entirely dictated by psychological impulses. The danger in the future seems to me to be that music is so vaguely infinite an art that it runs the risk of becoming the master and not the servant of mankind. The Richard Strausses of the world may create a monster which they will not be able to control. Emotion without reasoning powers leads to insanity ; music should not become an emotional stimulant only.

Even more severe is his condemnation of Tchaikovsky. He finds the *Pathetic* symphony sincere and human, but "its humanity and sincerity pall on one. . . . The whole symphony, with its bursts of commonplace, with its military and ballroom atmosphere, is the expression of an ordinary man—touching it may be, but also cloying, enervating, pessimism - breeding." In another chapter he dwells on the insanity, the morbid sentiment, and excessive and theatrical emotion of modern music—qualities which are "surely strangling" its growth. His admiration for Sir Edward Elgar—who certainly cannot be classed amongst the academics—is largely tempered with dissatisfaction. He finds the sentiment of both *Gerontius* and *The Apostles* "almost grovelling in its anguish of remorse," and unmanly in its hysterical prostration. The music is conditioned by "an anaemic sentimentality," which makes Mr. Baughan, "without having strong feelings in the matter, yearn for the breezy faith of a

Martin Luther." Lastly, on the subject of Wagner, Mr. Baughan carries his criticism to lengths that ten years ago would have been pronounced obscurantist. For example, he finds much exaggeration in the Wagner music even when Ternina sings it. Much allowance, however, must be made for the mood of the moment, as he himself claims in his Preface ; besides, as he remarks on p. 97, " I suppose a musical critic in time becomes either a nervous wreck or a solid and unsensitive Philistine." Still, when all allowance has been made for the hyperaesthesia produced by a surfeit of music, we cannot altogether acquit Mr. Baughan of inconsistency as well as ingratitude in belabouring the University musician for the possession of precisely those qualities the lack of which he finds so dangerous in the leading composers and executants of the moment. At their lowest they perform the function of a brake on the anarchical tendencies so much in vogue, and for this service alone they deserved more generous treatment at his hands.

June 30, 1906.

XXXII

MUSIC AT PUBLIC SCHOOLS

A FEW weeks ago we dealt with the estimate—in the main hostile—of the influence of " University musicians " given by Mr. Baughan in a recently published volume of musical essays. It has since occurred to us that whatever influence, for good or evil, is exerted by University musicians may be traced back, in part at least, to the musical education they have received at school, whether public or private. This obvious deduction naturally prompts a survey of the position of music in our secondary schools—an extremely interesting subject, but one for the adequate discussion of which the present writer is not fully equipped. Still, admitting the risk of generalising from imperfect and partial knowledge, it may not be amiss to set down a few notes based on individual experience and observation.

Are boys at public and private schools more

musical than they used to be, say, thirty years ago ? The question is not to be answered off-hand, but, within the limits imposed by personal knowledge, it ought not to be difficult to arrive at some general conclusions. The conditions under which boys are afforded opportunities for cultivating their musical taste remain tolerably constant at our public schools. First and fore-most, there is the school chapel ; second, there are the private lessons given by music masters ; and third, there are the various societies, choral and instrumental, in which they have the chance of taking part in concerted music. Dealing with the last-named category first, it is clear that there has been a great advance in the organisation of instrumental music at our public schools. The brass band or drum-and-fife band of a generation back has now in many cases been supplemented by a string band, which on occasions, and with the necessary professional stiffening in the wood and wind, gives performances of classical music. In regard to teaching, again, there has been a good deal of levelling up. More care is taken in the selection of music masters and organists, and the standard of efficiency in these respects has undoubtedly risen. The same remarks, we think, must be taken to apply to the services in school chapels. It is not that the boys join

s

more heartily in favourite hymns than their
fathers did, but that the musicianship of the
choir and the choice of church music show the
influence of the general progress in musical taste
and education which has taken place in the last
quarter of a century. Again, it has become the
practice—and a very excellent practice—at many
public schools to supplement the public entertainments organised for the benefit of the school
as a whole with concerts or recitals given by
distinguished artists, and thus to afford opportunities to boys while still at school of learning
what first-rate music sounds like when interpreted
by first-rate performers. What we have said,
however, of this improvement in teaching and
these improved facilities for hearing good music
must be taken as applying chiefly to public
schools. There *are* private schools where music
is well taught, but the high fees frequently
charged afford no guarantee of the efficiency of
the teacher.

In the last resort, the question how far music
enters into the life of an average English public
or preparatory school boy is largely a question
of time ; and here the conditions are much
the same as they were thirty years ago, if
indeed they are not less favourable. There is
this great difference between music in our primary

and secondary schools, that in the former, though
limited to choral singing, it forms part of the
obligatory curriculum, while in the latter music
has, with very rare exceptions, to be studied in
play-hours. In other words, all the time devoted
to music must be subtracted from that ordinarily
devoted to pastime. Now it cannot be said that
the competing attractions are less potent than they
were thirty years ago. The cult of games has
waxed rather than waned since 1880. Certainly
more games are played, to say nothing of the enhanced charms of bicycling, the enormous spread
of photography, and the increased attention very
properly paid in many schools to drill and rifle-
shooting. Again, schoolboys nowadays read the
newspapers and magazines much more than they
did thirty or twenty years ago. Taking all these
attractions and distractions into account, the
wonder is that so many boys are found ready
to sacrifice any of their playtime to music lessons
or practising, and it speaks a good deal for the
popularity or persuasiveness of music masters
that they are able to secure such creditable results.
The number of boys at public or preparatory
schools who attain any real proficiency as performers must always be small ; it is surprising
that it is not smaller. Out of school-time the
average boy, if he has any ambition, will naturally

exert himself mainly in such a way as to enhance his prestige with and win the applause of his fellows, and there is little of either to be gained by working at the piano or violin. Compared with the glory of appearing at Lord's or Prince's, or even of gaining his house colours, such reputation as he may attain sinks into insignificance ; and viewing the public-school system as a whole, we do not wish that it should be otherwise. To expect any radical change in the comparative values assigned to pre-eminence in art and athletics at our schools would be premature, to say the least of it. Nor are we prepared to assert that schoolboys of to-day are really more musical than those of the last generation. What we do assert is that they have more opportunities of hearing music, and that those who are prepared to make sacrifices are better trained and taught.

There are, however, two other factors in the situation which, though they have only recently made themselves felt, cannot fail to effect the whole question of musical education. The greater complexity of modern life is reflected at school as elsewhere. There are only twenty-four hours in the day, and the number of things to be done in it—whether needful or not—constantly increases. There are more subjects to be studied, more games to be played, more interests to cultivate ; and though there may be a greater readiness to recognise the humanising influence of music, on the other hand utilitarian educationists insist with ever-growing vehemence that we should concentrate our efforts on those subjects which make for national efficiency. In face of this strenuous cry, how can one expect that more time will be found for the cultivation of the musical taste? Simultaneously with this tendency we find the domain of music invaded by a host of time- and labour-saving mechanical substitutes for human performers. That their introduction must result, if it has not already resulted, in a diminution of the number of amateur executants is tolerably obvious, unless the testimonials of several eminent musicians are flagrantly insincere. As Professor Smart says, machinery has in many cases — *e.g.* the camera and pianola—raised the standard demanded of the human competitor. To keep up to this heightened standard requires further specialising of a sort impossible at a public school. In these circumstances, it is difficult to avoid the conclusion that in future fewer boys will learn musical instruments, and to this extent their practical musicianship is likely to diminish rather than increase.

There remains the question how far the

gramophone and pianola are to be regarded as *bonâ-fide* and desirable means of musical education. The question is worth considering, because there can be little doubt that many of the rising generation are likely to owe their first acquaintance with music, good, bad, and indifferent, to these momentous inventions. For ourselves, we have never sought to deny their efficiency or, within certain limits, their value. The repertory now available for mechanical performance is already very large ; it contains a great deal of classical music, and is obviously capable of lending considerable assistance by preserving accurate records of the renderings of great artists, and thus perpetuating the best traditions. As regards the pianola, it should be borne in mind that the more musical the operator, the better the results produced. On the other hand, it would be idle to deny that the more vulgar and trivial records are in the main the more popular. Furthermore, it may be contended that any device which leads to indefinite and mechanical multiplication must exert a sterilising influence on the creative side of art. What machinery has done for the plastic and pictorial arts, machinery is already doing for music. It may help to educate the masses, but its ultimate end is repetition, not creation.

Hence, as our public schools are a microcosm, it is only natural that in the sphere of music they should share the disabilities as well as the advantages of an age in which the progress of culture is largely affected by machinery.

August 25, 1906.

XXXIII

QUO MUSA TENDIS?

THE correspondent of an evening paper, *à propos* of the performances of German opera at Covent Garden, recently unearthed an amusing prediction from the *Athenæum* in 1874 to the effect that the British public would never stand two perform- ances of *Tristan und Isolde*. By that year H. F. Chorley had ceased to be musical critic of the *Athenæum*, but the paper had not abandoned its anti-Wagnerian attitude. Much water has flowed under the bridges since 1874, and *Tristan*, then anathema to those who stood upon the ancient ways, no longer suffices to fulfil the aspirations of some of the most advanced critics of to-day. Admittedly the last word in "sublimated eroticism," it fails, so we are told, to represent the dominating tendencies of contemporary music- makers, from whose most characteristic works the eternal duel of sex is excluded. Prophecy in matters musical is more than usually dangerous, and in what follows we propose rather to record some phases of criticism than to indulge in any forecasts of our own. But it is significant of the rapidity with which reputations are made and lost at the present day that even Richard Strauss, only a few years back the *enfant terrible* of the musical world, is already regarded in some quarters either as "representing a declining impulse by his excessive predilection for the dynamic element in life," or as having exhausted his creative powers and lapsed into the position of "an enormously clever man who was once a genius." The attitude of Strauss's admirers is indeed hardly less remarkable than his music. Of those who have recently expressed their opinions in England and in America, Mr. R. A. Streatfeild, the author of a brightly-written volume on *Modern Music and Musicians* (Methuen and Co., 7s. 6d.), is perhaps his only whole-hearted panegyrist. In spite of the episodes of the windmill and the bleating of sheep in *Don Quixote*, he declares that "the absurd attempts at realism to which some modern composers are addicted . . . would be as impossible to Strauss as to the austerest of his academic critics." He admires all his works without exception, but reserves his highest praise for the *Symphonia Domestica,* an "exquisite idyll of home life" which "has won Strauss more friends than anything he ever wrote." In particular, he describes the love scene as being "of such rapturous and exalted feeling, of emotion so sacred and tender, that it seems almost a desecration to speak of it in terms of ordinary criticism," and continues in the same vein of lofty panegyric :—

Since Beethoven wrote the finale to the Eroica Symphony, the love of man and woman has not been sung in accents of purer and nobler inspiration. In the closing movement we see the destiny of the child mirrored in the hopes of the parents. They seem to read the future with the piercing gaze of love and faith and hope. The music tingles, as it were, with fervour and enthusiasm. We are hurried from climax to climax till the work ends triumphantly in a broad sweep of impassioned exultation. Before such a work as this, so profound in feeling, so transcendent in scientific mastery of musical art, it is no wonder that many of Strauss's detractors have been reduced to silence.

What the effect of the symphony and the later works of Strauss has been on Strauss's detractors we do not venture to pronounce with Mr. Streatfeild's confidence. But it certainly has not reduced his admirers to silence. On the contrary, their dismay and indignation are lyrical in their intensity. Mr. Lawrence Gilman was, up to the

production of *Ein Heldenleben*—the noble conception, "marvellous richness and beauty," and
"sublime" ending of which move Mr. Streatfeild
to transports of enthusiasm—a thorough-paced
admirer of Strauss. But now—well, he had
better be allowed to speak for himself :—[1]

Eight years ago, when Strauss presented to a somewhat indifferent world that marvellous tragi-comedy in
tones [*i.e.*, "Don Quixote"], the few who gave attentive
and eager heed to it recognised in its creator a genius
who had achieved a quality of musical utterance quite
without any precise parallel—a fulfilment of the magnificent promise disclosed by the author of "Tod und
Verklärung" and "Zarathustra." "Don Quixote" is
indisputably one of the great things of music—a work
charged to the brim with humanity, with eloquence,
with commanding beauty : there is nothing quite like it
in the entire literature of the art. It marked the summit
of Strauss's achievements. But what has come over him
since ? "Ein Heldenleben," which followed "Don
Quixote" some years later, was marred, for all its
wonderful impressiveness, by evidences of a growing
tendency on the part of Strauss to prostitute his great
gifts—in the phrase of Mr. Newman, "to deface his
picture by some piece of malicious folly ; to thrust his
head through the canvas and grin at the public." Of the
incredible fatuity of the "Symphonia Domestica" one
has not the heart to speak—a work in which triviality
and ignoble burlesque do their utmost to obscure the
glimmering of a persuasive and lovely motive.

[1] *The Music of To-morrow.*   London : John Lane.   [4s. 6d. net.]

In regard to Strauss's other works this divergence of view is also noteworthy.   Thus, while Mr.
Streatfeild finds in his *Don Juan* the study of a
man " rioting in the lust of the eye and the pride
of life, a voluptuary and a cynic," Mr. Gilman pronounces it essentially non-erotic and non-romantic.
Mr. Gilman regards the *Don Quixote* as Strauss's
masterpiece, and *Till Eulenspiegel* as a riotous and
exhilarating burlesque ; *per contrà*, Mr. Streatfeild
holds that the former is not one of Strauss's
greatest works, and that the latter exhibits him
at his philosophic standpoint.   As Mr. Streatfeild
admits that he has not heard *Salome*, it is hardly
fair to quote Mr. Gilman's onslaught on the
" barbarousness and banality," the " barrenness
and flaccidity of thought," which mark every page
of this " dull and pretentious music."   Mr.
Gilman, it may be noted, finds the cause of this
degeneration in a flaw " more spiritual than
physical or psychic " :—

Is there not operative in Strauss some active principle
which corresponds to the philosophic attitude of Friedrich
Nietzsche, for whom Strauss has confessed, in more ways
than one, a fervent admiration ?   Is he not smitten with
that passion for personal aggrandisement, that vicious
" Titanism " of which Mr. Huneker speaks in his acute
analysis of Nietzsche's temperament and teachings : that
ruthless and strabismic individualism which, for all its
valuable potentialities, is, at bottom, irremediably false

and maleficent? It is, is it not, the fitting creed of such
an intelligence as could father that precious witticism in
the "Roving Expeditions of an Inopportune Philosopher":
"Kant, or *cant*, as an intelligent character"! The
Nietzschean proclivities which I have assumed in Strauss
find issue in a growing lust for mere enormity. He
seems to have been seduced by some perverted conception
of Nietzsche's spiritual magalomania. He would employ
an orchestra of a size and complexity hitherto unimagined
—an orchestra swollen out of all proportion to the
character of the musical thought it is intended to convey
(I am speaking, let it be remembered, of the later Strauss
—not the admirable Strauss of "Don Quixote"); he
would seek out the most brutal and abortive cacophonies;
he would burden his music-paper with a welter of poly-
phonic extravagances: he would, in short, impose himself
upon you by sheer magnitude of dimension and immensity
of mass. He has acquired all the Nietzschean arrogance
and contempt, forgetting that no artist may progressively
achieve save through humility and sacrifice, through
ceaseless self-scrutiny and rigorous self-discipline. Thus,
for him, mere perfection of expression has come to seem
almost negligible: the art of salient and vital utterance
which of old he knew so well how to exert has come
to withhold its secrets from him; he is no longer the
master, but the slave, of his temperament.

Strauss may have silenced his detractors, but
it is sufficiently clear from the foregoing extracts
that he has excited the gravest misgivings amongst
some of the ablest of those who hailed him as the
coming man. The most damaging criticisms of

his later works have come not from his enemies but his admirers.

Turning from the music of yesterday to that of to-morrow, we gather from Mr. Gilman's suggestive volume that it is not to Germany but to France that he looks for the most fruitful and significant developments of the youngest of the arts. Strauss is, in his view, too much under the tyranny of action—whether on the material or psychical plane—to be truly and fully representative of the time-spirit. "For all his truth and vigour of presentation, for all his intrepid and rich humanity, Strauss has never touched, has never attempted to touch, that region of experience which lies over the borderland of our spiritual consciousness ; and it is toward that region that all the finer and, as I think, more permanent elements in our modern art and thought are surely swerving." Mr. Gilman's mode of expression is open to a criticism that is more than merely verbal. A swerving motion is not indicative of a settled and irrevocable tendency. It rather expresses a deviation, and it is perhaps more as a deviation than an inevitable trend that we are justified in regarding the music of Debussy, the arch-hierophant of the music of to-morrow, and of other composers who admittedly derive their impulse from a literary source—the dramas and

poems of symbolists like Maeterlinck and Mall-
armé, and of "spiritual adventurers" into the
crepuscular world like Mr. Yeats.   Of Debussy,
in particular, Mr. Gilman speaks as "the subtlest
temperament in European music, who is employing
his luminous and recondite art in the weaving of
a hesitant mysticism into designs of impalpable
and iridescent beauty."   *Quo musa tendis?* asks
Mr. Gilman, and his answer is :—

To the search, I think, for a still more intimate,
luminous, and eloquent means of restoring to us that
sense of the invisible which music, pre-eminently among
the arts, is fitted to convey.   The element of mysticism
which has crept into its being in our time is not yet free
from sensuousness ; and it is overmuch preoccupied with
the merely fantastic, the consciously bizarre.   I believe
that it will shake itself clear of these things ; that it will
attain, too, an added fluidity and fineness of exceptional
texture ; that it will become continually less vehement,
violent, and assertive.   I can hear, in this supposititious
art that I like to imagine, supremely moving tone-
sequences, poignantly chromatic in their progress and
interrelation, yet wholly different (more supple and
various) from the formulas perpetuated in contemporary
music by those who have drunk too deeply at the
intoxicating spring of Wagner's genius.   I am aware of
a new voice and a new art, subtle yet commanding,
having strange and undiscovered potencies of communi-
cation, of revelation — a speech at once luminous and
esoteric, importunate and profound.   Its persuasions,

perhaps, shall lead us closer " to the gates of our being . . . where are the fountain-heads."

That such tendencies will be increasingly represented in the music of to-morrow we are not prepared to deny. The interval between literary movements and their corresponding musical reactions becomes shorter as the world advances ; but no one can contemplate the restriction of the function of the best music to the stimulating of the subliminal consciousness or the exploration of the crepuscular and astral life without a certain misgiving. If the two chief features of the civilisation of the future, as some think, are to be music and machinery, it is as well that the protest against materialism should be as effective as possible. But apart from that consideration, anything that tends to contract or blur the horizons of art is a matter for regret rather than satisfaction.

January 26, 1907.

XXXIV

COMEDY IN MUSIC

Much that concerns the nomenclature of music is perplexing and unsatisfactory—a not unnatural result when one reflects how much of its terminology is borrowed from other and earlier arts, and how largely in regard to titles composers draw upon literary sources. The drawbacks of this method are nowhere more conspicuously illustrated than in respect of the use of the words "comic" or "comedy." *Opéra comique* has come to have a purely technical meaning without any real reference to the content or spirit of the music, the specific connotation being opera in which the dialogue is spoken, not sung. Thus *Carmen* is called a "grand opéra comique," though no one who has read Mérimée's story is likely to regard it in that light, while the *dénoûement* of the story in its operatic version retains its essentially tragic complexion. However, we are not denying that a great deal of *Carmen* is bright, sparkling, and full of the meridional glamour which inspired Nietzsche to pen his strange eulogy of Bizet's masterpiece culminating in the phrase *il faut méditerraniser la musique*. The typical composer of *opéra comique* was Auber, and there was no lack of graceful comedy in the sprightly runnings of his Muse. If we are in search of serious abuse of the terms " comic " and " comedy " in connexion with music, we need not cross the Channel for offenders against the fitness of things. They abound in profusion in our own music-halls and theatres. The *lion comique* is happily a dead lion, but middle-aged men will remember his roars and be thankful that their children are delivered from his ferocious pleasantries. The great Vance is no more, though he has achieved an accidental immortality in the pages of *The Wrong Box*, where also may be found, amongst other delights, the *locus classicus* on the penny whistle. But the " dashing serio " (*i.e.* serio-comic), by turns strenuously sentimental and formidably arch, still warbles and prances nightly on a hundred platforms, and salaries exceeding the most avaricious dreams of journalists are drawn by the leading hierophants of musical comedy. It is true that the term " musical comedy " has of late fallen somewhat into abeyance ; but the particular sort of entertainment to which it was applied—viz. a more or less incoherent story, diversified with "turns" for popular performers, and lyrics, topical, facetious, and maudlin, set to appropriate music—still holds the boards, and provides opportunities for a coalition of talent ranging occasionally to sextuple collaboration. The aim of the musical accomplices is not very exalted. Indeed, it has prompted the desire, expressed in an ingenious gloss on " J. K. S.," for a transference to that happy shore where

> The Ivans cease to Caryll
> And the Rubens Paul no more.

But it would be altogether unjust to assert that the music specially composed to reinforce the vivacity of these entertainments never succeeds in fulfilling its object. There are at least half a dozen writers who make a speciality of purveying facile, tuneful, tinkling airs, and furnishing them with ingenious orchestral embroidery. Everybody can "score" nowadays. But the faculty of composing music that is intrinsically funny or humorous is seldom found. When music is commandeered in the interests of comedy or burlesque, it is too often relegated to merely ignoble functions, or at best employed to accompany rather than enforce a comic situation. Offenbach, for all his cynical *canaillerie*, had the gift. So had

Sullivan, though in his case wit was tempered by excessive geniality.   Sullivan was no pedant, but his sense of symmetry and love of beauty were so highly developed that even in jest he never sacrificed charm to characterisation.

Music that is intentionally humorous, or humorously allusive, of necessity appeals to a limited audience.   How many people, we wonder, were able to appreciate the exquisite satire of Hans von Bülow's comment on a shrieking operatic soprano who immediately preceded him in the programme of a miscellaneous concert given in America ?   Bülow's contribution was a classical piece, but before beginning he played, by way of criticism, the baritone solo, "O Freunde, nicht diese Töne," which follows the discordant fanfare at the beginning of the last movement of Beethoven's Ninth Symphony.   The humour of Beethoven himself—freakish, unexpected, and at times obstreperous—is not appreciated by all his admirers. But for this it is easy to find literary parallels. For example, *The Wrong Box*, mentioned above, which is a source of continual joy to many readers, is regarded by some devout Stevensonians as a piece of misguided frivolity wholly unworthy of their hero's genius.   Mozart wrote a delicious burlesque symphony called "The Village Musicians" containing a solo for the violin full of intentional

absurdities and lapses from the right key ; but
when, not many years ago, it was included in a
concert of humorous music, the audience entirely
failed to see its point, and expressed disapproval of
its sweet desipience as though the blunders had
been the fault of the performers, and not part of
the composer's satire.   But this misunderstanding
is not confined to the classical composers.   There
never was a composer about whose real intentions
a greater divergence of opinion prevailed than the
redoubtable Richard Strauss himself.   That he
has a strongly marked vein of fantastic humour
is incontestably shown by *Till Eulenspiegel*.   But
the musical pundits are greatly divided over
some of his late works ; indeed, some of his most
fervent admirers cannot altogether acquit him of
" pulling the leg " of the public in his *Symphonia
Domestica*, and this theory has found its most
pointed expression in the saying attributed to a
Straussian, *à propos* of his last opera, " unverschämte
Musik—aber es wirkt."

Parody in music is not unknown, though it has
been far less freely resorted to than in the domain
of letters, and so far at any rate has perhaps been
most strikingly illustrated by the unconscious
imitation of indiscreet disciples.   Many of the
great masters have passed through a stage of
assimilation, but with them it never lasted long.

On the other hand, the minor poets of the musical world have spent their whole lives in playing the sedulous ape to Mendelssohn, Brahms, and Wagner. Of deliberate and successful parody in music few examples have attained to more than ephemeral popularity. One recalls the "Humorous Meditations on a German Air" of Siegfried Ochs as a pleasant exercise in this *genre*, but here the effect is rather due to the ingenious but mechanical device of perverting melodies by various composers than to real imaginative parody of their respective styles. For the rest, musical parody has been chiefly practised, and for the most part in a perfectly legitimate way, by the school of entertainers started by John Parry— who began his career as a serious musician, and had for his most distinguished successor the late Mr. Corney Grain. Mr. George Grossmith and others still carry on the traditions of this school, which has served a useful purpose in pillorying the extravagances, the mannerisms, and the affectations of musicians. On the whole, the personal side of the subject-matter for musical satire is less liable to attack than in former years. But the extravagance of modern composers perhaps affords greater opportunities for the parodist than at any other time in the history of music, and a cordial welcome is due to the clever troupe of "The

Follies," headed by Mr. Pélissier, for their efforts in this direction. In their more ambitious efforts—*e.g.* the travesty of Wagnerian drama—their methods are somewhat crude. When Mr. Pélissier, clever pianist though he is, attempts to parody Chopin he does not even succeed in giving a colourable imitation of his model. But their burlesques of a musical comedy and a music-hall programme are not only intensely amusing, but admirable pieces of destructive criticism. Having served an arduous apprenticeship at the " Halls " themselves, Mr. Pélissier and his colleagues come to their task with an intimate inside knowledge, which they have turned to the very best account. The form of entertainment in which music is employed to reinforce the appeal of popular comedians to the heart of the great public has thus, by a curious irony, prompted a travesty which is not merely a piece of genuine musical comedy, but suggests further and wider application of the methods of musical satire.

June 29, 1907.

XXXV

THE RE-EMERGENCE OF THE PRIMA DONNA

THE autumn season at Covent Garden has been notable for an event of quite exceptional interest in the annals of opera—the advent of a star of the first magnitude who has created a real *furore* in the old-fashioned Italian operas of the early and mid-Victorian epoch. Since 1861, when, unheralded and unpuffed, Madame Patti sang for the first time in London, there have only been two of these immediate conquests of the public—by Madame Christine Nilsson in 1867 and by Madame Albani in 1872; for Madame Melba's sovereignty was hardly established in her first season in 1888. Madame Tetrazzini's achievement, then, is quite as remarkable as that of any of her predecessors, and for a variety of reasons. To begin with, the mere fact that she had been singing for at least a dozen years was scarcely a point in her favour, but rather the reverse, since we are prone to believe that first-rate singers are bound to gravitate to England without delay, and *per contra*, that their absence is a sign of inferiority, or, at any rate, of incapacity to please our taste. The newcomer, however, has had to overcome a still more serious obstacle in her choice of rôles, for instead of electing to be heard in the more modern or fashionable works, she has deliberately challenged attention in a type of opera which for the last dozen years has been steadily dropping out of the Covent Garden repertory, and indeed has come to be regarded in some quarters as dead beyond the possibility of resuscitation. It was not merely that the growing popularity of Wagner threatened to relegate *Traviata* and *Trovatore* to the dustbin, but that Verdi himself had eclipsed the product of his middle period by the far nobler and more distinguished works of his old age. To revive and lend new lustre to these faded scores, to crowd Covent Garden in the autumn season and send up the price of stalls to a premium of more than a hundred per cent,—all this is clear evidence of an exceptional equipment, of something much more than a beautiful voice and a flexible larynx. Madame Tetrazzini, so far as sheer beauty of *timbre* is concerned, need not fear comparisons with any living singer. Though her voice is not of exceptional volume, it has remarkable carrying-

power even in its *sotto voce* tones ; she sings with
delightful and effortless ease, and never attempts
more than she can perform. She has, in short,
precisely the endowment and the technique which
render the most trivial vocal frippery not merely
endurable but engaging. She is, moreover, as her
performance in the last act of *Traviata* shows, an
excellent actress on entirely conventional lines.
Small wonder, then, is it that the old guard of opera-
goers, who have been sorely depressed during the
past twenty years or more by what they would
call the tyranny of Wagner, should hail the newcomer's triumph as a convincing proof of the
abiding vitality of the old Italian opera.

The lesson of Madame Tetrazzini's success,
however, is not quite so simple as all this. To
begin with, one must allow something—in music
as well as politics—for the swing of the pendulum.
Wagner himself had a sincere admiration for
Bellini. Brahms wished that he had written the
" Blue Danube " waltz. To turn from composers
to peoples, nowhere was the Mascagni mania more
acute than in Germany. It is the old story of
extremes meeting, and although the audiences
which have been filling every corner of Covent
Garden during the last few weeks on Tetrazzini
nights differ clearly in their composition from those
which attended, say, the Wagner " cycles " last

summer, they probably contain a substantial proportion of cultivated amateurs who, for a while at any rate, welcome the change from complexity to lucidity, from infinite melody to clear-cut tune. We must remember, again, that a generation of opera-goers have grown up in the last twenty years many of whom have actually never heard *Traviata*, and to whom in consequence its ingenious morbidity has all the attraction of the unfamiliar. It is the simultaneous existence of the faithful old guard who have never been converted to Wagner together with enlightened modernists who are not altogether immune from reactionary tendencies and newcomers who have grown up during the Wagner régime and never heard the old operas before that constitutes the opportunity of a great singer like Tetrazzini ; and when all allowance is made for exaggeration and *réclame*, her triumph has been great and genuine enough to acquire a definite significance.

The influence exerted by the *prima donna* on the evolution of music has nearly always been reactionary. Even so great an opportunist as Handel was driven to threats of personal violence in order to secure her submission, and the greatest and most original composers have been precisely those who have treated her with the least consideration. Now, however, the *prima donna* has been more or less deposed from the special pinnacle which she once occupied in the popular estimation. She no longer reigns supreme even in the operatic firmament, where conductors have at last come by their own, and shares the homage of the masses with violinists, pianists, and (occasionally) ballad-singers. Frequenters of the opera during the past twenty years will readily recall a period, extending over several seasons, during which the brothers de Reszke quite eclipsed all feminine competitors for popular favour. The popular *prima donna* is still made the subject of a good deal of fulsome adulation in a certain section of the Press, but she no longer inspires the same fanatical heroine-worship exhibited by the admirers of Jenny Lind or Piccolomini. For instance we cannot imagine that anybody nowadays sits up till midnight in Kensington Gore to watch operatic stars driving home, as old-fashioned people tell us they did in the palmy days of Grisi and Mario. For that we have to thank Wagner and Richter, Bayreuth and symphony concerts. But with the relegation of the *prima donna* to a less exalted station in the musical world, she has become capable of rendering a real and valuable service to the art which in the days of her tyranny she did so much to hamper and retard. Nothing has been more remarkable in connexion with the performances of German opera in the last ten years than the improvement in technique and finish of the artists engaged. Hostile critics of the old school declared that Wagner's music was so essentially unvocal that it was impossible to apply the methods of the *bel canto* to it at all, and that the greatest singers abstained from it in self-defence and of necessity, if they wished to preserve the beauty and freshness of their voices. This view undoubtedly derived a considerable measure of support from the style of singing adopted by the leading Wagnerian singers of the last generation, who along with, and to a certain extent because of, their keen sense of dramatic effect, were over-prone to sacrifice charm to character, delicacy to declamation. Their intonation was often defective and their voice-production frankly detestable. Wagner himself, it should be added, never sanctioned the view that it was impossible to reconcile the *bel canto* with the adequate interpretation of the music-drama. On the contrary, he had the liveliest appreciation of the methods of Manuel Garcia—under whom his own niece studied —and actually invited him to undertake the training of the singers engaged for the opening performances at Bayreuth in 1876. But what, perhaps, did more than anything else to explode this fallacy was the practical illustration afforded by MM. Jean and Edouard de Reszke when, towards the end of their active career, they took to singing in Wagnerian opera, and showed, first, that Wagner's music sounded infinitely more beautiful when it was sung instead of being yelped ; and, secondly, that the singing of these tremendously long and exacting rôles did not impair the quality of the voice if it was legitimately produced and used. The co-operation of such singers has been invaluable, and has, we have no doubt, been largely responsible for the improvement, on the vocal side, of the interpretation of Wagner's operas, and the consequent increase in their popularity. But even singers who from lack of sympathy or consciousness of their limitations resolve to refrain from Wagnerian rôles are capable of exerting a stimulating influence on those who are mainly or wholly engaged in their interpretation. In other words, the more first-rate exponents of the *bel canto* we have, the higher is the standard of excellence likely to be achieved in the more dramatic and more interesting branches of operatic music. Shorn of her absolutism, the *prima donna* is no longer a menace to art. The deliberate cult of ugliness in instrumental music at the present day makes us doubly ready to greet singers, like Madame Tetrazzini, who never utter a sound that is not pleasant to hear.

November 23, 1907.

XXXVI

A SINGER ON HIS ART

THE career, the achievements, and the marked
individuality of the writer claim an attentive and
sympathetic hearing for Sir Charles Santley's
little book on *The Art of Singing*.[1] It is
more than fifty years since he made his first
public appearance, and he still maintains his position as the foremost figure amongst native singers.
Throughout his career he has fully justified the
title he gave to his earlier volume of reminiscences.
He has always been a student as well as a singer,
never content to rest on his laurels or proceed on
the lines of least resistance. He graduated in
opera when Mario and Grisi were names to
conjure with, and, abandoning the boards in the
"seventies" after the failure of a venture to
establish English opera, to further which he had
severed his connexion with the Italian lyric stage,

[1] *The Art of Singing and Vocal Declamation.* By Sir Charles Santley.
London : Macmillan and Co. [3s. 6d. net.]

he devoted himself to concert and oratorio work, with results which are happily familiar to the present generation of concert-goers. Throughout his career, again, he never sought to disguise his individuality or his nationality. Trained in Italy, and an excellent linguist, the core of the man was always British and manly, free from the affectations and mannerisms which many singers deliberately cultivate. This unaffected sincerity is one of the chief charms of this volume. Sir Charles Santley not only speaks from a ripe and almost unrivalled experience, but he speaks with a frankness which leaves nothing to be desired. The literary quality of the book is negligible, its vocabulary is curiously limited, and the author's outlook by no means devoid of prejudice, and even Philistinism. But, on the other hand, he utters a good many home-truths with refreshing bluntness, and his warnings on the subject of " production quacks " were never more needed than at the present day. Sir Charles Santley apparently accepts as correct the prodigious estimate of ten thousand as the number of those engaged in teaching singing in London alone, and even if we divide it by two, at least four out of that five thousand are wholly unfitted for the task. Sir Charles Santley, it is true, addresses himself primarily to students who intend to take up

singing professionally ; but while his remarks may
have the desirable result of discouraging a certain
number of incapables, they will be none the less
appreciated by serious amateurs who have no
intention of taking to singing as a livelihood.

The prime requisite in a singer, according to
Rossini, was a voice. Recently an able musician
declared that no singer was worth his salt unless
he sang with brains. Now comes Sir Charles
Santley, who pronounces patience to be the great
desideratum, while, of course, admitting the need
of natural resources and intelligence as well.
There are no short cuts to success in singing, and
he strongly emphasises the value of a deliberate
and leisurely preparation, insisting at the outset
that " the only adviser to be consulted is a conscientious, practical artist who has ' gone through
the mill ' and come out stamped ' genuine.' "
He is no believer in a singing-master who is not
or has not been a good singer. For the rest, he
attaches importance to vocal exercises, solfeggi,
etc., and the study of the work of the great artists
as opposed to the adoration of the idols of an
ignorant public. But practice and intelligent
imitation are not enough. The serious aspirant
must choose a singing-master, and here Sir Charles
Santley has some illuminating remarks on the
claims of those " who profess to teach the produc-

tion of the voice on scientific principles," showing that he would entirely endorse the satire implicit in the stanza about " the young lady of Brussels " of whom it is written that—

> When they asked " Can you sing ? "
> She said " My ! what a thing !
> But I'll tell you a lot about muscles."

According to his view, the more a master knows of anatomy, the less he will talk about it to his pupils :—

Manuel Garcia is held up as the pioneer of scientific teachers of singing. He was—but he taught singing, not surgery ! I was a pupil of his in 1858 and a friend of his while he lived, and in all the conversations I had with him, I never heard him say a word about larynx or pharynx, glottis, or any other organ used in the production and emission of the voice. He was perfectly acquainted with their functions, but he used his knowledge for his own direction, not to make parade of it before his pupils, as he knew it would only serve to mystify them, and could serve no good purpose in acquiring a knowledge of the art of singing. My experience tells me that the less pupils know about the construction of the vocal organs the better ; in fact, as I heard a master once remark, " better they should not be aware they had throats except for the purpose of swallowing their food."

In the chapters specially addressed " to the pupil " Sir Charles Santley inculcates self-denial and moderation in all things—food, drink, exercise,

sleep, and study.   His own experience inclines
him to regard tobacco as a valuable sedative ; but
he does not advocate smoking, while vigorously
deprecating the invectives of those who denounce
smoking as a filthy habit.   His remarks on
general culture are decidedly vague.   " A vocal
artiste "—Sir Charles Santley uses this detestable
form throughout—"must have a nodding acquaintance, at least, with the sister Arts, literature, prose
and poetry (especially the latter), and painting."
Languages are essential, especially Italian, " as the
best works as studies for a singer are written in
that language."   But he differs *toto caelo* from
those English singers who declare that Italian is
much easier to pronounce than their own language.
In his opinion, few foreigners ever acquire a pure
Italian pronunciation.   The upholders of the
Bohemian life as the only artistic existence are
dismissed with a flat denial.   " I never yet
encountered a great artiste who led a Bohemian
life, or was unsystematic in his work."   Much
less disputable than this peremptory assertion is
the statement that " you cannot be an artiste and
a votary of Society at the same time.   It has been
often tried and always proved a failure."   On
the subject of articulate enunciation Sir Charles
Santley's remarks are above reproach : " The
English-speaking peoples, more than any other,

require to pay strict attention to this study ; as a
rule, they are totally regardless of uttering a letter
or syllable clearly in ordinary conversation, and so
acquire a slipshod, inelegant enunciation which
requires patient, persevering study to correct
and fit them for public speaking." This, as he
further notes, is not the fault of the language,
but of those who speak it without learning how
it should be spoken.   Here we may quote an
interesting personal experience of the writer :—

I was present at a performance of *The Merchant of
Venice* at the Princess's Theatre.   Carl Formes, the once
celebrated bass singer, played Shylock.   He always preserved a strong German accent in conversation ; but
though all the other characters in the play were sustained
by Englishmen, the only one who recited his lines to be
understood was Formes.   The reason was obvious ; he
pronounced the letters, divided the syllables, and accented
the accented syllables, so that, though now and then his
pronunciation of a word was not quite English, his
enunciation was perfectly distinct.   I did not miss a
single syllable throughout his entire performance.

The recent performance of the *Ring* in English
at Covent Garden furnishes a confirmation of this
criticism.   The foreign singers who took part,
though not always intelligible, were on the whole
much more articulate than their British colleagues.
The bulk of Sir Charles Santley's advice to
young singers is tolerably obvious, but some of

his sayings combine practical wisdom and good feeling to an extent on which it would be hard to improve. Thus, after impressing on his readers the need of patience and courtesy, of conquering shyness and giving full play to artistic feeling whilst preserving modesty of demeanour, he enlarges on the value of keeping a silent tongue :—

Never discuss the talents of your fellow-artistes nor your own prospects, your prospective engagements or the remuneration you expect to receive from them ; they are your business only, and once you confide them to your bosom friend, they will soon be everybody's business, and probably end in no business at all.

He might have added that the singer who can only talk "shop" of this sort is one of the worst of bores. Excellent also is his caution with regard to the choice of agents :—

Have nothing to do with those who tell you that the only way to make a name, and so procure engagements, is to give a concert or recital in which you would have an opportunity to display your talents in their various phases and obtain notices of your performance in the public journals (the quality of which they, the agents, can command), which will spread your name far and wide, together with sundry similar chimerical advantages.

Another valuable hint is addressed to the singer who has secured an operatic engagement, and has been cast for a part :—

Do not wait for your music to be sent to you ; go at once to the librarian and procure it ; and learn it by heart in anticipation, in order that during the rehearsals you may direct your whole attention to the development of the character you have to represent ; and to the assimilation of your part with those of your fellow-performers, that you may do your share in carrying out the interest of the drama.

Lastly, we may quote, from his chapter on the stage, his condemnation of experienced actors who abuse their position to play practical jokes on " greenhorns " :—

When you arrive at being an old stager do not play tricks on the inexperienced—it is bad manners, unkind, and instead of enhancing your reputation, will lessen you in the estimation of those among your audience and comrades who are aware of your disloyal conduct.

The value of the book has already been illus-trated. Some of its blemishes remain to be indicated. The tone throughout is that of the *laudator temporis acti*. Not only is there no mention of a single living singer, or, indeed, of any one later than Sims Reeves or Gardoni, but the general impression conveyed is that singers holding the first rank at the present day are ignorant of the very foundations of the art which they practise. There is no acknowledgment, again, of the immense improvement in the choice of songs at modern concerts and recitals as compared with, say, thirty years ago, or of the value to the musical community of good amateurs. Indeed, the possibility of an amateur being an artist seems to be flatly negatived by the contemptuous reference on p. 22. These omissions, and the somewhat bitter tone of certain passages, are to be regretted in a singer who has so little cause to complain of generous recognition as Sir Charles Santley. The book abounds in good advice, but it is not so much from singer to singer as from the old man to the young, and much of it is sententious in form as well as trite in matter. It lacks organic cohesion, and is rather a series of *obiter dicta* on various aspects of singing than a connected treatise. His exposure of quackery, charlatanism, and faddism is as well timed as it is vigorous. There is, indeed, hardly a word with which one can disagree ; but he does not tell us enough. It is an ungrateful task, however, to criticise the work of a great man who has rendered such splendid service to his art, though we are sure that, as he has never minced his own words, he will be the last to resent outspoken criticism. For the rest, we have only to add that young singers who do not go and hear Sir Charles Santley while there is yet time will miss an invaluable opportunity of completing a liberal musical education. He is still a giant amongst singers. He still personifies, as he has done from his early days, all that is virile, sound, and sincere in the art of song, and such an experience will do far more good to the aspirant than the study of his book, excellent and timely though it is.

September 19, 1908.

XXXVII

THE MODERN ORCHESTRA

No one who has watched the course of music in the last twenty or thirty years can fail to realise the enormous change that has been wrought by the multiplication of orchestral concerts. Good music still costs a great deal too much to hear in England, and in certain of its manifestations, notably opera, it is beyond the reach of those who enjoy it most. But there has been a considerable improvement in this respect, and with the growth of opportunity a large section of the public, formerly content perforce with such fare as ballad concerts and occasional oratorios, has come to take its chief pleasure in listening to orchestral music. The change can be illustrated in a variety of ways, many of them beneficial and admirable. No one is likely to deny, for example, that to prefer Tchaikovsky's *Casse Noisette* suite or the *Siegfried Idyll* to the lyrics of Stephen Adams marks a genuine advance in culture amongst the musical masses. The development of the power of appreciating the different *timbres* of the different voices of the orchestra is another outcome of these altered conditions. For instance, the amateurs who to-day could distinguish blindfold a clarinet from a flute or a horn from a trombone must be treble the number of those who could have satisfied such a test twenty years ago. This education in orchestral acoustics has all sorts of curious results. One is constantly noting strange resemblances ; as, for example, a calf has been known unconsciously to simulate the tone of a bass clarinet, and some motor-cars have horns which remind one of a saxophone. Even those who are unable to follow a symphony with a score can pick up a good deal of knowledge empirically by keeping their eyes open and learning to recognise the origin of various sounds—harp harmonics, muted horns, soft pizzicato notes on the basses—by watching the orchestra. All this knowledge adds to the interest and pleasure of concert attendance, apart from the general educational advantage derived from hearing representative symphonic works of various schools. Again, instrumentalists and conductors have come to their own, and the prima donna and the pianist no longer enjoy a monopoly of adulation. But while the modern cult of the orchestra from the point of view of the audience makes in the main for a deeper and more intelligent appreciation of the music that counts, it is not so easy to express unreserved satisfaction with the results in so far as they affect composers and conductors. The greater the number of people who enjoy the technique of orchestration, the greater is the inducement to composers to lavish their energies on non-essentials. Not long ago an English statesman observed that any fool could annex. Varying the formula, it is hardly too much to say that nowadays almost any clever pupil can score for a full orchestra. A lack of ideas matters little if you can show off the band, pile up sonorous climaxes, exploit the eccentric tones and extreme registers of special instruments, and, above all, create an atmosphere. What a writer in the *Observer* last Sunday said rather unfairly of Debussy—that his music is "all adjectives, and it is left to the interpreter to supply the noun"—can certainly be predicated with considerable truth of a good deal of modern impressionistic music. Debussy, unlike many of his contemporaries, has shown that he can produce remarkable and impressive results with the limited resources of a small orchestra. Most of the ultra-moderns depend largely on their big battalions. The ordinary full orchestra does not content them, and whole groups of instruments have to be enlarged or doubled, or non-orchestral instruments specially imported, to satisfy their demands. There is no inherent virtue in this worship of mammoth dimensions — Jumbomania, as an American critic once happily designated it—and it is a fashion which reacts to the disadvantage of aspiring composers who follow it, since it is a rudimentary law of musical economics that the bigger the score, the greater is the cost of production.

The foregoing remarks are illustrated, and, we venture to think, confirmed in many respects, by the appearance of Dr. Coerne's treatise on *The Evolution of Modern Orchestration*.[1] Dr. Coerne is an American composer who, as Mr. H. E. Krehbiel, the well-known New York critic, informs us in a brief Introduction, has achieved the distinction—unique amongst natives of the United States—of having had an opera performed at a European opera-house. He is, moreover, the only person on whom the University of Harvard has bestowed the degree of Ph.D. for special work in music. So much for his technical qualifications, which are beyond cavil. The time chosen for the publication of his book is opportune, since the audience is assured, and all the materials are available for such a survey as that which he

---

[1] *The Evolution of Modern Orchestration.* By Louis Adolphe Coerne, Ph.D. London : Macmillan and Co. [12s. 6d. net.]

has attempted. Yet, in spite of some excellent qualities, Dr. Coerne has only achieved a partial success. He is handicapped by a ponderous style and a fatal fondness for polysyllables—*e.g.* when the word expansion is quite adequate to express his meaning, he always prefers the monstrous form "expansibility." His criticisms are occasionally impaired by an inappropriate choice of adjectives—as when he applies the word "sturdy" to Grieg, the composer of whom Debussy wittily said that to listen to his music inspired the sensation of eating pink bonbons stuffed with snow. Again, his laudable desire to be fair and generous to everybody results too often in undiscriminating praise.

Dr. Coerne has perhaps not made it sufficiently clear that in a work of this sort, in which the evolution of technique of expression is the prime matter of inquiry, the importance of certain composers is out of proportion to their intrinsic merit as creators. We cannot better illustrate this defect than by quoting some extracts from the section on Richard Strauss. After endorsing the view that Strauss is the most commanding figure in the musical world of to-day, crediting him with genuine inspiration, describing the *Heldenleben* as a noble creation, and declaring that *Salome* has "universally created a sensation to which nothing

in the annals of the musical stage furnishes a
parallel unless it be the initial performances of
Tristan und Isolde in Munich in 1865," he nevertheless qualifies his praise with the following
significant reserve :—

> His synthesis of thematic counterpoint in all the
> voices of the different choirs is at times so reckless that
> the euphony of its harmonic corollary is endangered and
> the resultant effect presents a chaos of cacophony unless
> the auditor accustom himself to follow the Melos not
> vertically but horizontally.

When Dr. Coerne comes to close quarters with
Strauss he seems altogether hypnotised by the
marvellous subtleties of Strauss's instrumentation,
by his "superb command of dynamics" and his
"colossal orchestral language,"—in a word, he
becomes a Jumbomaniac of the deepest dye.   Yet
in an excellent appreciation of Brahms he specially
commends him for combating "the ever-increasing
inclination of the ultra-modern school to enslave
music in the throes of what has been called 'a
thrice-intensified *Weltschmerz*,'" and adopts an
equally sane view of the mission of music in the
concluding passage of his final chapter :—

> The ideal mission of music, therefore, ever has been
> and surely should continue to be that of uplifting.   It
> should present a moral synonymous for the æsthetic, the
> pure, the spiritual.   It should reveal the highest ideals of

the living soul. It should, according to Browning, express truth, not of the mind—knowledge, which is absolute, but of the soul—shifting. Music above all other arts interprets the innermost thoughts of the soul. It is being constantly re-created, whereas all other arts are but the images of what is already created. The imitative arts—sculpture and painting, can no longer be all-satisfying to the self-consciousness of an age influenced by the subjective thought of such men as Goethe and Schiller. Why, therefore, should modern music be reared solely upon a similar realistic basis of imitation instead of upon an idealistic one of representation ? The fundamentals of music rest upon an acoustic element dependent upon absolute pitch. Since, however, an isolated tone cannot suggest a definite idea or image, it is necessary, in order that music should mean something, to connect a series of tones so as to produce melody, to combine several tones so as to form chords, and to group these chords so as to obtain contrasts of tonality and modes. This accomplished, there must be added rhythmic life, variety of tone-colour, and dynamic contrast. Finally, the whole fabrication must be fitted into a framework of structural form based upon the science of logic. But all this is not enough. There exists an underlying psychological principle that cannot be disregarded. Appreciation for acoustic effects and the realizations of intellectual reflection are but the stepping stones to something higher. The first requirement of a composer is intuition or the spontaneous expression of musical instinct—an element more essential to musical creation than to any other branch of art. Further requisites are imagination, emotion, inspiration, and above all spirituality. There is a tendency among recent exponents of the most advanced school to declare that the possibilities of purely æsthetic music have been exhausted. Morbidness and pessimism dominate the creative conceptions of these recent experimentalists. They are leaning more and more toward the expression of concrete ideas concealing vague abstractions. The present writer is heartily in sympathy with the most catholic application of all legitimate resources so long as the primary object of musical utterance be not lost sight of. It goes without saying that descriptive, imitative, realistic and even morbid music has its proper place in the poetic conceptions of our contemporary tone-masters. Exception only is made to music that is primarily intellectual or pessimistic. On the other hand, it need not be primarily pleasure-giving. In a word, all such objectives should be made subjective to a purer motive. The portrayal of lesser sentiments and passions is legitimate only in so far as to form a background for the nobler, which are thereby thrown into relief. The ideal mission of music is to reflect the loftiest sentiments of the composer's soul, and to awaken similar experiences in the mind of the auditor so as to inspire and uplift him. Such were the ideals of Beethoven. May his example continue to be emulated !

We may note in conclusion that while the prevailing tone of Dr. Coerne's work is genial, he speaks with a certain bitterness of the unfavourable conditions under which serious American composers pursue their career. If his account be true, native talent is more consistently discouraged in the States than in any other country.

November 21, 1908.

XXXVIII

VETERANS OF THE ORCHESTRA

It is not altogether easy to find analogies in other spheres of activity for the position of the leading members of our great orchestras. They might, however, not inaptly be compared to leader-writers, in that, like them, they are practically anonymous, and, barring an occasional cadenza or *obbligato*, enjoy no opportunity for personal display, but form part of a great organism and express themselves in accordance with the desires and indications of a dictator. But just as journalism has been described as the grave of literary ambition, so the orchestra has occasionally entombed or submerged a promising talent. The conditions under which orchestral players practise their art are not favourable to creative originality. It is a great thing for a composer to have played in an orchestra, just as it is for a playwright to have been on the stage. But he ought not to remain

too long in it.   To be perpetually interpreting the
works of others is not the best preparation for
asserting one's own individuality.   Yet if they
cannot be accorded the highest place in the musical
hierarchy, leading orchestral players are none the
less highly important and valuable members of the
musical world.   They are better paid than they
used to be, but it cannot be contended that they
are overpaid, when one considers the amount of
work they do—the strain imposed on them at
Festivals, for example, is very great—or compares
their earnings with those of successful soloists.
They seldom taste the sweets of publicity, are
rarely alluded to in the Press, and it is only of
late years that their names have become known
outside a very limited circle of enthusiasts.   But
the measure of musical accomplishment exacted of
them is exceedingly high, and in mere musicianship they are immeasurably superior to the great
majority of professional singers.   The opportunities for display that fall to them are few and
far between.   Yet many of them fully deserve the
much-abused title of artist, some of them are great
artists, and most of them are very good fellows.
Of course they have their foibles and their weaknesses, though we are not prepared to say that
there is any solid basis for the innuendo conveyed
by a famous conductor, who, while rehearsing the

Venusberg music, once said to his band : " You play it as if you were teetotalers—which you are not." And their judgment on the abiding value of a new work is not infallible for two reasons : first, because they cannot gauge the total effect as it strikes the audience ; and second, because they are inevitably impressed by technical considerations and the interest of their own individual parts. Still, the applause of the orchestra is always very dear to the composer, and is an unfailing testimony to his musicianship.

The great orchestral players have often been men of a striking or picturesque personality. Mr. White, the double-bass player, was a very handsome old man and looked the image of an old soldier ; and there was something leonine and patriarchal about the elder Wotton, one of the finest bassoon-players in Europe. Even if he has never spoken to any one of them—and they are excellent company and full of good stories of conductors and composers—the assiduous concert-goer comes to feel a great kindness towards the men who, year in year out, have ministered so loyally and efficiently to his pleasure. He sees Mr. Malsch among the oboes, and he knows in advance—if Beethoven's C minor or Schubert's Unfinished Symphony is in the programme— that the famous passages for that poignant orchestral voice will lose none of their " proposed effect." One gets to know the personal traits of some performers, and in some cases even to recognise their instruments. Thus there is a well-known double-bass player with a fine Maggini, the scroll of which is surmounted with a Turk's head, which you can see with an opera-glass right across Queen's Hall. But when the time comes for these veterans to rest from their labours, when they drop out of the ranks or pass away from our midst, the recognition of their exertions is too often limited to their colleagues instead of being shared by the general musical public. Happily there are exceptions to this rule. For example, at Blackheath a testimonial concert was recently held in honour of Mr. Alfred Burnett, so familiar to Festival-goers for many years as the cheery, indefatigable, enthusiastic leader at the Birmingham and Three Choir meetings. But Mr. Burnett's career has many other interesting and distinguished entries. He played for twenty-three years in the Royal Italian Opera orchestra under the baton of Costa, and for twenty-two years under Manns at the Crystal Palace, and he took part on many occasions at the "Pops." with Joachim, Piatti, Madame Schumann, and his master, Wieniawski. He has been attached to the staff of both the Academy and the Royal College of Music, and for thirty-five years has taken a foremost part in organising and directing the chamber, choral, and orchestral concerts in Blackheath. And all along he has been the heartiest, most genial and essentially manly of men—as the best musicians are—radiating sunshine and good humour wherever he went. On Mr. Burnett in his honoured and vigorous old age there recently fell a well-nigh irreparable blow—the theft of his fine Carlo Bergonzi violin. This is one of the losses that can never be replaced, but, as Mr. Burnett himself observed at the close of the concert, "that which looked to me some few months back as a calamity, a disaster from which I should find it difficult to recover, has turned out to be one of the happiest accidents of my life." It occurred to his friends and neighbours in Blackheath that this was a fitting opportunity for showing their appreciation of his lifelong labours and their sympathy with him in his loss. Though started in Blackheath, the scheme of organising a concert in his honour met with general support, leading singers and instrumentalists gave their services, and one-fourth of the excellent full orchestra which took part in the concert were past or present pupils of Mr. Burnett, and had in many cases come from considerable distances to assist at this tribute to their old master and friend. The real value of such a tribute, though we are delighted to see that on the present occasion it had its tangible side as well, resides in the sentiment of which it was the practical expression—the spontaneous desire to make fitting recognition of a long and honourable career spent in unobtrusive but highly efficient service on behalf of the serious side of art. Benefits and testimonials are not invariably bestowed on the most deserving objects, but where, as in this case, character and ability are combined in the recipient, one can only congratulate all concerned on the prosperous accomplishment of a happily conceived design. Such an event is *optimi exempli*. It is good to see honest effort appreciated, and the veterans of the orchestra, who bear the brunt of the work of interpreting the music that really counts, have for the most part hitherto had far less than their due share of public gratitude.

March 20, 1909.

XXXIX

BEETHOVEN'S LETTERS

GREAT men, even great authors, do not always proclaim their greatness in their letters, and conversely some of the greatest masters of the epistolary form have reached in it a level unattained by them in more formal manifestations of their creative powers. The letters of Beethoven,[1] of which a representative collection is now available in an English dress, make no pretence to literary finish. It is safe to say that no one ever put pen to paper with less thought of the possibility of ultimate publication. He was not a scholar, and, in so far as literary expression went, was never preoccupied by the choice of the sovereign word or any of the deliberate niceties of composition. More artless effusions it would be difficult to imagine. Yet it

---

[1] *Beethoven's Letters.* Critical Edition, with Explanatory Notes by Dr. A. C. Kalischer. Translated with Preface by J. S. Shedlock, B.A. 2 vols. London : J. M. Dent and Co. [21s. net.]

is not too much to say that he hardly ever wrote even the briefest note that was not characteristic of his deep, sincere, and passionate nature. One need not lay stress on his shortcomings in spelling or punctuation, because they were common amongst men of ability in the eighteenth and early nineteenth century.——Disraeli, it may be remembered, was by no means immaculate in this respect, for all his literary experience.——Beethoven's handwriting, though often almost illegible, had nothing commonplace or petty about it, and now and again his signature, as in the letter acknowledging the gift of the piano from the firm of Broadwood, had a splendid and sweeping boldness. Models of calligraphy, however, these letters are not, any more than models of literary expression. Their interest lies in the entire fidelity with which they reflect the mood of the moment, ranging from black despondency to unbridled farce, from passionate devotion to furious irritation.

Beethoven had a genius for friendship, but it was an imperfect genius. He was constitutionally incapable of serenity, his deafness made him morbidly sensitive, and he was such a strange mixture of helplessness and independence that he put a tremendous strain on the loyalty of his most devoted admirers. But the inner nobility of the man shines through all these angularities and

excrescences. It is a curious fact that Beethoven
—a convinced democrat—seems to have been
unable to make friends with, or inspire attachment
in, his social inferiors. His relations with his
servants were deplorable, and the continual misery
which he endured in this regard finds expression
in scores and scores of his letters. The number
of his high-born friends was legion, and he associated with them on terms of the frankest intimacy,
without any trace of the courtier or sycophant.
Indeed, whatever may be urged against the
Viennese nobles of that age, their liberal patronage
of Beethoven must be remembered to their
eternal credit. True, he said that he could not
get on with the "princely theatre rabble," but his
letters abound in acknowledgment of the services
rendered by Prince Lichnowsky and other great
aristocrats. If we except those addressed to the
Archduke Rudolph, Beethoven writes on the
terms of the frankest equality to his exalted
correspondents. He calls Count Franz von
Brunswick "brother," and displays an inexhaustible fertility of humorous invective in his letters
to the faithful Baron Zmeskall—the "dinner
Count," "music Count," or "pious sheep," as he
called him. "Dearest scavenger of a baron" is
only one out of many such fantastic openings to
letters which, when not full of high-spirited

fooling, almost invariably contain commissions for clothes or quill pens ("His Highness von Zmeskall is requested to hasten somewhat with the plucking out of his feathers"), or pathetic appeals for assistance in the choice, regulation, or dismissal of servants. Although in the later years of the great composer's life Zmeskall was superseded in the post of Beethoven's chief Good Samaritan by Nanette Streicher, the admirers of Beethoven must always have a very warm corner in their hearts for this faithful worshipper and butt. There must have been something amiably comic about a man who prompted Beethoven to write so much excellent nonsense,—by no means an easy thing, as Edward Lear himself observed. This extravagant humour was revealed to many others besides the "music Count," and it explodes in the letters to the gifted Countess Marie von Erdödy, who, though crippled by ill-health, busied herself constantly in his behalf. All the members of her household had their nicknames, and were the victims of Beethoven's inveterate habit of punning. This freakish vein found vent even in his business letters, notably his communications with the music-publishing house of Steiner and Co., in which Beethoven employs a series of whimsical military aliases to denote himself and the various members of the firm. His relations with other publishers were not always so happy ; but it must not be forgotten that on his death-bed he made special acknowledgment of his indebtedness to the firm of Schott. Schindler's letter to them is well known, but we cannot resist quoting one passage : " He then, once again, begged me not to forget Schott, also again to write in his name to the Philharmonic Society to thank them for their great gift, and to add that the Society had comforted his last days, and that even on the brink of the grave he thanked the Society and the whole of the English nation for the great gift. God bless them." Beethoven, if one of the most exacting of friends, could never be accused of ingratitude. His treatment of Neate, perhaps the most loyal of his English friends, was inconsiderate and tactless ; but it is good to know that at the end England was amongst the last thoughts of the dying Beethoven.

Beethoven, as we have said, was no scholar ; but he was a man of wide reading, and expressed his conviction that a composer ought to be acquainted with the best poetry, classical and modern. His own letters abound in allusions to classical or mythological personages, though he regretted that he could only read Homer in transla-tion. Latin quotations and tags occur frequently, and show that he must have had a fair working knowledge of that tongue, though he begs Baron Gleichenstein to get for him, along with a new hat, a German translation of Tacitus. Besides Homer, he specially mentions Ossian, and, above all, Goethe and Schiller, as his favourite poets. Towards his musical predecessors Beethoven was animated by a generous appreciation—above all, towards Bach, the great "forefather of harmony." Handel he also reverenced highly, and Haydn with reservations ; and the success of a performance of Mozart's *Don Juan* pleased him as much as if it had been a work of his own. He was conscious of his own greatness, but there was nothing thrasonical or boastful in the expression of this conviction ; he always took care to measure human achievement with the perfect wisdom of God. In one of his most exuberant letters to Zmeskall he makes the remarkable observation : "*Power* is the morality of men who stand out from the rest, and it is also mine" ; but Dr. Kalischer is right in refusing to regard this Caesarian *obiter dictum* as a true and essential criterion of Beethoven's ethical view of life. It was only the accident of the moment. The real Beethoven *moral* is rather to be found in the charming letter to a little girl of eight, where he wrote : ' I know no other excellencies in man than those which cause him to rank among better men ; where I find this, there is my home."

The letters of Beethoven are profoundly interesting, but as his bodily ills increase and aggravate his loneliness they grow sadder and sadder. There is something profoundly touching in this wounded Titan begging his good friend Frau Streicher that she will "sometimes remember a poor sick Austrian musician," or asking Zmeskall what it costs to have boots vamped, or entreating him to look out for a servant who could do a bit of tailoring. Yet it would be the greatest mistake to suppose that Beethoven was neglected. Much of his misery was inherent in his temperament and his physical afflictions, and nothing could have exceeded the delicacy or devotion of his friends. It is remarkable, too, how at the end he turned to the companions of his early days. Of the letters written in the last few months of his life, none are more tender or affectionate than those addressed to his "old, honoured, beloved friend" Dr. Wegeler, the husband of Eleonora Breuning, the playmate of his youth. And the Baron Pasqualati's persistent and considerate generosity, so touchingly acknowledged by the dying composer, has earned for him an eternal place in the golden book of Beethoven's friends.

We have refrained from commenting on the

classic places of the Beethoven literature—such as the letters to "the Immortal Beloved One" (identified by Dr. Kalischer with the Countess Giulietta Guicciardi), those addressed to Bettina v. Brentano, and the famous Testament inscribed to his brothers—aiming rather at giving a general impression of the cumulative effect of a perusal of Beethoven's ordinary correspondence. Though some of the letters are printed for the first time in Dr. Kalischer's collection, they do not add anything of serious importance to our knowledge of Beethoven. Where Dr. Kalischer differs from Nohl, Thayer, and other experts as to dates or the identity of Beethoven's correspondents, he does so on good grounds, and his notes, though somewhat ponderous in expression, show a pleasant combination of careful research, good feeling, and enthusiasm. He does not profess to give us *all* Beethoven's letters, but a complete and carefully collated collection of all those which have already appeared in book form, *plus* a considerable number which have not hitherto been printed. To the English edition Mr. Shedlock has added a few more new letters and a brief Introduction. The translation has been done in a straightforward fashion, but we regret to have to say that it is disfigured by a good many misprints in addition to the long list of *corrigenda* given in the first volume.   The printing and general get-up of the work are excellent, and its attractiveness is much enhanced by a number of interesting portraits and facsimiles.

April 24, 1909.

XL

NEW LIGHTS ON HANDEL

THE present writer was recently moved to
discuss the contention—put forward by a writer
in the *Cornhill*—that music was essentially an
aristocratic appanage. Since then Sir Hubert
Parry, at the Authors' Club, has stated the
contrary proposition with the utmost vigour, and
congratulated the present musical generation on
its emancipation from the tyranny of rank or
wealth. And now we have Mr. Streatfeild
proclaiming in his new and suggestive study of
Handel[1] that in the case of his hero it was the
great middle class who saved the situation when
he had been deserted by his aristocratic patrons.
To quote his own words—

The turning-point of his career was when in 1747 he
threw aside his subscription and appealed to the public at

[1] *Handel.* By R. A. Streatfeild. With 12 Illustrations. London :
Methuen and Co. [7s. 6d.]

large. The aristocracy had failed him and he turned to the middle class. There he found the audience that he had sought in vain in the pampered worldlings of the court. The splendid seriousness of Handel's music, its wide humanity, its exaltation of thought, its unfaltering dignity of utterance, had fallen on deaf ears so long as he appealed only to an aristocratic audience. It was in the heart and brain of the middle class that Handel found at last an echo to his clarion call. For fifty years he had piped in vain to princelings ; he turned to the people and found at once the sympathy that he sought.

As we read this spirited onslaught we are reminded of a debate held not many years ago, in which the misdeeds of Sovereigns formed the congenial theme of several highly-coloured orations. But when special attack was made on the late King Louis of Bavaria, this proved too much for Mr. Bernard Shaw, who happened to be present. While so many other Monarchs were, as he put it, "available for obloquy," he deprecated any insistence on the shortcomings of a King who, after all, had been Wagner's most munificent patron. Handel had as little cause as Wagner to abuse crowned heads. George I. treated him with undoubted consideration in overlooking his truancy from Hanover. Under George II. the temporary hostility of Prince Frederick of Wales to Handel was purely political, while their reconciliation led to a lasting friendship. With this exception, the attitude of

Y

the Royal family to Handel was one of unqualified support, and, as Mr. Streatfeild himself admits, Handel drew a pension of £600 a year from the Court for the best part of forty years. Certainly Handel had no legitimate cause for complaint with the monarchical system. When we come to his relations with the aristocracy, we find ourselves at once on very delicate ground. It has been recently announced by a high legal authority that if you circulate statements about a Duke and are then proved to have misrepresented the facts, it is not necessary to apologise so long as you have not charged the Duke with rapacity. This only shows how hard it must be to adduce any evidence that can tell in favour of a class who are *ex hypothesi* debarred from the consideration due, say, to a ticket-of-leave man. But assuming for the moment the rôle of the *advocatus diaboli*, we may be allowed to point out that Handel was mixed up with Dukes all through his life, and to urge the following extenuating circumstances on their behalf. It was the Duke of Manchester, Ambassador at Venice from 1707 to 1708, who first invited Handel to London. Handel's engagements would not allow him to accept the engagement at once, "but there is no doubt," observes Mr. Streatfeild, "that the Duke's amiable suggestion first turned his thoughts in the direction of England." In 1718 Handel became musical director to the first Duke of Chandos at Canons, and, whatever Swift may have thought or Mr. Winston Churchill may think of the origin of the Duke's wealth, the fact remains that we owe the splendid series of " Chandos " anthems to this engagement, during which, also, Handel's first English oratorio, *Esther*, and *Acis and Galatea* were composed. From Canons Handel went in 1719 to take up the post of principal musical director to the new Royal Academy of Music, a company formed under Royal patronage for the production of Italian opera, with the Duke of Newcastle as chairman. The capital subscribed was £50,000, and whatever were the faults of the aristocratic directors, they lost every penny they put up before the scheme came to an end. Handel was not a diplomatist, and the salaries of his " star " singers, though trifling in comparison to what are paid nowadays, ate up a large proportion of the takings. As an *impresario* on his own account Handel was no more successful, in spite of Court support an the King's liberal subscription of £1000 a year. Fashion *plus* Farinelli proved too formidable an opposition. But in the hour of defeat and embarrassment it was once more a Duke who held out a helping hand. It is perhaps overstating the

fact to say with Mr. Streatfeild that the sole claim
to immortality of William Cavendish, fourth
Duke of Devonshire, was that he invited Handel
to Dublin. He survives in the fine compliment
paid him by Sir Robert Walpole's brother Horatio,
who, when asked what he thought of Devonshire
House, replied : " Why I think it something
like the master ; plain and good without, but one
of the best inside houses in Britain."   Anyhow,
as Mr. Streatfeild readily admits, the Duke
appreciated Handel, and it was in response to a
definite invitation from Dublin Castle that Handel
started on the historic journey which had its
climax in the production of the *Messiah* at the
Fishamble Street Theatre on April 13th, 1742.
One more Duke and we have done.   There can
be very little doubt that but for the issue of
Culloden Handel's *Occasional Oratorio* would never
have been produced.   And there is no doubt
whatever that Handel composed *Judas Maccabaeus*
to celebrate the triumph of the Duke of Cumber-
land.

That the English aristocracy as a whole had the
bad taste to prefer Bononcini and the *Beggar's
Opera* to Handel may be true enough.   None the
less Handel's indebtedness to individual noblemen
and to the Court was immense, and this incontestable fact must be set against Handel's cavalier

treatment of his noble patrons. Mr. Streatfeild, we regret to see, lapses almost into the Limehouse vein in his eulogy of Handel's independence. " Here was a man who, while every other musician in the land remained at an angle of forty-five degrees in the presence of his princely patrons, resolutely stood upright, went his own way, and snapped his fingers in their ducal faces." Yet only a few pages later we read how Handel tuned his lyre to celebrate the " butcher " of Culloden ! The musical taste of the British aristocracy has often been very bad ; but without the assistance and encouragement of members of that class Handel would never have come to England, or gained a hearing at all. The inability to appreciate Handel at his true value was not confined to Peers and Peeresses. Some of the most distinguished men of letters joined in the attack on him, and, as Mr. Streatfeild reminds us, Pope's splendid tribute in the *Dunciad* was not inspired by direct admiration. It was the result of Pope's consulting his friend Arbuthnot :—

Pope knew little and cared less about music, but he was under no illusions as to his ignorance, and was content to accept the opinion of an expert. He asked his friend Arbuthnot what was Handel's real value as a musician. " Conceive the highest that you can of his ability," replied the doctor, " and they are much beyond

anything that you can conceive." Pope laid the words
to heart, and a scathing passage in the *Dunciad* pilloried
Handel's enemies for all time. The genius of Italian
opera, "by singing Peers upheld on either hand," is
pleading her cause before the throne of Dulness :—

> " But soon, ah soon, Rebellion will commence
> If Music meanly borrows aid from sense.
> Strong in new arms, lo ! Giant Handel stands
> Like bold Briareus with a hundred hands ;
> To stir, to rouse, to shake the soul he comes,
> And Jove's own Thunders follow Mars's Drums.
> Arrest him, Empress, or you sleep no more——"
> She heard, and drove him to the Hibernian shore.

Mr. Streatfeild's book is brightly written, and
is inspired by a generous and whole-hearted hero-
worship. He has compressed the facts of Handel's
life into an animated narrative, and without adding
substantially to the labours of his predecessors, he
has cleared up some disputed points of chronology
and incorporated in his work some of the most
fruitful researches of recent musical investigators.
The book, in short, is so good that it is a great
pity that the writer should have impaired its value
by the controversial attitude he assumes with
regard to Handel's sacred music. Mr. Streatfeild
conceives it to be his mission to explode the
traditional view that " Handel was the musician in
ordinary to the Protestant religion. . . . He had
been taken over bag and baggage by the Church

of England." He takes as his standpoint
FitzGerald's remark that " Handel was a good old
Pagan at heart, and till he had to yield to the
fashionable piety of England, stuck to opera and
cantatas, where he could revel and plunge and
frolic without being tied down to orthodoxy."
It is Mr. Streatfeild's ambition to strip from the
" real Handel " the " black gown and white tie
in which his ecclesiastical friends have disguised
him." Now, with all respect to FitzGerald, was
piety so fashionable in the mid-eighteenth century ?
FitzGerald's view implies disparagement of the
oratorios, in which Mr. Streatfeild would by no
means agree. Besides, on the pagan hypothesis,
Handel, on whose seriousness and sincerity he
frequently lays stress, stands convicted of a most
cynical exploitation of the genuine wave of religious
feeling awakened by Wesley, to which Mr. Streatfeild bears emphatic witness. To those who hold
with Berlioz that Handel was a mere materialist,
an *homme de ventre*, as compared with Gluck, the
homme de cœur, it may be easy to acquiesce in
such a view. But for an enthusiast like Mr.
Streatfeild, who claims that " of all who have
written music Handel was the greatest man," and
who endorses Samuel Butler's tribute to his
supreme poetic qualities, the attitude ascribed to
Handel illustrates the awkward consequences of

riding a theory to death.   Nobody wants to regard Handel as a sort of musical Chadband.   But matters are not greatly mended by representing him in the light of a genuine pagan masquerading in the garb of Pecksniff.

November 27, 1909.

XLI

THE REVIVAL OF GLUCK'S "ORPHEUS"

THE annals of opera have no more glorious entry than that which records the production of Gluck's *Orpheus* at Vienna in 1762. For the work is not only marked by that "grand simplicity" which Gluck declared it was his chief endeavour to attain, but it was the first notable effort to free the lyric drama from the false traditions and fettering conventions which threatened to stunt its growth and bar its progress. Gluck had to consent to compromise, like most efficient reformers, and the curious may find parallels between his concessions and those of Wagner, just a hundred years later, when *Tannhäuser* was produced in Paris. But with all deductions, *Orpheus* marks an astonishing advance on the old operatic formulae, which were dominated by a slavish deference to the equipment and caprices of the *bravura* singer.

The title-part, as is well known, was originally written for Guadagni, a male contralto. When the work was produced in Paris twelve years later, the part was transposed for Legros, a counter-tenor, and it was sung by high tenors until the historic revival by Pauline Viardot in 1860, who reverted to the original contralto version. Viardot's name at once suggests another interesting fact about *Orpheus*—its association with artists and musicians of altogether uncommon gifts and intelligence ; singers who transcended the limitations of their calling, prima donnas who were void of the weaknesses of prima - donnadom. High sopranos rarely show any marked intelligence, still more rarely any great dramatic aptitude. It is in virtue of the law of compensation that the operatic rôles which make the greatest demand on intelligence and dramatic instinct are out of the mental reach of the bird-like " star " soprano. Indeed, we have heard it crudely expressed that all the greatest singers had nondescript voices. Many vocal purists and precisians denied that Pauline Viardot was a great singer. It was said by some critics that her voice was indifferent in quality and her style exaggerated, and the formidable Fétis actually excluded her from his Pantheon —the *Biographie universelle des Musiciens* ! But whatever the experts may have thought of the limitations of her larynx, Pauline Viardot was a woman of genius. The ordinary prima donna is fifty years behind the enlightened taste of her day ; Madame Viardot was well abreast of it alike in her encouragement of the moderns and in her revival of a classic masterpiece like *Orpheus*. She had already been twenty-one years on the stage before embarking on this venture, in which, by the way, she had the enthusiastic assistance of that most redoubtable of Gluckists, Hector Berlioz, and she was at the zenith of her powers when she achieved what some consider the greatest triumph of her life. For it did not merely involve a wonderful display of art and energy and passion ; it meant a conquest of public opinion. The atmosphere of the Second Empire was not favourable to serious art. Offenbach's vogue was at its height, and it is curious to think that, by an inversion of the normal practice in regard to burlesques, *Orpheus* was produced two years *after Orphée aux Enfers*. As a contemporary writer observes : " En voyant un nombreux auditoire captivé par ce sujet mythologique, l'auditoire de nos salles de spectacle, si mêlé, si distrait, si frivole, transporté moralement sur la scène, on reconnaît la puissance réelle de la musique."

In the explanatory remarks prefixed to the programme at the Savoy, M. Cammaerts refers to

Miss Brema's illustrious predecessors in the rôle of Orpheus — Pauline Viardot, Marie Delna, Rose Caron, and Giulia Ravogli. Mlle. Giulia Ravogli's memorable performances at Covent Garden will not soon be forgotten. For a short space they achieved the miracle described by the French writer quoted above ; but the effect was only transitory, and we have since witnessed the long domination at the Opera of *bravura* tempered by realism, as illustrated in the works of Mascagni, Leoncavallo, and Puccini. Before we pass from the former interpreters of *Orpheus*, we may note that M. Cammaerts has overlooked the name of Mlle. Hastreiter, an American contralto who greatly distinguished herself in the part some twenty years ago. In a volume of letters printed privately in 1893 there is an excellent description of this remarkable artist written from Rome in January 1889 :—

I have been hearing a great deal of music, public and private. The most remarkable revelation was *Orfeo*, with a German - American *prima - donna*, Hastreiter. She embodies the part in the noblest, most stately, authoritative way, commands the stage, and seems to tower quietly over her fellow - artists and her audience. . . . Fancy those ingrained and conceited idiots *encoring*, if you please, an orchestral and pantomimic passage where Orpheus with eager strained gestures has to go round a group of Elysian heroines, feeling them over, and rejecting them as not Eurydice, and then falling into a half Bacchante, half Antinous-like plaintive attitude. She is absolutely plain, according to her portraits, but her commanding gestures and rich *contralto* voice make her a wonderful and noble embodiment of Gluck's conception.

Miss Brema's association with *Orpheus* is no sudden fancy, but an attachment of many years' standing. The work was revived for her in London for two seasons, and she sang in it for three seasons in Brussels, to say nothing of appearances in Paris, New York, and Germany. The mounting and scenery of *Orpheus* at the Théâtre de la Monnaie in Brussels were, we believe, of uncommon excellence ; but what lends special interest to the present revival is that the production has been directed and supervised in every detail by Miss Brema herself. The grouping and gestures of the chorus were of her devising, and the same careful and intelligent attention to detail was shown in the costumes and scenery. We have never seen a better-trained or more intelligent chorus. The dances of the Furies, planned and led by Miss Margaret Morris, were executed with wonderful spirit, and had just the right quality of weirdness and disquiet suggestive of tortured spirits. These dances too often verge on the ridiculous ; but at the Savoy they were quite impressively uncanny. The scene in the first act reminded one of a Burne-Jones stained-glass window. The scene in the Elysian Fields, again, was a beautiful picture, the effect of which was enhanced by the graceful movements of the Happy Spirits. In short, nothing was left undone to convey the spirit of Virgilian serenity which breathes from Gluck's golden music. It is an open secret that months of patient, laborious rehearsal were devoted to this revival ; but there was no sense of machine-like precision about actors or dancers. They had clearly been infected with enthusiasm for their work, and went through it with an obvious sense of enjoyment as if it were a labour of love and not a professional engagement. To have inspired her associates with such a spirit is a great achievement for any artist, and for a prima donna it is well-nigh unique. Not one in a hundred of that class could be entrusted with the " produc- tion " of an opera without the most disastrous results. But then Miss Brema belongs to the exceptional category already mentioned—the class of singers who think more of the music than of themselves. Her singing and impersonation of the part retain their fervour, if they have lost somewhat of their charm ; but when one considers the manifold and important functions she has also filled in this revival—as producer-in-chief, choir-trainer, and, above all, as a focus of the enthusiasm which animated all concerned—one is tempted to regard this as the most remarkable exploit of a remarkable career. Former revivals have suffered from the inadequacy of the Eurydice ; but Miss Viola Tree bore herself with a gracious simplicity, and sang with a fresh and ingenuous charm. Dr. Michael Balling, of Bayreuth, conducted a highly efficient orchestra, and the revival, taken all round, is a beautiful and satisfying act of homage to the genius of Gluck. And it gives us an excellent excuse for quoting the fine tribute with which Mr. Ernest Newman, a critic not overprone to eulogy, closes his study on *Gluck and the Opera* :—

Year after year the language of the art grows richer and more complex, and work after work sinks into ever-deepening oblivion ; until music that once thrilled men with delirious ecstasy becomes a dead thing which here and there a student looks back upon in a mood of scarcely tolerant antiquarianism. In the temple of the art a hundred statues of the gods are overthrown ; and a hundred others stand with arrested lips and inarticulate tongues, pale symbols of a vanished dominion which men no longer own. Yet here and there through the ghostly twilight comes the sound of some clear voice that has defied the courses of the years and the mutations of taste ; and we hear the rich canorous tones of Gluck, not perhaps with all the vigour and the passion that once was theirs, but with the mellowed splendour given by the touch of time.   Alone among his fellows he speaks our modern tongue, and chants the eternal passions of the race.   He was indeed, as Sophie Arnould called him, "the musician of the soul" ; and if we have added new strings to our lyre, and wrung from them a more poignant eloquence than ever stirred within the heart of Gluck, none the less do we perceive that music such as his comes to us from the days when there were giants in the land.

April 23, 1910.

XLII

ACCOMPANISTS AND SINGERS

THE recent jubilee concert of Mr. Henry Bird
sets the middle-aged amateur thinking on the
extraordinary development of the art of accompanying that has taken place in the last thirty or
forty years. It was not that there were no good
accompanists in the old days. *Vixere* (piano) *fortes
ante*—Henry Bird. In the early days of the
" Pops " Sir Julius Benedict was the regular
accompanist, and his qualifications were of course
above cavil. But for many years this duty was
performed in an irregular and unofficial way by a
variety of musicians who seldom rose above the
level of bare efficiency. Old frequenters of the
" Pops " can recall a performance of Brahms's
Meine Liebe ist grün in which the accompanist,
thinking that he had done his duty when the voice
part ended, burked the brief but passionate concluding symphony and ended " bang ! bang ! "

z

with two abrupt chords.   Undoubtedly the notion
prevailed that accompanying was subsidiary, subordinate, not to say menial, work, and for the
most part it was done by musicians who were
artisans rather than artists.   There were, of course,
bright exceptions.   The present writer remembers
a concert at Oxford more than thirty years ago at
which Mr. F. H. Cowen accompanied the singers
with real skill and delicacy.   But the average
professional accompanist was a most inadequate
performer.   There was one, a foreigner, of whom it
was cruelly said that his face resembled a meat-pie
in the window of an eating-shop in the Tottenham
Court Road, and there was certainly not more
soul in his playing than in a meat-pie.   He was
really a very bad player, and even in accompanying
old-fashioned operatic arias gave a very sketchy
and scratchy outline of the pianoforte part.
There were also Italians of the old school—noisy,
showy, florid players whom one associates with a
class of benefit concert happily well-nigh extinct,
at which one never heard any great and seldom any
good music ; concerts held in the old banqueting-
hall at St. James's Hall and other dismal
nondescript places, at which worn-out operatic
stars re-emerged—a rather piteous spectacle—and
indifferent violinists played the same show-pieces
by Vieuxtemps and Wieniawski, and perhaps a

stout lady would whistle. The standard of execution required of the accompanist was certainly not very high, for one seldom heard any modern music more difficult than Gounod's, but he rarely acquitted himself with more than adequacy. Accompanying was in those days one of the refuges of the mediocre, or even incompetent, alien musician. In the famous phrase, "they played the easiest passages with the greatest difficulty." This state of affairs was partly due to the fact that people very rarely sang difficult songs, or songs with difficult accompaniments, thirty or forty years ago ; partly to the rather snobbish view of the function of the accompanist as being derogatory to the prestige of any one who had any pretensions to be a soloist. The elimination of the incompetent accompanist has been due to the progress of musical taste, to the exacting quality of modern music, and to the general recognition of the fact that there is scope for artistic distinction in this department. In other words, people have come to admit that a first-rate accompanist is a most important person, almost, if not quite, as essential to the interpretation of the greatest songs as a first-rate singer.

The ideal relation of singer and accompanist is well expressed in a letter of Jenny Lind's. Writing of the musician who afterwards became her husband, she says : " Herr Goldschmidt is our accompanist, and whether he accompanies me or I accompany myself, it is absolutely the same thing." For many years Mr. Henschel has been a living example of the successful union of both functions. To hear him sing to his own accompaniment has always been a liberal education in both arts, and if one might generalise from individual instances, the obvious advice to singers would be always to play their own accompaniments. This, however, is clearly a counsel of perfection. To begin with, Mr. Henschel is a man of remarkable talent and singular versatility, and the number of singers who are able to render full justice to the accompaniments of modern songs —from Schubert to Strauss—to say nothing of their ability to sing them, is extremely limited. And there remains what is perhaps the greatest difficulty of all—the physical difficulty of making the most of your voice when you are sitting down and facing the audience sideways. It is all very well for society " entertainers "—disciples and followers of John Parry—who rely more on articulate utterance than singing for their chief effects, but artists who aim at the serious interpretation of great vocal music must ninety-nine times out of a hundred have recourse to an accompanist. The case of Mr. Henschel is not one of practical musical politics : it is rather a delightful but inimitable exception. Happily, as we have already seen, the singers of to-day are far better off than their predecessors, and if they are bent on singing good music, have no difficulty in finding people who are able to play it for them as it should be played. Composers are not always the best performers of their own music—neither Berlioz nor Wagner was an executant—and the good accompanist need not be a creative musician, or possess that genius of which Liszt truly observed that it "cannot exist with impunity." The essential quality required in an accompanist, besides precision and adequate technique—including the power of transposition at sight—is sympathy. But we believe that all artistic singers will readily admit that, while a certain measure of subordination is necessary, they by no means wish their accompanists to carry it to the extent of entire self-effacement. In the interludes and the opening and closing symphonies of many songs there is considerable scope for individuality, even for virtuosity. But apart from that, singers are dependent on accompanists to keep them from unduly slackening the *tempo*. The good accompanist has a stimulating and inspiring effect on the sensitive artist, just as the wooden, inelastic player will abate his energy and damp his enthusiasm.

In short, the co-operation is so close and vital that the best singers cordially recognise their debt to their accompanists, and it is a much more common occurrence now than it was formerly for a singer in acknowledging a call to bring on his accompanist with him. As a well-known singer has put it, " the really first-rate accompanist is the biggest asset in a singer's success next to his own magnetism. He is in all essentials the blood-brother, not the servant, of the singer, and has often and often pulled the latter triumphantly through when without him he would have failed dismally. But to attain this level the accompanist must have, what is just as much a gift as voice or ' magnetism' itself, a real genius for his work. Without that all the efficiency in the world is of little avail."

But it is not to be supposed that a perfect mutual understanding between singer and accompanist is a result arrived at—like the dancing of heroines in mid-Victorian novels—by the light of Nature without any training or preparation. Both must have the artistic temperament, must be good musicians, and even then cannot expect to achieve the ideal *entente* without careful rehearsals. In old programmes the pianoforte accompanist was nearly always described as a " conductor," and all that has been said above is applicable, with the necessary modifications, to orchestral accompanying. But the greatest orchestral conductors are not invariably above reproach in this regard. They may be admirable in opera, but their efficiency in this department is not always a certain guarantee of their success in accompanying detached songs. Sometimes they show a laudable loyalty to the intentions of the composer when the singer drags the time or seeks to prolong effective high notes, but occasionally it is hard for them to sink their individuality in a true co-operation, and keep the orchestra down to the proper level. It is certainly a great advantage for a conductor to officiate occasionally as a pianoforte accompanist —like Herr Nikisch.

It would be a difficult and invidious task to attempt to decide who was the pioneer of what may be called the new school of accompanying. But few would be prepared to deny that the appointment of Mr. Bird as accompanist to the "Pops," and his appearance in the same capacity at the recitals of Messrs. Borwick and Plunket Greene, marked the beginning of a new chapter in the annals of accompanying, and erected a new standard of efficiency from which there has been no falling away. A noteworthy and satisfactory fact about this development is that we are entirely indebted for it to native talent. The leading accompanists of the last twenty years—Mr. Henry Bird, Mr. Sewell, Mr. Waddington Cooke (who, however, has long abandoned accompanying for solo work), Mr. Liddle, Mr. Harold Samuel, and Mr. Hamilton Harty, to mention no others—are all British by birth and training.

August 20, 1910.

XLIII

THE BALLAD INDUSTRY

In the lucid and judicial survey of music in the reign of King Edward VII. taken by Sir Walter Parratt in his address to the Authors' Club on November 21st, 1910, he failed to mention one branch of native art which owes little or nothing to foreign influences, though some of its most successful exponents have worn foreign names—we mean the ballad industry. This omission has been made good in the handsome volume which Mr. Harold Simpson has now given to the public.[1] With a commendable modesty, he declares in his Preface that his work "does not aim at being either critical or instructive, but only entertaining." We agree as to the negation of the first and the application of the last epithet, but demur to the withholding of the second. For the book is not only instructive, it throws a positive flood of light on one of the most remarkable aspects of English music.

[1] *A Century of Ballads, 1810-1910: their Composers and Singers.* By Harold Simpson. London : Mills and Boon. [10s. 6d. net.]

In a succinct historical retrospect Mr. Simpson helps us to recognise how many generations had to elapse before the manufacture of the modern ballad was placed on a basis which afforded a proper scope for the talents of the lyric-writer and the tune-coiner. The English ballad started on lines which gave no earnest of its ultimate developments. There is no tinge of parlour pathos in " Sumer is icumen in." The word itself was indistinguishable from ballet, and indicated a song to be danced to—a thing which would never do in the Albert or Queen's Hall. The ballad as we now know it was long overshadowed by the madrigal, the words of which were generally informed by a pastoral sentiment or conveyed the praises of a Sovereign in terms which would be regarded as unduly fulsome in a democratic age. Still, even in those benighted days there were signs and symptoms of progress, and Bishop Hall in his " Martin Marsixtus," published in 1592, declared that " scarce a cat can look out of a gutter, but out starts a halfpenny chronicler, and presently a proper new ballet of a strange sight is indited." But the world had to wait for a hundred and thirty years for a real revulsion of popular taste. " *The Beggar's Opera* [1727] revived the old tunes of England. To its success is due the birth of Ballad operas, operas

into which a number of songs were introduced
which had nothing to do with the plot, somewhat
after the style of our modern musical comedies."
Many a weary year, however, had yet to pass
before the emergence of the real modern ballad,
with its wide appeal and gigantic circulation. Dr.
Arne compromised himself by setting Shakespeare's
songs instead of encouraging contemporary talent,
and Wagner's enthusiasm for the melody of
" Rule, Britannia ! " is, to say the least, a disputable testimony to its merit. Carey and Dibdin
wrote voluminously, but their earnings were
miserable when compared with the profits of
modern publishers. Still, there was an advance ;
and such places of popular resort as Vauxhall,
Ranelagh, and the Marylebone Gardens " did
much to foster public appreciation of ' popular '
ballads, and may be said, in fact, to have been
forerunners of the ballad concerts of to-day."

With the nineteenth century the popular
ballad at last began to come by its own. This
was the golden age of Balfe and Fitzball, Bunn
and Wallace, Haynes Bayly (to whose chaste
Muse Mr. Andrew Lang once consecrated an
inimitable essay), Crouch, Knight, and Wade, the
author of " Meet Me by Moonlight." But the
most notable landmark in the history of the ballad
in the early Victorian epoch is connected with the

name of Madame Vestris, who demanded "a sum
of £20 from Charles Dance, a composer, as a
royalty for continuing to sing his song, being
apparently the first singer to introduce this
practice," a happy modern adaptation of the devotion to Royalty displayed by the old madrigal
writers. This was a period enriched by such
masterpieces as "The Village Blacksmith," which
is "still being sung by Hayden Coffin and other
popular singers"; "The Banks of the Blue
Moselle" and "Many Happy Returns of the
Day," by John Blockley, which is "still sung
at birthday parties"; "My Pretty Jane," and
"I'm Saddest when I Sing." Bishop, Balfe, and
Wallace were competent musicians; but the
methods of some of the ballad composers are
picturesquely described by Willert (not Willett)
Beale in "The Light of Other Days," quoted by
Mr. Simpson on p. 102. Beale wrote a number
of songs under the alias of Walter Maynard, but
he was acquainted with a certain composer "who
used to whistle a tune to him, and get Maynard
to write it down and put it into shape, adding the
proper harmonies and accompaniments," the song
when completed being always claimed by the
whistler as his own. Another notable landmark
in the evolution of the popular modern ballad was
the introduction of the cornet accompaniment in

"The Light of Other Days " and "When Other Lips," though John Hullah, in a fit of ungracious veracity, described the instrument as "a cheap and nasty trumpet." But Hullah, Hatton, and, to a greater extent than either, Sterndale Bennett, failed to assist in the development of the ballad on the lines laid down by Balfe. The commercial instinct seems to have been sadly imperfect in Bennett, and Hatton sold the entire copyright of "Simon the Cellarer" for only twice what Milton received for *Paradise Lost*. With Henry Russell we enter on a new phase of the ballad—the descriptive and didactic "Cheer, Boys, Cheer" was described by the *Daily Telegraph* as "the anthem of optimism," and it held the town for two years, when it was superseded in popularity by "Pop Goes the Weasel." The genius of Ascher, the author of "Alice, Where art Thou ?" exhausted itself in that supreme effort ; but "Claribel," who disputes with Madame Vestris the honour of having been the first to introduce the royalty system, and Virginia Gabriel were voluminous composers of songs which linger in the memory of the middle-aged. Mr. Wilhelm Ganz, a still flourishing veteran, now enters on the scene, and a tragic contretemps is associated with one of his early successes—"Forget-Me-Not." It was a favourite of Madame Patey's, and once when on tour with Sims Reeves she sang this song at the beginning of the programme and secured an encore : "Reeves was quite upset about it, as he disliked any one being encored before he appeared." A whole chapter is devoted to Sullivan's "Lost Chord," of which half-a-million copies were sold in twenty-five years. "A recent writer" describes it as "probably one of the six most popular songs ever penned," and the composer, writing to Madame Antoinette Sterling shortly before his death, said : "I have composed much music since then, but have never written a second 'Lost Chord.'"

As we reach the "seventies" and "eighties" the fame of the ballad-writer reaches its zenith. "Millions of copies" of "Jack's Yarn" are said to have been sold. "In the Gloaming" was published in 1877, and has since been used as a hymn tune in the Rocky Mountains and a school song in the Australian bush. Hamilton Aïdé, Odoardo Barri (who *inter alia* composed a vocal waltz called the "Song of the Gout"), Marzials of "Twickenham Ferry" fame, and Hope Temple were already celebrated ; and among the lyric-writers, Clifton Bingham (who has written one thousand five hundred and fifty songs), Michael Watson, and, above all, F. E. Weatherly, appealed most effectively to the musical million. Mr.

Clifton Bingham, it must not be forgotten, is the author of "A Greenland Lullaby," which contains a couplet enshrining an interesting zoological discovery :—

> Thy father hath gone in his boat to the sea
> To bring home a necklace of coral for thee.

Mr. Simpson tells us in reverential accents the romantic genesis of that "great song," "Whisper and I Shall Hear," by Piccolomini, *alias* Henry Pontet, and "The Garden of Sleep," by Isidore de Lara, who also wrote "All of My All," and "is said to have given over two hundred recitals in ten years." Mr. F. E. Weatherly is the hero of the chapter entitled "An Harmonious Quartet," and Mr. Simpson has been fortunate in securing from this indefatigable lyrist a paper of reminiscences embellished with complimentary facsimile letters from Mr. Gladstone and Mr. Swinburne. When Mr. Weatherly began writing songs "no programme ever included anything approaching a humorous song," but he changed all that with "The Three Old Maids of Lee." Of "Nancy Lee," composed by "Stephen Adams" and described in a musical journal of 1878 as "the greatest song of the day," no fewer than seventy thousand copies were sold in eighteen months, and its popularity was only equalled by that of "The

Midshipmite," another product of the same collaboration. Mr. Weatherly has been writing songs for forty-three years, and "no one is more astonished than I at the fact, and at the variety of songs I have written." He is unable to state the exact number, but "in one ottoman I have fifty-one volumes of eighteen to twenty songs each." Unfortunately he omits to mention how many ottomans he possesses. It is, however, pleasing to learn that, although he has never written a sea song at sea, he wrote his version of the *Siciliana* (in *Cavalleria Rusticana*) "when shut up in the train in a black fog between Wimbledon and Waterloo." No surroundings, however depressing, can shackle the wings of soaring genius.

With the inauguration of the St. James's Hall Ballad Concerts the ballad industry entered on its most prosperous phase. Mr. Simpson gives us a list of "some of the famous names that float across the mental vision in looking back at the ballad concerts of that day "—*i.e.* 1870-1890—in which, curiously enough, we find that of Clara Novello placed between Madame Alice Gomez and Miss Margaret Macintyre. But these later chapters, notably those on "Songs of To-day and Yesterday" and "Modern Ballads and Composers," are rich in surprises. For example, we learn that

"In Old Madrid," though the first big success of its composer, H. Trotère, was not his first but his twenty-ninth song. The divine afflatus descended on the composer while he was playing in the orchestra at the Royal Aquarium, of which he was at that time a member. "He rushed out between the performance into a little refreshment-room and asked for some notepaper. They had nothing but a Meredith and Drew biscuit-bag, and on this he wrote down the melody of 'In Old Madrid.' Afterwards it struck him that it would make a good song, so he put it into song form and sent it to Clifton Bingham, with the result that every one knows," no less than twenty-eight different editions—all pirated—having been published in America, while over two million copies have been sold of this song and "Asthore," his next popular song. The music of "Go to Sea," again, was composed first, "the idea coming to Trotère on the top of a 'bus, a favourite place for composers [? ballad composers] to find inspiration." It will thus be seen that the modern ballad composer no longer whistles the tune for his "ghost" to transcribe or harmonise. The method of the lyric-writer, too, has changed. Thus Mr. Teschemacher, the author of nearly six hundred published songs, writes the majority of his lyrics "actually at the piano." "When I want a new lyric," he says, "I sit down to the piano and improvise, just play anything that comes into my head, and in a little while I get an idea, and then it clothes itself in words, and the lyric is there, in my brain, ready to be put on paper." In dealing with the galaxy of living composers, male and female, whose formidable output is one of the most striking proofs of the prosperity of the ballad industry, Mr. Harold Simpson shows an even more undiscriminating enthusiasm than marks his treatment of their predecessors. The volume is profusely illustrated with excellent photographs of nearly fifty celebrities, and equipped with an Index (in which the number of references to Mr. F. E. Weatherly stands easily first), and an alphabetical list, occupying ten pages, of songs and ballads, including " Ma Curly-headed Babby," " I Want Somebody to Love Me," " Hullo, Tu-tu," and " Hello, Martha." Mr. Simpson's artlessness is quite engaging, and he has unconsciously composed a musical " Dunciad " which ought to be of considerable service to any one who wishes to compile a list of the Hundred Worst Songs in the world.

December 3, 1910.

XLIV

MUSICAL ENGLAND

A CERTAIN section of the English musical world is periodically smitten with a desire to feel its pulse and inquire into its condition, activity, and progress. Personally, we own to a certain prejudice against these recurrent moods of national introspection. If a people are really musical they do not need to discuss whether they are or not. But in so far as the discussion causes us to take stock of the situation and compare the opportunities we enjoy with those of a previous generation, it may prove interesting, and even amusing. The subject came up at the preliminary meeting held at the Mansion House, on the 15th February 1911, in preparation for the International Musical Congress, Lord Plymouth taking the occasion to observe that we could not be called unmusical or unappreciative of good music, in view of our record in the past or the present. Lord Plymouth supplemented this excellent sentiment with something in the nature of a home truth, observing that we were uncritical as a public ; that we were inclined to mistrust our independent judgment and to follow tradition and fashion in our musical likings.   Lord Redesdale, who followed, eloquently pleaded for the representation of Japan at the Congress, on the ground that she had abandoned the Oriental system, embraced the cult of Wagner, and had, in short, entered the comity of music as well as of nations.   Diplomacy is a great and valuable calling, but it is compatible with a fundamental ignorance of the evolution of art. Sir Hubert Parry, speaking later on, expressed the sensible and proper hope that the Orientals would go on with their own music : " The world was not going to gain anything if they got all the musicians in China to play Richard Strauss." Nor will it, let us add, if all British composers play the sedulous ape to the calculated eccentricity of foreigners or disguise their poverty of invention with pseudo-Oriental upholstery.   Sir Hubert Parry, however, succumbed to the temptation of alluding to the eternal question, observing that we had " an inexhaustible passion for the music of foreigners, yet foreigners declared that we were an unmusical nation," adding that it was hardly necessary to follow out the inference to its logical

conclusion.   Still, we can forgive his indiscretion
for the stimulus it applied to the writer of a
memorable article in the *Daily Telegraph* of the
following day — an article, if we may adapt a
metaphor from the tea trade, recalling the delicious
leonine flavour of five-and-twenty years ago, and at
the same time espousing the cause of modernity
in music with an antinomian audacity. (It is hard
to write on the subject without being infected
by a Telegraphese passion for polysyllables and
periphrasis.)

On the great question the *Daily Telegraph*
is, of course, resonantly, stridently optimistic.
England unmusical? Perish the thought! Whatever may have been the shortcomings of the past,
we are now in the mid-stream of musical culture.
The enormous value of music as a factor in
national organisation is developed in an impressive
passage, in which the example of Germany is held
up to our imitation : " Wagner was supplementary
to Bismarck, just as Shakespeare was to Burleigh.
This is a lesson we are learning again, though
late, and if time be given to us by Providence
to repair some disastrous and sterilising errors
of national thought, we shall again be a greater
people because of the renaissance of the artistic
sense, and of all forms of what we may call
educated emotional enthusiasm that is stirring on

every side in the England of to-day." The precise nature of the "educated emotional enthusiasm" that the *Daily Telegraph* has in its mind may be gathered from its proud boast that though we are "fettered by prudery," still "we are as well able as any people, probably, to keep pace with Richard Strauss," whose *Salome* was "for many of us a mind-changing event." That it was a mind-changing event, in a sense undreamt of by the *Daily Telegraph*, is shown by the criticisms of Mr. Newman, formerly one of Strauss's most enthusiastic admirers. Writing of the *Rosencavalier* in the *Nation* of February 18th, 1911, he observes :—

My own opinion is that it marks a further stage in that slow deterioration of the musical faculty that has been apparent at some point or other in all Strauss's work of the last few years—apparent, that is to say, to every one but the uncritical thurifers who believe that Strauss can do no wrong. There were things in the *Symphonia Domestica*, *Salome*, and *Elektra* that made one ask in wonderment whether those works were not really written by two different men, so enormous was the distance between the best and the worst parts of them. In *Der Rosencavalier* the stigmata of degeneration are both more pronounced and more numerous.

But while the *Daily Telegraph* entertains high hopes of our ability "to keep pace with the Strauss of *Salome*," and so to resist the sterilising

tendencies of Free Trade and other lapses from
national sanity, it gives a terrible picture of the
benighted musical condition of England twenty-
five years ago. At that time "Beethoven could
seldom be heard worthily done." With all respect
for so puissant an authority, Beethoven was both
frequently and worthily done in those dark days
by Manns at the Crystal Palace and Charles Hallé
in Manchester. And to speak of "high-class"
music in Manchester as though it were solely
associated with the *régime* of Dr. Richter is an
aspersion on the splendid achievements of his
predecessor which Dr. Richter would be the first
to repudiate. The *Daily Telegraph* belittles the
past in order to glorify the present. After all,
the world went very well in the middle "eighties,"
before critics found "stigmata of degeneration"
in new compositions, but confined themselves for
the most part to belittling Brahms and abusing
Wagner. In this controversy the *Daily Telegraph*
ranged itself staunchly on the side of the ob-
scurantists. To middle-aged observers its resort
to Strauss as a sort of test by which to measure
our capacity for "educated emotional enthusiasm"
is one of the most humorous things in the annals
of journalistic inconsistency. It is only fair to
say, however, that this is not a solitary case.
Twenty-five years ago the majority of musical

critics were, if not exactly reactionary, at least frugal in their applause of those who trod the new paths. The pendulum has now swung far in the opposite direction, and the Press, as a whole, delights to advertise its emancipation from tradition, to scrutinise established reputations, and to exalt new-comers at the expense of the old masters. Still the Homeric vaunt that we are better and better off than our fathers is not always allowed to pass unchallenged, and a notable expression of the minority view is to be found in a recent issue of the *Manchester Guardian*, where a contributor to the London Letter of that journal writes as follows :—

A distinguished foreign musician who has for many years made his home in London expressed to me the other day his opinion that there was considerably less musical feeling in England to-day among the general public than there was a few years ago. I ventured to remark that there were far more concerts, four first-class orchestras in London where there had been none before, and that all foreign musicians come to London as a matter of course. But he answered : "No, you have no real devotion to great music as a nation. Things were at least better in the old days of the 'Pops.' Where is that audience now in which one came to know every face ? No concert hall is ever filled to hear chamber music now. It is only a sensation that attracts the great public—a daring opera by Strauss, a solo by Pachmann or Kreisler. For the greatest music, as music, no crowd,

no enthusiasm.   A low commercial spirit has arisen
which did not exist before.   Agents boom those who
give the most money.   Pretence succeeds as often as real
merit.   Foreign musicians come.   Yes.   They will not
believe it.   I tell my friends over and over again—
'Leave England at once, you will get no support here.'
They only think I fear their competition, but they learn
that I was right.   It is very sad.   I feel it very much.
I love English life so much that I have refused high
positions in my own country.   But I do not deceive
myself.   The love of music is dying out among you."

There is much in this indictment which it is
difficult to gainsay.   The number of good quartets
is legion, but how little they are encouraged
by private engagements !   There is no more delightful form of entertainment than to sit in a
comfortable armchair—not a concert-room stall—
and listen to a good string quartet.   The cost is
negligible, but most of the people who can afford
the luxury cannot or will not afford the time.   The
growth of competing distractions is never-ending.
In the last twenty-five years we have witnessed
not only the universal incursion of golf, but the
development and, let us add, the improvement of
the music-halls, the tyranny of " bridge," the
coming of the motor, and the winter sports craze.
How on earth can rich and fashionable people
find time for music, unless it is sensational,
aggressive, and unorthodox ?   Concert givers,

again, suffer from the competition of mechanical substitutes—the pianola and the gramophone—as well as the lack of satisfactory concert-halls. There are no end of halls, but very few really meet the requirements of performers of chamber music, and the gap caused by the demolition of the old St. James's Hall, with all its drawbacks, has never been filled. The dominion of din grows greater and is more intrusive. Formerly audiences were disturbed by an occasional post-horn or muffin-man, but now the motor-horn furnishes an almost continuous *obbligato*. Musicians have, moreover, to reckon with the exacting attitude of *blasés* amateurs who have grown surfeited with symphony concerts and can only listen to music that is violent or highly spiced. The musical atmosphere has grown heated by the violence of partisanship, and while literary criticism is in the main lax and "sloppy," Bludyer seems to have re-emerged in that of music.

But the worst feature of modern musical England is the tyranny of the royalty ballad. A portly volume was written the other day with the object of representing it in the light of a benevolent and wholly admirable *régime*. To the majority of British concert-goers songs are still the only things in music that really count, and music publishers practically force on the public songs of a type designed to satisfy the meanest intelligence and the most grovelling aspirations, by making it worth while for really good singers to sing them. Thus the good singing of indifferent music creates a demand for it, and the mischief goes on in a vicious circle. Another unsatisfactory aspect of modern British music is this, that the only concerts—if we except those given by two or three favourite artists—which at the present day are securely established are symphony and ballad concerts. The rest rely more or less on " paper." Some years ago a well-known German musical critic remarked that in Berlin a new class of professionals was coming into existence—those who were ready to listen to music " for a consideration." This class is not confined to Berlin. The question of audiences and payments is one of the most serious of all. Far too many of those who can afford to pay for their musical entertainment will only go to concerts as " deadheads." On the other hand, at any hour of the working day there seems to be an almost unlimited paying audience for cheap music-halls and " cinema " theatres amongst the working classes. When will some dispassionate and industrious investigator give us a book on the economics of national amusement ?

Thus far we have endeavoured to set forth the case for dissatisfaction with the present condition of music in England. That grounds for a reasoned optimism exist we are far from denying. Foremost among the improvements of our time are the multiplication of opportunities for hearing great instrumental music at reasonable prices. These advantages are not confined to the well-to-do classes or to London. The taste for classical chamber music has spread to the masses, as any one will admit who has attended the concerts at the South Place Institute. Mr. Fuller Maitland, in his new and excellent study of Brahms, tells a delightful story of a working man who, after listening to a Beethoven quartet at a concert given by the People's Concert Society, at Holloway, observed : " That's all very well, but give me my Brahms." Another healthy sign of the times is the decentralisation which gives us, to mention only one instance, the Bournemouth Municipal Orchestra. The enterprise of its conductor, Mr. Dan Godfrey, and the splendid encouragement he has lent to the work of British composers, deserve a wider recognition than he has yet received. We have spoken elsewhere on the immense advance in the art of accompanying, and this remark applies in general to the raising of the standard of execution in all instrumental works. The number of good quartet parties now resident in London is quite extraordinary, and when one considers how small is the remunerative demand for their services, their devotion to this arduous and noble branch of this art is all the more admirable. This raising of the standard is also markedly shown in the choice of the songs sung at recitals and also in the quality of the music heard at the music-halls. Leaving the question of his humour aside, Harry Lauder has a delightful voice, perfect diction, and an exceptionally good sense of rhythm ; while every good musician should take off his hat to Mr. Pélissier and his company for the admirable ensemble maintained by the Follies in their concerted music, and the cleverness and charm of the music itself. Mr. Pélissier's " Baked Potatoes " quartet—to take only one example—is a little masterpiece of atmospheric effect and melodic appropriateness.

February 25, 1911.

INDEX

THE END